VOX GRAECA

VOX GRAECA

A GUIDE TO
THE PRONUNCIATION OF
CLASSICAL GREEK

BY

W. SIDNEY ALLEN

*Professor Emeritus of Comparative Philology
in the University of Cambridge*

Third edition

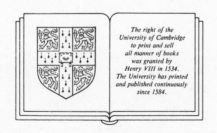

The right of the
University of Cambridge
to print and sell
all manner of books
was granted by
Henry VIII in 1534.
The University has printed
and published continuously
since 1584.

CAMBRIDGE UNIVERSITY PRESS

CAMBRIDGE

NEW YORK   NEW ROCHELLE   MELBOURNE   SYDNEY

Published by the Press Syndicate of the University of Cambridge
The Pitt Building, Trumpington Street, Cambridge CB2 IRP
32 East 57th Street, New York, NY 10022, USA
10 Stamford Road, Oakleigh, Melbourne 3166, Australia

First published   1968
Second edition   1974
Reprinted   1981
Third edition   1987

Printed in Great Britain
by the University Press, Cambridge

British Library cataloguing in publication data
Allen, W. Sidney
Vox Graeca: a guide to the pronunciation
of classical Greek. – 3rd ed.
1. Greek language – Pronunciation
I. Title
481'.52   PA267

Library of Congress cataloguing-in-publication data
Allen, W. Sidney (William Sidney), 1918–
Vox Graeca: a guide to the pronunciation of
classical Greek.
Bibliography.
1. Greek language – Pronunciation.   I. Title.
PA267.A4   1987   481'.52   86–31063

ISBN 0 521 33367 9 hardcovers
ISBN 0 521 33555 8 paperback

UP

Je ne croy pas qu'il y ait personne qui ne voye quelle misère c'est de ne rien comprendre en cette Langue que par les yeux.

(C. Lancelot, *Nouvelle Méthode pour apprendre facilement la Langue Grecque*)

CONTENTS

CONTENTS

FOREWORD TO
THE THIRD EDITION

The need for a further reprinting of this book provides the opportunity for making a number of additions and amendments.

In the foreword to the first edition I referred to the desideratum of a 'New Meisterhans' to provide fuller documentation of the Attic inscriptional material; and in a supplementary note to the second edition I mentioned that the Harvard dissertation of Leslie Threatte raised hopes that this need might be met in the near future. These hopes have since been amply fulfilled by the publication in 1980 of Part I (Phonology) of Threatte's *The Grammar of Attic Inscriptions*. As a result it is now possible to describe a number of phonetic changes with greater detail and accuracy than hitherto, and a majority of the revisions make reference to this work. In this respect at least the present edition may be considered more definitive than its predecessors.

Since the second edition there has also appeared the work by Sven-Tage Teodorsson, *The Phonemic System of the Attic Dialect 400-340 B.C.* (1974), which was followed by his *The Phonology of Ptolemaic Koine* (1977) and *The Phonology of Attic in the Hellenistic Period* (1978) (= Studia Graeca et Latina Gothoburgensia 32, 36, 40). Teodorsson's extensive collection of material is of particular value in regard to orthographic variation; but his interpretation of the variants is often surprising, leading as it does to the conclusion that by the mid-4th century B.C. the vowel system of Attic was already virtually that of modern Greek. Teodorsson gives more weight to relatively infrequent 'progressive' variants than to more numerous 'conservative' forms, taking the view that the latter represent the speech of only an educated minority. He has to recognize, however (1977, p. 256), that this was the standard of Attic administration and of the Attic Koine adopted by peoples outside Attica: only thus is he able to explain the fact (p. 257) that 'some of the phonological changes that had already taken place in Attic before Alexander were accomplished only one or two centuries later in Egypt'. No one would deny the existence of linguistically conservative minorities or the tendency of orthographies themselves to be conservative; but it is possible to overvalue the evidence of occasional variants, which may have a number of explanations, including dialectal influence; and some of Teodorsson's arguments are of dubious validity. This is not the place for a detailed critique of his views; but I find myself largely in agreement with the opinions of C. J. Ruijgh in his review of Teodorsson's first-mentioned book, in *Mnemosyne* 31 (1978), pp. 79–89.

I have also now added an appendix on the names of the letters of the Greek alphabet, to provide a parallel and a historical background to the similar appendix in the second edition of *Vox Latina*.

I am grateful to the C.U.P. for agreeing that the total amount of material additional to the first edition now makes it desirable to incorporate it in the main text, rather than relegate it (as in the second edition) to supplementary notes at the end.* I have in particular revised the section on stress in classical Greek to take account of my more recent thinking on this question. The discussion inevitably requires rather greater technicality than is general in this book; but since it does not significantly affect the practical recommendations (cf. pp. 114 f., 138 f.), it need not unduly concern the less theoretically inclined reader. The chapter on quantity has also been extensively recast.

Cambridge   W. S. A.
November 1984

* Forewords to the previous editions are reprinted unamended, but two additional points call for mention. In the discussion of types of evidence in the foreword to the first edition (p. xiii) there should be included under (3) representations of foreign words in Greek; further evidence is also provided by Indo-European comparisons. And for dialectal variation in modern Greek (p. xiv, n. 6) Thumb's information may now be usefully supplemented by that of Newton (see Bibliography).

As in previous editions, works appearing in the Bibliography are referred to by the author's name only, with an identifying letter where necessary; and the two more frequently cited works of the present author simply by *VL* (*Vox Latina*) and *AR* (*Accent and Rhythm*).

FOREWORD TO
THE SECOND EDITION

Since this book first appeared a number of further studies relevant to Greek pronunciation have been published or have come to my attention, and the need for a reprinting has provided an opportunity for taking account of these. In the meantime there has also appeared my *Accent and Rhythm* (C.U.P. 1973), which suggests a reinterpretation of various 'prosodic' phenomena (such as syllable, length, and quantity) and further develops the ideas on stress in classical Greek briefly mentioned on pp. 120 ff. of the present work. References to *Accent and Rhythm* are abbreviated as *AR*.

In order to save expense and at the same time to avoid changes in pagination, the new material has been added as a supplement rather than incorporated in the main text (which remains unchanged, with a few minor corrections). An obelus in the margin indicates the existence of a relevant supplementary note.

The Select Bibliography has also been revised and enlarged.

Cambridge W.S.A.
February 1974

FOREWORD TO
THE FIRST EDITION

In its purpose, principles, and general arrangement, the present book forms a companion volume to *Vox Latina* (Cambridge, 1965), to which there are several cross-references (abbr. *VL*). It does not, however, assume a prior reading of the earlier book, and a certain amount of duplication on some of the more general topics is thus inevitable; in particular, the Phonetic Introduction is repeated, though with some modification. A select bibliography is added (apart from detailed references in text and notes, which, though more numerous than in *VL*, are limited to the most relevant studies);[1] as in *VL*, the classificatory arrangement of the contents makes an alphabetical index superfluous—the items most likely to be consulted in such an index would be the individual Greek letters, and full references to the detailed discussion of these are given in the summary of recommended pronunciations; straightforward statements of classical or recommended values are further picked out by underlining in the text.

As in the case of Latin, there prevailed until quite recent years a peculiarly English pronunciation of ancient Greek, which has now been generally superseded by a reform which approximates to that of the original language, but seldom transcends the limitations of native English speech-habits. In some cases there are practical pedagogical advantages in replacing the correct rendering by a more familiar sound; but it is desirable in such cases that the proper value should be known—and this usually is known within limits as narrow as those which apply to our phonetic reconstruction of Latin.

In general the conclusions agree with those of Sturtevant's *Pronunciation of Greek and Latin*, and particular attention is paid to any points of difference. A book intended not only for the

---

[1] Works appearing in the bibliography are elsewhere referred to by author's name only, with an identifying letter where necessary.

academic scholar but also for the general reader and student is not the place for presenting the results of new and possibly controversial lines of research; it did, however, seem reasonable to incorporate a revised description of the Greek tonal accent, which rationalizes rather than contradicts previous accounts; and also to refer briefly to the results of a study, recently published elsewhere, on stress in ancient Greek, a subject which has hitherto been virtually ignored but which may be particularly relevant to certain metrical phenomena.

In making practical recommendations, realism has seemed a better counsel than perfection, and, with one exception, no revolutionary proposals will be found. The exception concerns our English treatment of the Greek accents, where the balance of argument seemed to favour the abandonment of present practice and the adoption of one which enjoys wider acceptance and better historical precedents. Such a recommendation is, of course, only made after detailed historical, analytical, and practical discussion.

The results of any historical study are only as valid as the evidence upon which they are based; and a major portion of the book is therefore taken up with the presentation and evaluation of this. The principal types of data employed in phonetic reconstruction are: (1) statements by contemporary or near-contemporary grammarians and other writers, (2) word-play of various kinds, contemporary etymologies, and onomatopoeia, (3) representations in other ancient languages, (4) subsequent developments, (5) spelling conventions and variants, (6) the internal structure of the language itself, including its metrical patterns. These are the same classes of evidence as were used for Latin; but in one respect the two tasks of reconstruction are very different. Variations in Latin are largely a function of the time-dimension (early—classical—late), and the time-span of the language is relatively short. At any given period of its life one can say without gross inaccuracy, and more particularly of the written language, that 'Latin is Latin is Latin' regardless of where it is found. The end of its life as a vernacular language is marked by a process of fission into a number of progressively diverging dialects which quite soon acquired the status of distinct languages; and the techniques of comparative linguistics often enable us to utilize this diversity to establish the *état de langue* immediately prior to fission.

Greek, on the other hand, presents a very different picture. At the time of our earliest records it is already far advanced in the process of divergence,[2] being represented by a number of widely differing dialects—all certainly recognizable as Greek,[3] but some of them very unlike one another, even at the same period; as Meillet (p. 79) has commented, 'it must have been difficult for Greeks from different cities, speaking different dialects, if not to grasp the general sense, at least to understand one another exactly'.[4] For example, an unsophisticated Attic visitor to Gortys in Crete might well have perused the famous Law Code without it being clear to him that, if he were unfortunate enough to be caught in adultery and remain unransomed, his captors could do with him '*as they pleased*'—in the words of the Code, επι τοις ελονσι εμεν κρεθθαι **οπαι κα λειοντι**. In some cases, moreover, as Meillet also observed, written forms might conceal yet further differences in speech—θ, for example, in the Cretan κρεθθαι probably stood for a sound unfamiliar to Attic ears.

Later a single form of speech, the 'Koine', becomes dominant, and the other dialects, with rare exceptions (as Laconian), gradually die out. The survivor follows the normal processes of linguistic change,[5] including 'borrowing', but does not itself branch out into a series of new languages—some dialectal variation has of course occurred,[6] but it is relatively slight compared with that of the Romance field, and there is a generally accepted norm.

[2] Even Mycenaean, in spite of its early date, comes nowhere near to representing an undifferentiated 'Proto-Greek'.

[3] Cf. Herodotus, viii. 75: τὸ Ἑλληνικὸν ἐὸν ὁμαιμόν τε καὶ ὁμόγλωσσον.

[4] Greek sources themselves, however, scarcely refer to the question of mutual (un)intelligibility: as an isolated exception Mr J. B. Hainsworth draws my attention to Pausanias, ix. 22. 3 (referring to Corinna).

[5] So far as the colloquial language is concerned: we are not here concerned with the artificialities of the 'Katharevusa'.

[6] The phonetic details are best studied in Thumb, Part I.

In a much simplified diagram[7] the patterns of development in Latin and Greek, from their earliest attested stages, may be contrasted as follows:

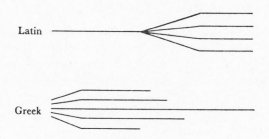

In describing the pronunciation of ancient Greek a choice thus has to be made not only of time but also of place; and, not surprisingly, it is fifth-century Attic that we select as the goal of our inquiry—though, as an aid focusing upon this point in the continuum, we shall often have occasion to refer to other dialects and to earlier and later stages of Attic. It is not of course suggested that literature of other periods and dialects should not be read aloud—but it is assumed that it will be read approximately as it would have been by a fifth-century Athenian; in the case of later literature this is inevitably an artificial procedure, but the differences between fifth- and fourth-century Attic are in any case negligible, and for phonetic purposes both may be included under the cover-term of 'classical Greek'. For later stages a reasonable amount of information is given, so that the purist who is so inclined may take the necessary precautions to avoid anachronism; such information may also be of interest as providing links with the modern language. In one case, however, rather more attention has been paid to a non-Attic form of speech in its own right— namely the Homeric 'dialect', for the reason that an Attic rendering in some respects fails to account for certain metrical

[7] E.g. disregarding phenomena of convergence in Greek, which may have been particularly marked in the period preceding elimination of dialects in favour of the Koine; cf. Chadwick, p. 4.

peculiarities; it is not proposed that a 'Homeric' pronunciation should be attempted, but sufficient explanation is given to make these phenomena intelligible.

For the Attic inscriptional material I have relied primarily on the examples in Meisterhans–Schwyzer, cross-checked in the *CIA*; but as the *SEG*, *inter alia*, bears witness, a mass of new material is now available, which often provides better examples and evidence for more accurate dating of phonetic changes. I have in some cases been able to incorporate such findings, but until we have a 'New Meisterhans' the exploitation of much of the newer material is a time-consuming and haphazard business.

With regard to inscriptional evidence in general, it should be mentioned that a change of sound must commonly have antedated its first indication in spelling, let alone the general adoption of a new spelling; for, as English orthography most eloquently demonstrates, spelling tends to conservatism and to fossilization by grammarians. For this reason, and also because many changes are likely to have been resisted longer in actual speech in the more literate circles of the community, it is to the less well educated of ancient scribes that we are indebted for much of our knowledge of pronunciation.

I am grateful to the Syndics of the Cambridge University Press for encouraging me to undertake this further study; to John Chadwick for reading the whole of it in draft and suggesting a number of improvements; and to Professor Homer A. Thompson and the American School of Classical Studies at Athens for the photographs facing p. 70 and permission to reproduce them.

Cambridge   W.S.A.
January 1967

ABBREVIATIONS

1. Journals, series, etc.

AC	*L'antiquité classique*
AJA	*American Journal of Archaeology*
AL	*Acta Linguistica*
ArchL	*Archivum Linguisticum*
BCH	*Bulletin de correspondance hellénique*
BSOAS	*Bulletin of the School of Oriental and African Studies*
BZ	*Byzantinische Zeitschrift*
CHL	*Commentationes Humanarum Litterarum (Societas Scientiarum Fennica)*
CIA	*Corpus Inscriptionum Atticarum*
CIL	*Corpus Inscriptionum Latinarum*
CJ	*Classical Journal*
CP	*Classical Philology*
CQ	*Classical Quarterly*
CR	*Classical Review*
DAWB	*Deutsche Akademie der Wissenschaften zu Berlin*
GG	*Grammatici Graeci* (Teubner, 1867–1910: repr. 1965)
GL	*Grammatici Latini* (Teubner, 1857–1880)
HSPh	*Harvard Studies in Classical Philology*
ICPS	*International Congress of Phonetic Sciences*
ICS	*Illinois Classical Studies*
IG	*Inscriptiones Graecae* (Berlin)
IGA	*Inscriptiones Graecae Antiquissimae* (ed. Roehl)
JA	*Journal Asiatique*
JHS	*Journal of Hellenic Studies*
KZ	(*Kuhns Zeitschrift* =) *Zeitschrift für vergleichende Sprachforschung*
MF	*Le Maître Phonétique*
MH	*Museum Helveticum*

NTS	*Norsk Tidsskrift for Sprogvidenskap*
PhW	*Philologische Wochenschrift*
REG	*Revue des études grecques*
RhM	*Rheinisches Museum für Philologie*
RIL	*Rendiconti dell'Istituto Lombardo (Cl. di Lettere e Sc. Mor. e Stor.)*
RL	*Richerche linguistiche*
SbAWB	*Sitzungsberichte der k. Preuss. Akademie der Wissenschaften zu Berlin, phil.-hist. Kl.*
SbAWW	*Sitzungsberichte de k. Akademie der Wissenschaften zu Wien, phil.-hist. Kl.*
SC	*Studii Clasice*
SEG	*Supplementum Epigraphicum Graecum*
SIFC	*Studi italiani di filologia classica*
TAPA	*Transactions of the American Philological Association*
TCLP	*Travaux du Cercle Linguistique de Prague*
TLP	*Travaux Linguistiques de Prague*
TPS	*Transactions of the Philological Society*
WSt	*Wiener Studien*
YClS	*Yale Classical Studies*
ZPh	*Zeitschrift für Phonetik*

2. Editions of grammatical and technical works

C M. Consbruch (Hephaestion, *Enchiridion, cum commentariis veteribus*. Teubner, 1906).

H A. Hilgard (*Scholia in Dionysii Thracis Artem Grammaticam = GG*, i. iii)

A. Hilgard (Theodosius, *Canones*; Choeroboscus, *Scholia in Theod. Can.*, i = *GG*, iv. i. Choeroboscus, *Scholia*, ii = *GG*, iv. ii).

K H. Keil (*GL*, i–vii)

L A. Lentz (Herodianus Technicus = *GG*, iii. i/ii)

M H. S. Macran (Aristoxenus, *Harmonics*. Oxford, 1902)

S R. Schneider (Apollonius Dyscolus, *Scripta minora = GG*, ii. i)

U   G. Uhlig (Dionysius Thrax, *Ars Grammatica*; *Supplementa Artis Dionysianae vetusta* = *GG*, I. i)

        G. Uhlig (Apollonius Dyscolus, *De Constructione* = *GG*, II. ii)

UR   H. Usener & L. Radermacher (Dionysius of Halicarnassus, *Opuscula*, ii. Teubner, 1904–29)

WI   R. P. Winnington-Ingram (Aristides Quintilianus, *De Musica*. Teubner, 1963)

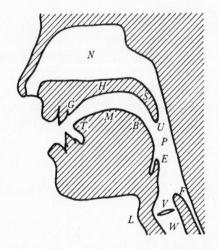

Fig. 1. The organs of speech.

B	Back of tongue	N	Nasal cavity
E	Epiglottis (drawn over	P	Pharynx
	windpipe when swallowing)	S	Soft palate (velum),
F	Food-passage		in lowered position
G	Gums (alveoli)	T	Tongue-tip
H	Hard palate	U	Uvula
L	Larynx, with 'Adam's apple'	V	Vocal cords (glottis)
M	Middle of tongue	W	Windpipe

[After Ida C. Ward, *The Phonetics of English*]

PHONETIC INTRODUCTION

(i) Syllable, vowel and consonant

In any extended utterance, in any language, there is an alternation of sounds having more and less acoustic power, or 'sonority', so that a diagrammatic representation of the utterance would comprise a succession of high and low points. These points would occupy various levels on a scale of sonority, but it is only their relative positions compared with preceding and following sounds that are immediately relevant.[1] The number of SYLLABLES in an utterance generally corresponds to the number of high points. The sounds which habitually occur at these points are termed VOWELS, whilst those which habitually occur at low points are termed CONSONANTS.

Some types of sound, however, may occupy either high or low points relatively to their neighbours; such sounds are classified as vowels in their former ('nuclear') function, but are generally termed SEMIVOWELS, and classified with the consonants, in their latter ('marginal') function. Many languages employ different symbols to indicate this distinction of functions (thus English *y* and *w* for the consonants corresponding to the vowels *i* and *u*); in classical Greek, however, the marginal function of ι and υ is very restricted, much more so than in English or Latin, and no special symbols are used to indicate it.

Finally, two successive vowel-sounds may occur as independent syllabic nuclei, the necessary margin being created by some diminution of energy between them, even though they may have the same degree of inherent sonority, as e.g. in ὄγδοος, Διί, inscr. αθηναα (though this situation is less common in Attic, being often resolved by 'contraction' into a single syllable, as ᾿Αθηνᾶ).

---

[1] It should also be mentioned that we are at present concerned only with the *inherent* sonority of the sounds, ignoring such 'prosodic' factors as stress, pitch, and duration, which also contribute to overall prominence (cf. Jones (*a*), §§ 208 ff.; Gimson, pp. 216 ff.).

An alternative approach to the definition of syllable, vowel, and consonant is discussed in detail in *AR*, pp. 40 ff. This is the 'motor' theory developed by Stetson (see Bibliography), which approaches the problem from the standpoint of the physiology of the syllabic process rather than its acoustic results. Whilst much of the detail of Stetson's experimentation has been considered suspect, the theory nevertheless provides a powerful theoretical model for the explanation of such 'prosodic' features as length, quantity, and stress, and helps towards an understanding of various metrical phenomena.

Briefly the main features of the theory are as follows. The syllable is generated by a contraction of one set of chest muscles, which superimposes a 'puff' of air on the larger respiratory movement ('like a ripple on a wave'): the syllable is consequently termed by Stetson a 'chest-pulse'. The action is of 'ballistic' (as opposed to 'controlled') type, which means that the 'release' is followed by a period of free movement, and terminated by an 'arrest'. The arrest may be effected either by the contraction of an opposed set of chest muscles or (or mainly) by a complete or partial closure in the mouth which blocks the egress of air. The release may also be assisted by means of an oral closure, which causes a rise in air pressure and so effects a more energetic release when the closure is relaxed.

The outflow of air during the free movement (the 'peak' of the syllable) normally sets the vocal cords in vibration, and the glottal tone thus generated is modified in various ways by oral filtering, giving rise to the different vowel sounds; and the various types of oral closure associated with the arrest of the syllabic movement, or with assisting its release, give rise to the different consonants.

(ii) Consonants

A primary classification of consonants is into the categories of VOICED and VOICELESS. Voiced sounds involve an approximation of the two edges of the vocal cords, so that when air passes through them it sets up a characteristic vibration, known technically as 'glottal tone' or VOICE; voiceless sounds involve a clear separation of the cords, so that no such vibration occurs. The difference may be exemplified by the English (voiced) z and (voiceless) s. If the ears are closed, the vibration of the former can be clearly heard by the speaker; the vibration can also be felt by placing a finger on the protuberance of the thyroid cartilage ('Adam's apple').

Sounds may be further classified according to the position or organ involved in their articulation. Thus LABIAL (or BILABIAL) involves the articulation of the two lips (e.g. English p), LABIO-DENTAL the articulation of the upper teeth and lower lip (e.g. English f), DENTAL the articulation of the tongue-tip and upper teeth (e.g. English *th*), ALVEOLAR the articulation of the tongue-tip and upper gums (e.g. English t), PALATAL the articulation of the mid-part of the tongue and the hard palate, VELAR the articulation of the back of the tongue and the soft palate or 'velum' (e.g. English k).

If the speech-organs form a complete closure, during which air is prevented from passing until the closure is released, the resulting sound is termed a STOP. Stops are further subdivided into PLOSIVES and AFFRICATES. English has the plosives p, b (bilabial, voiceless and voiced), t, d (alveolar), and k, g (velar). For affricates, see under fricatives below.

If the vocal cords are left open for a brief period after the release of a stop, producing an audible type of 'h-sound' immediately following, the stop in question is described as ASPIRATED: there is clear aspiration of voiceless stops, for example, at the beginning of stressed initial syllables in English. In French, on the other hand, the vocal cords are approximated almost simultaneously with the release, and the result is a relatively UNASPIRATED sound.

Consonants other than stops are broadly classifiable as CONTINUANTS, and may be of various types. If the tongue or lips form a closure, but air is allowed to escape via the nasal passages (by lowering the velum), the result is a NASAL consonant (sometimes, as in *VL*, referred to as a nasal *stop* on account of the oral closure). In most languages the nasals are

3

all inherently voiced; English has the nasals *m* (bilabial), *n* (alveolar), and as *ng* in *sing* (velar).

If the organs are not completely closed, but if the channel between them is so narrow as to cause an audible effect as the air passes through it, the resulting sound is termed a FRICA-TIVE. English examples are *f* and *v* (labio-dental, voiceless and voiced), dental as in *thin* (voiceless) and *then* (voiced), *s* and *z* (alveolar), and 'palato-alveolar' as in *ash* or *passion* (voiceless) and *pleasure* (voiced); a voiceless velar fricative is heard in Scottish *loch*. The ASPIRATE, *h*, is sometimes called a 'glottal fricative'. A fricative effect is also produced by the gradual release of a stop, and it is this which characterizes the affricates; English examples are palato-alveolar as in *chest* (voiceless) and *jest* (voiced).

If one side of the tongue forms a closure, but the other side permits air to flow freely,[2] the result is a LATERAL consonant, such as the English *l*. Such sounds are sometimes classed with the *r*-sounds as 'liquids' (see p. 39 f.).

(iii) Vowels

Variations of vowel-quality are effected primarily by the raising of different portions of the tongue's surface towards the palate, and by different degrees of such raising resulting in different degrees of aperture between tongue and palate. Vowels may thus be classified according to (*a*) how far FRONT or BACK they are articulated (i.e. involving more forward or more backward areas of the tongue and palate), and (*b*) how CLOSE or OPEN they are (i.e. involving greater or lesser raising of the tongue): the terms HIGH and LOW are also commonly used.

The relations of the vowels to one another may then be conveniently represented in terms of a two-dimensional dia-gram. When so represented they tend to fall into a quadrilateral or triangular pattern,[3] such as:

---

[2] Alternatively there may be a central closure, with air-flow on both sides.

[3] Such patterns are actually based on a mixture of auditory, acoustic, and articulatory criteria: cf. P. Ladefoged, *Preliminaries to Linguistic Phonetics*, pp. 67 ff.

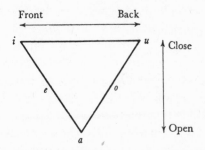

Vowels intermediate between front and back are referred to as CENTRAL, and vowels intermediate between close and open as MID (the so-called 'neutral' vowel of standard southern British English, as at the end of *sofa* or *finger*, is a mid central vowel).

Associated with the features already mentioned are various degrees of lip-ROUNDING; generally speaking back vowels are associated with rounding and front vowels with its absence (lip-spreading). Thus the English *u* and *i* in e.g. *put*, *pit* are respectively close back rounded and close front unrounded. Sometimes, however, rounding is associated with a front vowel and spreading with a back vowel—thus the French *u* and German *ü* are front rounded vowels, whilst back unrounded vowels occur in some languages.

Vowels are normally articulated with the nasal passages closed (by raising the velum), but if they are left open the result is a NASALIZED vowel (as e.g. in French *on*, transcribed phonetically as õ).

DIPHTHONGS are formed by articulating a vowel and then, within the same syllable, making a gradual change of articulation (or 'glide') in the direction of another vowel. Most commonly, but not inevitably, the first element of a diphthong is more open than the second. Thus the diphthong of English *high* involves a glide from *a* towards *i*, of *how* from *a* towards *u*, and of *hay* from *e* towards *i*. Considerations of the phonological structure of a language sometimes make it appropriate to interpret a diphthong as a combination of a vowel and a semivowel (*y* or *w*).

In many languages vowels fall into two degrees of LENGTH,

LONG and SHORT. By and large the difference corresponds to a greater as opposed to a lesser duration—but not invariably so. Other features, notably differences of tenseness and quality, may be at least as important (they are, for example, in distinguishing the so-called 'short' vowel of English *bit* from the so-called 'long' vowel of *beat*).

Length may also be related to the syllabic process. A chest arrest (see above), being a relatively slow movement, involves a continuation of the vowel whilst it takes effect—and so may be associated with long vowels. An oral arrest, on the other hand, is a relatively rapid movement and so is associated with short vowels (if the vowel were prolonged, it would give time for the chest arrest to intervene, and the oral articulation would not then provide the arrest: cf. p. 91).

Short vowels may also be associated with a type of movement in which the release of the following syllable overtakes the arrest of the preceding, rendering it effectively unarrested: for further details see *AR*, pp. 62 ff.

Differences of quality may be correlated with differences of duration because the shorter the duration the less time there is for the organs to move from their 'neutral' position to the 'optimal' position for a particular vowel.

(iv) Accent

In addition to the vowels and consonants of which a word is constituted, a particular segment of the word (e.g. syllable or vowel) may be characterized by a superimposed feature which sets it off against the other segments not so characterized. Such a feature is referred to as an ACCENT, and is sometimes said to have a 'culminative' function, as forming, so to speak, the phonetic climax of the word.

The accent may be either FIXED or FREE. The former type is exemplified in such languages as Czech, Icelandic, or Hungarian, where the accent normally falls on the first syllable of each word; Armenian, where it falls on the last syllable; or Polish, where it mostly falls on the penultimate. The Latin accent is also fixed, though it is regulated by a more complex formula (cf. *VL*, p. 83). The free accent is typical, for example, of English or Russian, where it is not bound to a particular place in each word;[4] and this freedom of location makes it capable, unlike the fixed accent, of differentiating the meanings of otherwise identical words: thus e.g. English *ímport* (noun), *impórt* (verb);[5] *fórbears, forbéars* (and *fóur béars*); Russian *múka* 'torment', *muká* 'flour'; *pláču* 'I weep', *pláčú* 'I pay'.

Physically the accentual feature may be manifested in either of two ways, by variation in the PITCH of the voice ('MELODIC accent') or by STRESS ('DYNAMIC accent'). Stress, however, though primarily effected by an increase in muscular effort, is a complex phenomenon, in which factors of pitch and duration may also play an important role.

It is essential to distinguish melodic accent from INTONA-TION. The former refers to the pitch-patterns operative within individual words, whereas 'intonation' refers to the pitch-pattern operative over the whole clause or sentence. However, there may be, and there usually is, considerable interaction between these two patterns; thus the pitch-pattern of a given word may vary greatly in accordance with the pitch-pattern of the sentence (as also of other words in the environment); such an effect is sometimes referred to as a 'perturbation' of the word-melodics.

The term 'melodic' in this connexion should also, strictly speaking, be distinguished from 'TONAL', since the latter is often used in linguistics with a specialized connotation, referring to languages 'having lexically significant, contrastive, but relative pitch *on each syllable*', as e.g. Chinese (K. L. Pike, *Tone Languages*, p. 3).[6]

---

[4] When grammatical considerations are taken into account, however, as in transformational-generative phonology, the English accent is very largely predictable by rule—though the rules are of great complexity: see especially N. Chomsky & M. Halle, *The Sound Pattern of English*.

[5] More often, however, English spelling also masks differences of vowel(s) as between homographic verbal and nominal forms, e.g. in the first syllable of *convict*, in both syllables of *present*—and in all four of *analyses*.

[6] Cf. E. Fischer-Jorgensen, *AL*, 6 (1950), pp. 54 f.

(v) Speech and writing

In the study of a 'dead' language there is inevitably a main emphasis on the written word. But it is well to remember that writing is secondary to speech, and, however much it may deviate from it, has speech as its ultimate basis. The written symbols correspond, in a more or less complete manner, to phonological or grammatical elements of speech; and, as André Martinet has pointed out, 'vocal quality is directly responsible for the linearity of speech and the consequent linearity of script'.[7] It is therefore in a sense misleading to speak of written symbols as being pronounced—rather it is the other way round, the symbols representing spoken elements. But when, as in the case of ancient Greek, our utterances mostly involve reading from a written text, the traditional terminology of 'pronouncing letters' may reasonably be tolerated, and is in fact maintained in this book.

In ancient Greek, as in modern European languages, the correspondence is between symbols (letters) and phonological elements, and is much more regular than in some languages, such as English or French or Modern Greek (or Irish or Tibetan), which notoriously use different symbols or combinations of symbols to indicate the same sound.

It is sometimes stated that an ideal writing-system would have a symbol for every sound—that it would in fact be a kind of 'visible speech'. Since, however, the number of sounds in a language is infinite, and the 'same' sound probably never precisely recurs, this requirement is quite impracticable. It is also unnecessary, as alphabets from earliest times have recognized. The number of symbols can be reduced to manageable proportions without any resultant ambiguity by a process which has long been unconsciously followed, though its theoretical basis has only been worked out during recent decades.

What is required is not one symbol per sound, but one symbol (or combination of symbols) per PHONEME. A 'phoneme' is a class of similar sounds that are *significantly* different from other

[7] *A Functional View of Language*, p. 25.

8

sounds, e.g. the class of *t* sounds in English *tin*, *hat*, etc., or the class of *d* sounds in *din*, *had*, etc. The (voiceless) *t* phoneme and the (voiced) *d* phoneme are different phonemes in English, and so require distinct symbols, because *tin* has a different meaning from *din*, *hat* has a different meaning from *had*, etc.; in technical terminology, the members of the *d* and *t* phonemes are in 'parallel distribution'—i.e. they can contrast significantly with one another, and with members of other phonemes, in otherwise identical immediate environments, such as (–)*in*, *ha*(–), etc.

On the other hand, the fact that an initial *t* in English (as in *tin*) is more strongly aspirated than a final *t* (as in *hat*) is not responsible for any difference of meaning, since the two varieties occur only in different environments, and so cannot contrast with one another—they are in 'complementary' and not parallel distribution. They are thus both members (or 'allophones') of the same *t* phoneme; only one symbol is required to write them, since the difference in sound is predictable from their environment, i.e. initial or final position as the case may be. It should be noted, however, that the phonemic distribution of sounds varies from language to language; in a language such as Hindi, for example, aspirated and unaspirated *t* sounds belong to separate phonemes, since the occurrence of one or the other is not predictable from environment and they may contrast significantly (e.g. *sāt* 'seven', *sāth* 'with').

The number of phonemes in a language varies; the number of consonants, for example, varies from 8 in Hawaiian, through 24 in English and 32 in Sanskrit, to 55 in the East Caucasian Tabasaran and 80 in the West Caucasian Ubykh. Latin, according to different analyses, has from 15 to 18 consonant phonemes in native words, and classical Greek from 14 to 18.[8] In languages with very large consonant systems the number of vowel phonemes tends to be correspondingly small (1 or 2 in some Caucasian languages), since numerous environmental (allophonic) variants are needed for each vowel phoneme in

[8] Depending on whether the ŋ sounds (see p. 39) are established as a separate phoneme, whether ı and ʊ in their non-syllabic function are treated as consonants (pp. 47 ff., 81 ff.), and whether the rough breathing is treated as a consonant or as a modification of the vowel (p. 53).

order to provide additional cues for the recognition of some of the otherwise very fine consonantal distinctions. The analytical segmentation into discrete phonemes in fact masks much of the complexity of actual speech. Human language has been evolved for use in less than perfect acoustic conditions, and to this end possesses a high degree of inbuilt 'redundancy'; so that even in a language like English the distinction between e.g. *cat* and *pat* depends not simply upon the consonantal difference but largely also upon variation in the transitional phases of the following vowel—to the extent that the wrong vowel-variant is liable to cause misinterpretation of the consonant and, conversely, the correct vowel-variant may induce identification of the consonant even if the latter is deleted.[9]

This 'phonemic' principle, then, is an economic principle, reducing redundancy and employing the minimal number of symbols that is consistent with the unambiguous representation of speech.[10] And the post-Eucleidean spelling of Greek (see p. 17) comes reasonably near to being phonemic. The principal shortcomings are (*a*) in the vowels, failure to distinguish between short and long α, ι and υ (but see pp. 90 ff.); and (*b*) in the consonants, the use of special symbols ('monographs') to represent some combinations of two phonemes, viz. ζ, ξ, ψ (pp. 56 ff.).

When indicating particular sounds in a phonetic notation it is customary to enclose the symbols in square brackets, e.g. [tʰ] to represent the initial sound of English *tin*; phonemic symbols, on the other hand, are conventionally set between obliques, e.g. /t/ for the phoneme which includes the initial sound of *tin* and the final sound of *hat*. In a book intended primarily for the

[9] Cf. Carol D. Schatz, 'The role of context in the perception of stops', *Language*, 30 (1954), pp. 47 ff.

[10] The possibility of further reduction by 'morphophonemic' methods (cf. Allen, *Sandhi*, pp. 16 f.; E. P. Hamp, *CP*, 62 (1967), p. 44; also p. 39 below) is here ignored to avoid undue technicality.

Transformational-generative grammar dispenses with an autonomous phonemic level of statement, and represents its phonological component in terms of sets of 'distinctive features'. Whatever the validity and value of this method, however, in an integrated grammar, it would lead to an intolerable and unnecessary complication in the present work—quite apart from the fact that there is as yet no general agreement on the inventory of 'features'.

classical and general reader rather than the technical linguist and phonetician it has seemed desirable to keep phonetic symbols to a minimum. Partly for the same reason the conventions of the International Phonetic Alphabet have in some cases been modified in the direction of (for English classical readers) more familiar forms—e.g. by the use of [y] instead of [j] for the palatal semivowel, and by the use of the macron instead of the colon for vowel-length.[11] In any case, regrettably or not, the IPA has no canonical status; it is not in fact true (as stated by one reviewer of *VL*) that 'the use of IPA symbols is standard'—certainly not, for instance, in the U.S.A.; what matters is not so much the shape of the symbol as the definition of its value.

Note: Where English equivalents are given for Greek sounds, the reference, unless otherwise stated, is to the standard or 'Received Pronunciation' (RP) of southern British English. The choice of this form of English as a basis of comparison is made on purely practical grounds. It is impossible to cite examples that will be equally applicable to all nationalities and dialects of English; one must perforce select a standard, and 'RP' is by far the best documented and most familiar of such standards.

[11] In discussing the Greek vowel-systems and their development there are positive advantages in using the same basic symbols, with appropriate diacritics, for all mid front vowels and for all mid back vowels (rather than e.g. IPA [eː], [ɛː]).

CHAPTER I

CONSONANTS*

Before discussing the individual consonant-sounds in detail it is necessary to emphasize that wherever the normal spelling writes a *double* consonant, it stands for a correspondingly lengthened sound.[1] This is most clearly seen from its effect on the quantity of a preceding syllable, the first syllable of e.g. ἵππος or ἐννέα being always 'heavy' (see p. 104) although the vowel is short. And potentially the distinction between single and double consonants may be responsible for differences of meaning, as in ὄρρος 'rump' beside ὄρος 'mountain', or ἐκαλύπτομεν 'we concealed' beside ἐκκαλύπτομεν 'we reveal'. In English double consonants are pronounced as such only when (as in ἐκκαλύπτομεν) they are divided between separate words or elements of a compound word—e.g. *hip-pocket, leg-glide, disservice, unnamed* (distinct from *unaimed*). In other contexts the written double consonants have no function except to indicate that the preceding vowel is short—e.g. in *sitting, shilling, penny, copper*.[2] It is, therefore, the compound type of word in English that provides the model for the pronunciation of double consonants in Greek.

In early Greek inscriptions the double consonants are written single (cf. *VL*, p. 11); but at Athens the double writing makes its appearance by the end of the 6 c. B.C.

In pure Attic dialect the geminate σσ does not occur except in compounds such as συσσιτεῖν (from συν-σιτεῖν). For in some words, where various other dialects have σσ, Attic (like Ionic) has simplified this to σ: e.g. ἔσονται, κατεδίκασαν, μέσος beside

---

* An asterisk after a term indicates that it is explained in the phonetic introduction.

[1] Inscriptional spellings often show doubling of the first consonant of a group, particularly if this is σ (e.g. 5 c. B.C. Attic μαλισστα); but such doubling is not distinctive; its purpose is uncertain, and it may be intended only to show that the group is divided between two syllables.

[2] In Middle English long vowels were generally shortened before two consonants (cf. *wisdom* beside *wise*); and in Early Modern English double consonants between vowels were simplified. Since, however, the double writing served to indicate the shortness of the vowel, it was retained and further extended to words which originally had a single consonant (as *peni, coper*).

Lesbian εσσονται, κατεδικασσαν, μεσσοσ;[3] and in other words, where most other dialects have σσ, Attic (like Boeotian) shows ττ: e.g. γλῶττα, τέτταρες, πράττειν beside Ionic γλῶσσα, τέσσερες, πρήσσειν. But, like many literary languages, literary Attic was subject to influences from outside the restricted area of the spoken dialect, most particularly from Ionic. And one of the most characteristic features of this influence is the substitution of forms with σσ for the ττ of 'pure' Attic as exemplified by the inscriptions.[4] In fact in tragedy, and in prose works up to and including Thucydides, the ττ of Attic is almost entirely avoided. Even though normal Attic grammar was used, and Attic phonology generally adopted, it seems that the ττ was felt as something of a provincialism by contrast with the σσ of most of the rest of the Greek-speaking world—all the more to be avoided as a characteristic of the speech of the 'συοβοιωτοί'; and even false Ionicisms (notably ἡσσᾶσθαι as against Attic ἡττᾶσθαι and Ionic ἐσσοῦσθαι) were liable to be perpetrated in avoidance of this shibboleth.

Although the Attic forms came more and more to gain literary acceptance (and not only in comedy and oratory, where local forms would be particularly appropriate),[5] it was not long before the influence of the Koine began again to reinforce the claims of the general Greek σσ. Thus, whereas Xenophon had favoured the ττ forms, already in Aeneas Tacticus (4–3 c. b.c.) one finds 78 cases of σσ as against 24 of ττ; and, in spite of the

[3] Inscriptional forms are rendered, as in the original, without accents or breathings, or distinction of final ς; current word-divisions are however employed.

[4] From the beginning these show ττ except in non-Attic names such as (5 c. b.c.) ηαλικαρνασσιοι. In the 4 c. there begin to appear a few forms with σσ: e.g. in 338 one instance of θαλασσα (but θαλαττα still general in the 3 c.), and towards the end of the century the Koine word βασιλισσα, which is always so written. Otherwise Attic inscriptions continue to show ττ up to the time of Augustus. The θαλασσα example, however, is in a decree containing an oath required by Philip of Macedon from members of the League of Corinth after Chaeronea, and Threatte (p. 538) suggests that the form is due to the 'international character' of the text. Other 4 c. -σσ- forms are found in contexts of poetic diction.

Even after Augustus -ττ- forms continue to appear in some words: e.g. φυλαττειν beside θαλασσα c. a.d. 150.

[5] In oratory Pericles is said to have been the first to adopt the ττ forms (Aelius Dionysius, fr. 298 Schwabe), allegedly for reasons of euphony (cf. Plato Comicus, fr. 30 Kock: ἔσωσας ἡμᾶς ἐκ τῶν σίγμα τῶν Εὐριπίδου, with clear reference to *Medea*, 476 f.). See also Stanford, pp. 7 f., 53 f.

artificial revival of ττ by the 'Atticists', the Koine itself shows few examples of it (most notably ἡττᾶσθαι; note also modern Greek πιττάκι from Attic πιττάκιον); indeed, even the Atticists were liable to overlook an occasional σσ when their attention was concentrated on other matters.

The ττ of pure Attic is part of an isogloss having its probable point of origin in Boeotian (which even has e.g. μεττω, εψαφιττατο beside Attic μέσου, ἐψηφίσατο). This ττ does not derive directly from the σσ shown by other dialects; but both ττ and σσ are separate developments from an earlier more complex sound, and this fact has given rise to some speculation about the nature of the sounds which they represent. The matter is discussed in more detail below (pp. 60 f.).

The value of orthographic γγ is separately discussed under γ = [ŋ] (pp. 35 ff.), and that of ρρ under ρ (pp. 41 ff.).[6]

(i) Voiceless* plosives*

In Greek, as in a number of modern languages, there were two distinct varieties of voiceless plosive, unaspirated* (π, τ, κ) and aspirated* (φ, θ, χ). Their distinctiveness is demonstrated by minimally different pairs such as πόρος/φόρος, πάτος/πάθος, λέκος/λέχος. Similar oppositions are found in Sanskrit and the modern languages derived from it (e.g. Hindi kānā 'one-eyed'/khānā 'to eat'), and there extend also to the voiced plosives (e.g. Hindi bāt 'thing'/bhāt 'cooked rice'). Both aspirated and unaspirated plosives are indeed also found in English; the initial t of top, for example, is clearly aspirated, but the t of stop is not. Here, however, the contrast is not distinctive—it is not 'phonemic' but merely 'allophonic' (see p. 9); for the two varieties never occur in identical environments, the non-aspiration being a special characteristic of the position after s (unlike in classical Attic, where e.g. both στένω and σθένω occur).

[6] Note, however, that RP provides no model for a double [r] sound (the difference between e.g. four elms and four realms is comparable with that between an ocean and a notion: cf. pp. 101 f.).

14

The two varieties were categorized by the Greek grammarians as (γράμμα) ψιλόν ('smooth, plain', i.e. unaspirated) and δασύ ('rough', i.e. aspirated). The expected Latin translation of these terms would be (*littera*) *lenis* and *aspera* (as in the case of *spiritus lenis/asper* translating πνεῦμα ψιλόν/δασύ for the 'smooth' and 'rough' breathings). But in fact the Latin terms, as found e.g. in Priscian, are *tenuis* and *aspirata*; and *tenuis* is still occasionally encountered as a term for the voiceless unaspirated plosives in modern works of a conservative kind.

(a) Unaspirated*

The fact that aspirated and unaspirated plosives were distinguished in Greek means that aspiration must be suppressed in the latter if confusion is to be avoided; such a pronunciation comes more readily to native speakers of e.g. French than to those of English or German, where voiceless plosives, more particularly in initial position, are generally aspirated. Apart from the evidence of its differential function, the unaspirated pronunciation of π, τ, κ in Greek is strongly suggested by the term ψιλόν, and further supported by statements that those consonants are 'smooth' 'which occur without the expulsion of breath' (†Ps.-Aristotle, *De Audibilibus*, 804 b, 8–11)[7] or 'which gently propel the air' (†Aristides Quintilianus, *De Musica* ii. 11, p. 76 WI.; cf. †i. 20, p. 41).

All this evidence is comparatively late, but the same pronunciation is indicated for a very early period by the operation of what is termed 'Grassmann's Law',[8] whereby the first of two originally aspirated syllable-initials in a word loses its aspiration. In the case of an initial vowel, a form such as (present) ἔχω [ekhō] involves loss of the initial aspiration [h] ('rough breathing') by comparison with (future) ἕξω [heksō], where there is no aspirated consonant following. The same law as applied to an initial voiceless plosive produces contrasts of the

---

[7] Texts of references marked thus (†) are given on pp. 162 ff.

[8] After its discovery in 1862 by the mathematician and linguist Hermann Grassmann.

type (gen. sing.) τριχός: (dat. plur.) θριξί. Thus τ is to θ as zero is to [h]—in other words τ stands for [t] as θ stands for [th], i.e. τ is unaspirated, and is therefore appropriately described by the same term (ψιλόν) as the 'smooth breathing'.

Finally the unaspirated pronunciation is entirely in accordance with related forms in Sanskrit: thus e.g. πατήρ = Skt. *pitấ* where *p* and *t* are known from the ancient Indian phonetic treatises to have been unaspirated[9] (Sanskrit in fact also has its own version of Grassmann's Law, giving alternations such as (pres.) *budhyate*: (fut.) *bhotsyati*).

The voiceless unaspirated plosives, like the other plosive classes, occur with bilabial* (π), dental* (τ), and velar* (κ) articulation. They are described by Dionysius of Halicarnassus, for example, as being produced respectively 'from the extremities of the lips', 'by the tongue being pressed against the front of the mouth at the upper teeth', and 'by the tongue rising to the palate near the throat' (†*De Compositione Verborum* xiv, p. 56 UR).

τ The description of the dentals as being produced 'κατὰ τοὺς μετεώρους ὀδόντας' is rather imprecise and could possibly refer to an alveolar* rather than a purely dental contact. But modern Greek shows a dental pronunciation, and in relatively ancient times this receives support from transcriptions into Prakrit (Middle Indian) on coins of the Greek kings of Bactria and India in the 1 and 2 c. B.C. For in Prakrit (as in Sanskrit and the modern Indian languages) there is a characteristic distinction between dental consonants (romanized as *t* etc.) and 'retroflex' consonants (*ṭ* etc.), the latter being articulated with the inverted tongue-tip on the gums behind the upper teeth. When English words containing alveolar plosives are spoken by Indians or borrowed into modern Indian languages, the English sounds in question are normally rendered by the Indian retroflexes: thus e.g. Eng. *station* becomes Hindi *sṭeśan*. But the Greek τ, θ, δ regularly appear as Prakrit dentals and not

---

[9] The Sanskrit grammarians describe the aspirated and unaspirated plosives as '*mahāprāṇa*' and '*alpaprāṇa*', i.e. 'having big/little breath' respectively: cf. Allen, pp. 37 f.

16

retroflexes—e.g. *Evukrātidasa*, *Agathukreyasa*, *Diyamedasa* = Εὐ-κρατίδου, ᾿Αγαθοκλέους, Διομήδου; they are therefore likely to have been true dentals, as e.g. in French, and not alveolars as in English.

κ As in many languages, the precise point of articulation of the velar series may have varied to some extent according to the following vowel, i.e. further forward before a front* vowel and further back before a back* vowel. Such variation would, of course, be non-distinctive and so, by phonemic principles, would not demand symbolization, but would be liable to be indicated if, by historical accident, a symbol happened to be available (cf. *VL*, pp. 14 f.). Thus in the oldest Attic inscriptions one finds before the vowel o the symbol Ϙ (κόππα), which had represented the Semitic uvular plosive [q] (*'qōf'*): e.g. (pre-550 B.C.) ευδιϙοσ, but ανδοκιδεσ. This practice, however, ceased at an early date, and with the official adoption of the Ionic alphabet in the archonship of Eucleides (403–2 B.C.) the sign no longer existed (except as a numeral = 90,[10] where it retained its original alphabetical position between π = 80 and ρ = 100, with various later shapes, as e.g. ꝗ, ϛ, ꙯). It survived in the west Greek alphabet, and thence as the Q of Latin (cf. Quintilian, i. 4. 9).

There is no evidence in ancient times for the 'palatalized' pronunciation of κ as [kʸ] before front vowels which is normal in modern Greek.

κ occurring at the end of the preposition ἐκ seems to have been assimilated to the type of consonant which followed, i.e. voiced* or aspirated (cf. Threatte, pp. 579 ff.). Hence we regularly find in 5 c. Attic inscriptional spellings of the type εγ βυζαντιο, εγ δελφον, εγδοι (= ἐκδῷ), εγ λινδο, εγλεγεν (= ἐκλέγειν), and, less regularly, e.g. εχ θετον (= ἐκ θητῶν), εχ φυλεσ. The latter practice, however, ceases at the beginning of the 3 c. B.C., and εκ also becomes normal before voiced initials from the 1 c. B.C. The writing of εκ before both voiced and aspirated consonants is likely to be normative rather than phonetic (just as in English we generalize the use of *s* for the plural, even after voiced

[10] See further p. 47, n. 85.

sounds, e.g. in *dogs*, where it is pronounced [z]; this normative spelling is regular in our texts, but probably misrepresents the actual pronunciation, viz. as [eg] before voiced[11] and [ekh] before aspirated consonants (other than χ).[12]

(b) Aspirated*

The evidence for this category is required primarily to show that in classical Attic the sounds written φ, θ, χ were aspirated plosives, like the *ph*, *th*, *kh* of Sanskrit and the modern Indian languages (and similar to the initial *p*, *t*, *k* of English or German), and not fricatives* as in modern Greek (where φ = labio-dental* [f] as in English *foot*, θ = dental [θ] as in English *thin*, and χ = velar [x] or palatal* [ç] like the German '*ach*' and '*ich*' sounds respectively). There is no doubt that at a later date the aspirated plosives did develop to fricatives (see pp. 23 ff.), and so the main task will be to prove that this had not happened as early as the 5–4 c. B.C.

The earliest evidence from ancient descriptions lies in the use of the term δασύ, as against ψιλόν for the unaspirated series (see p. 15). It is first found in the passage from the *De Audib*. cited above,[13] where the sounds to which it applies are described as 'expelling the air immediately with the sounds';[14] but the use of the term may well go back further than this. An interesting point about the choice of the terms δασύ and ψιλόν is that the same binary opposition is found in non-technical, material uses—e.g. Hdt., iv. 175, where a wooded ridge is contrasted with the treelessness of the rest of Libya; similarly iii. 32 contrasts a lettuce-stalk with and without its leaves, and iii. 108

---

[11] Other than ρ—but in fact as an initial this was probably voiceless (see pp. 41 f.). Before σκ the κ seems to have been lost altogether (thus εσκυρου = ἐκ Σκύρου, 329 B.C.), but was also analogically restored (hence e.g. ἐκσκαλεύω).

[12] See p. 27.

[13] The terms δασύτης and ψιλότης are indeed found in Aristotle, *Poetics*, 1456b, but the passage is probably an interpolation.

[14] The words used are 'εὐθέως μετὰ τῶν φθόγγων'. If the work is of early authorship (? Straton), μετά with the genitive should mean 'with', not (as Sturtevant, p. 77) 'after', and this might be interpreted as implying simultaneous breath, i.e. friction. But the use of the adverb εὐθέως makes this interpretation improbable (the genitive is found with μετά meaning 'after' in Byzantine Greek).

the presence and absence of fur on an animal. In all such cases it is a 'privative' opposition, contrasting the presence with the absence of an additional discrete feature, rather than one inherent quality with another; Dionysius (*De Comp.* xiv, p. 57 UR) does in fact refer to the category of δασέα as having 'τὴν τοῦ πνεύματος **προσθήκην**'. Such a terminology would be eminently appropriate to the opposition of aspirated and unaspirated consonants, but hardly to the distinction between fricative and plosive, i.e. between incomplete and complete closure of the organs. Moreover, the same terminology is employed to distinguish the 'rough' from the 'smooth' breathing[15] (cf. p. 15), and there is no doubt that this is a privative opposition of the aspirate [h] to zero (see pp. 52 ff.).

The grammatical tradition divides the consonants into two primary categories, ἡμίφωνα and ἄφωνα, corresponding to continuants* and plosives respectively; thus e.g. Dionysius Thrax, *Ars Gramm.*, p. 11 U, 'ἡμίφωνα μέν ἐστιν ὀκτώ· ζξψλμνρσ... ἄφωνα δέ ἐστιν ἐννέα, βγδκπτθφχ'. In Aristotle, *Poetics*, 1456b the latter are described as 'having contact' (μετὰ προσβολῆς) like the former, but as not being pronounceable without a vowel. The allocation of φ, θ, χ to the category of ἄφωνα is a fair indication of their plosive, non-fricative nature, since fricatives would be classifiable with σ as ἡμίφωνα, being continuants and so 'independently pronounceable'. The same allocation is found even at a much later date in e.g. Aristides Quint. (*De Mus.* ii. 11, p. 76 WI), who further speaks of the δασέα as being pronounced 'ἔνδοθεν ἐκ φάρυγγος'—which would be a commendable description of aspirates but completely inappropriate to fricatives, since these do not involve any difference in glottal activity but only in oral aperture.

Other clear evidence comes from the language itself. When a final voiceless unaspirated plosive (π, τ, κ), as in e.g. οὐκ or elided ἀπ', κατ', stands before an aspirated vowel (i.e. initial [h]), it is changed to φ, θ, χ; which can only mean that φ, θ, χ here stand for aspirated [ph], [th], [kh],[16] and not for

---

[15] E.g. *Suppl. Artis Dionysianae*, p. 107 U.

[16] Mention may here be made of the forms οὐθείς, οὐθέν, μηθείς, μηθέν etc. which

fricatives.[17] In such cases a spelling of the type καθ' ἡμέραν, with the aspiration also marked on the following vowel, is, strictly speaking, redundant, since the aspiration is transferred to the consonant; it is a normalizing tradition originating in Byzantine practice, but is not general in those inscriptions which otherwise indicate the rough breathing (see p. 52), just as it is not in compounds such as καθημέριος. A similar transfer of aspiration is found in crasis, e.g. τῇ ἡμέρᾳ → θἠμέρᾳ, καὶ ὅπως → χὤπως (note also, with intervening ρ, the compound προ-ὁδος → φροῦδος: cf. p. 43); but here the Byzantine tradition also omits the original vowel-aspiration and marks the combination by the sign κορωνίς, having the same shape as the apostrophe (and, in modern printing, as the smooth breathing). In the case of compounds and established formulae the effects of elision and crasis do not of course necessarily prove the aspirated, non-fricative nature of φ, θ, χ for the 5 c. B.C., but only for the period of formation; but the continuation of this pronunciation is indicated by the same effects in the case of independent words.

Further indications for an early period are provided by Grassmann's Law (see p. 15), which proves that at the time of its operation the relationship between the values of e.g. θ and τ was the same as that between [h] and zero, i.e. presence and absence of aspiration. The law applies particularly clearly to verbal reduplication. Reduplicative syllables normally repeat the initial consonant of the root—e.g. πέ-πω-κα; but if the root-initial is φ, θ or χ, the reduplicative initial is π, τ or κ—e.g. πέ-φευγ-α, τί-θη-μι, κέ-χυ-μαι. The important point here is that the reduplicative initial is a *plosive*, which would not be expected if the root-initial were a fricative (roots beginning with σ, which *is* a fricative, form their reduplicative syllables with initial σ,

replace οὐδείς etc. in Late Attic and the Koine (though οὐδεμία etc. remain unchanged). This presumably indicates a devoicing and aspiration of the final consonant of elided οὐδέ: it is improbable that (as Threatte, p. 472, suggests) the θ here stands for a *voiced* aspirate [dh], since such a consonant would be quite isolated in Greek (and indeed in all IE languages other than Sanskrit and possibly Armenian). The -θ- forms first appear and become normal in inscriptions in the 4 c. B.C., but are again replaced by the -δ- forms in the 1 c. B.C. (as in Modern Greek δεν).

[17] The fricative pronunciation of a comparable junction of plosive + *h* as in e.g. [gouθəm] for *Gotham*, N.Y., is a '*spelling* pronunciation', based on the non-junctional value of the digraph *th* in English (contrast [gotəm] for *Gotham*, Notts.).

[h] or zero: e.g. σέ-σηρ-α, ῐ-στη-μι, ἔ-σταλ-μαι). Evidence for the continuation of the aspirated plosive pronunciation into the 5 c. B.C. and later is provided by occasional new recurrences of this type of dissimilation, as revealed by inscriptional spellings—e.g. 4 c. αρκεθεωροσ beside αρχεθεωροσ. Similar indications are given by occasional *as*similations such as late 5 c. *h*εχον for ἔχον, with extension of aspiration to the initial[18] (for details see Threatte, pp. 455 ff.).

Further evidence comes from the procedure of 'expressive doubling' of consonants (as in e.g. 'familiar' ἄττα, 'hypocoristic' Δικκώ, 'imitative' ποππύζω). For when the doubled consonant is φ, θ or χ, the resulting form shows πφ, τθ, κχ—e.g. ἀπφῦς, τίτθη, κακχάζω. Such a spelling indicates that the lengthening of these consonants consisted in a stop* element (π, τ, κ), which would not be appropriate if the original sound were a fricative but entirely so if it were a plosive: thus [ph, th, kh] → [pph, tth, kkh]. Here again, however, the proof only refers to the time at which the doubling took place, and in many cases this must have been long before the 5 c. B.C. Similar evidence is provided by the apocopated forms of prepositions, as in Hom. κὰπ φάλαρα, where the assimilation of the final consonant to the following initial produces a stop.

When in Attic the nasal ν was followed by the fricative σ, the nasal was generally lost or assimilated to the fricative—thus e.g. συν + σιτεῖν → συσσιτεῖν, συν + στέλλειν → συστέλλειν. Inscriptions show that this was not simply an ancient feature inherited in compounds, since they also apply it at the junction of separate words—e.g. 5 c. B.C. εσ σανιδι, ε στελει (= ἐν στήλῃ). This, however, does *not* occur before φ, θ, χ, but the ν is either retained or changed in type (to μ, γ before φ, χ: cf. p. 33) in the same way as before an unaspirated plosive: thus e.g. τημ φυλην (376 B.C.) as τεμ πολιν (416), *h*ιερογ χρεματον (410) as τογ κηρυκα (353). This treatment contrasts with that of modern Greek, where before the now *fricative* φ, θ, χ a final ν is lost in the same

---

[18] It does not affect the significance of such evidence that spellings of this type may indicate not so much phonetic assimilation as an analysis of aspiration as applying to a sequence rather than to individual sounds (theoretical discussions by Z. S. Harris, *Language*, 20 (1944), pp. 181 ff.; Allen, *BSOAS*, 13 (1951), pp. 939 ff.; H. M. Hoenigswald, *Phonetica*, 11 (1964), p. 212).

way as before σ and other continuants—e.g. acc. sing. τὸ φίλο as τὸ σουγιά and *unlike* e.g. τὸν πατέρα (= [tombatéra]).

Some further confirmation of the plosive value of φ in classical times is perhaps provided by the presumably onomatopoeic πομφόλυξ, πομφολύζειν, for the sound of bubbling; and by the surely deliberate use of π and φ in Pindar's description of a volcano (*Pyth.* i, 40 ff.; esp. ἀλλ᾽ ἐν ὄρφναισιν πέτρας φοίνισσα κυλινδομένα φλὸξ ἐς βαθεῖαν φέρει πόντου πλάκα σὺν πατάγῳ).

Finally, when in e.g. Attic tragedy a short vowel is followed by a group comprising a plosive followed by a liquid, the syllable containing the vowel may be treated as light (see further pp. 106 ff.). It is, therefore, highly significant that the same option exists in the case of φ, θ, χ + liquid, as e.g. Sophocles, *O.C.*, 354–5, ...Καδμείων λάθρᾳ | ἃ τοῦδ᾽ ἐχρήσθη... The same is also true of voiceless plosives with nasals, and here again the option also exists in the case of a form such as σταθμός, whereas it does *not* where a fricative (σ) is followed by a nasal as in e.g. κόσμος.

The evidence thus seems conclusive that in 5 c. Attic φ, θ, χ represented *plosives* (as π, τ, κ) and NOT *fricatives* (as σ, or as φ, θ, χ in modern Greek).

The continuation of the plosive pronunciation into a later period is shown by the fact that Latin renders Greek φ at first as a simple *p*, later as *ph* (e.g. *Pilipus, Philippus*), but never in classical Latin times as *f*, which would have been appropriate for a fricative pronunciation. The fact, on the other hand, that e.g. Latin *Fabius* is rendered in Greek as Φάβιος is no counter-indication even for the period of such transcriptions; for Greek had no other way in which to represent the Latin *f*, and in such circumstances it would be quite normal to represent it by the symbol for the nearest available sound in Greek, even though this were still a plosive [ph]. For although fricatives and aspirates are not identical, they are phonetically (and often historically) *related*—in fact the ancient Indian phoneticians apply the same term[19] both to the air-stream of the fricatives and to the aspirated release of the plosives. There is an exact parallel

---

[19] *ūṣman*, lit. 'heat, steam, vapour', glossed in this use as *vāyu*, 'wind'; cf. Allen, p. 26.

to this in modern times, when unsophisticated speakers of an Indian language like Hindi borrow English words containing an *f*; for, having no fricative [f] in their own speech, they substitute for it the aspirated plosive—thus e.g. English *film* is rendered by *philam*. It was presumably in such a context that Cicero ridiculed a Greek witness who could not pronounce the first consonant of the name *Fundanius* (†Quintilian, i. 4. 14).

However, there is no doubt that, as modern Greek shows, the aspirated plosives did eventually change to fricatives. Evidence is sometimes quoted which would suggest that the beginnings of such a change could be traced to the 2 c. B.C. As mentioned above, the Greek grammarians generally agree in allocating φ, θ, χ to the same category of ἄφωνα as π, τ, κ, β, δ, γ, and not to the category of ἡμίφωνα (as σ). Sextus Empiricus, however, (*Adv. Gramm.* = *Math. I* 102) mentions that 'some people' classify φ, θ, χ with the ἡμίφωνα; he is himself writing in the 2 c. A.D., but Diogenes Laertius (vii. 57) seems to attribute a system of only six ἄφωνα (π, τ, κ, β, δ, γ) to the Stoic Diogenes Babylonius of the 2 c. B.C., thereby implying a classification of φ, θ, χ as ἡμίφωνα. But other evidence is against so early a development, and the classification may simply be a Stoic aberration. It is true that Plato in the *Cratylus* (†427 A) classes φ with σ in a category of 'πνευματώδη'; but he is here mainly concerned with the needs of his 'gestural' theory of the origin of language,[20] and the classification provides no grounds for assuming a fricative pronunciation of φ (cf. also p. 22 with note).

With one problematic exception (*Fedra* in *CIL* I², 1413: cf. Schwyzer, p. 158) the first clear evidence for a fricative pronunciation comes from the 1 c. A.D. in Pompeian spellings such as *Dafne* (= Δάφνη), and is particularly compelling in view of the form *lasfe*: λασφη (= λάσθη). For the interchange of dental and labial is only likely to take place in the case of fricative articulations, [θ] and [f], which are acoustically rather similar (compare the substitution of Cockney [f] for RP [θ] (*th*), or the Russian substitution of ф for Byzantine and

---

[20] Cf. Allen, *TPS*, 1948, p. 51.

modern Greek θ). From the 2 c. A.D. the representation of φ by Latin *f* becomes common, and Latin grammarians have to give rules when to spell with *f* and when with *ph*.[21] In the 4 c. Wulfila renders Greek φ and θ by Gothic *f* and *þ* (e.g. *þaiaufilus* = Θεόφιλος);[22] χ is normally rendered by *k*, but in any case Gothic probably had no [x] (velar fricative) except as a non-syllable-initial allophone of *h*.

It is possible that in some quarters the labial φ may have developed its fricative pronunciation earlier than θ or χ; for in the inscriptions of the Jewish catacombs in Rome from the 2–3 c. A.D. φ regularly appears as *f*, but θ appears as *th* and χ as *ch* or *c*. This in itself would not be conclusive proof of a plosive pronunciation for θ and χ, since Latin had no sign for a dental or velar fricative (though the alveolar* *s* might occasionally have been expected for the dental);[23] but in Greek inscriptions from the same source χ tends to be confused with κ (e.g. χιτε = κεῖται) and θ with τ (e.g. εθων = ἐτῶν, παρτενοσ = παρθένος), whereas no such confusion is found in the case of φ and π.[24] These features may of course be dismissed as peculiarities of the dialect of the Jewish community; however, such a phased development as these inscriptions suggest is not improbable in a more general context, since labial plosives in a number of languages show a greater tendency to lose their stop articulation and develop to fricatives than do plosives of other series. In Ossetic, for example, (an Iranian language spoken in the Caucasus) Old Iranian *t* and *k* have developed initially to the aspirated plosives [th] and [kh]; but Old Iranian *p* has gone beyond the [ph] stage to give a fricative [f], e.g. (western dialect) *fidæ* 'father' from Old Iranian *pitā*,[25] as against *kænun* (= [khənun]) 'to do, make' from Old Iranian *kunau-*.[26]

[21] Thus Caper, *GL*, vii, p. 95 K; Sacerdos, *GL*, vi, p. 451 K; Diomedes, *GL*, i, p. 423 K.

[22] The Gothic letter-forms in question, on the other hand, are not derived from the Greek; but this need not be for phonetic reasons.

[23] As in the form *Apollopisius* = -*Pythius* found in the *Notae Tironeanae*: cf. also p. 26.

[24] Cf. H. J. Leon, *TAPA*, 58 (1927), pp. 210 ff.

[25] Armenian has gone a stage further, with *hayr* from Indo-European *pətēr*, and Celtic still further with (Old Irish) *athir*.

[26] Cf. H. Pedersen, *Die gemeinindoeuropäischen u. die vorindoeuropäischen Verschlusslaute* (Dan. Hist. Filol. Medd., 32, no. 5), p. 13.

On the fricative pronunciation of φ it should finally be noted that none of the evidence enables us to say with certainty whether at a particular period it was a *bilabial** fricative (phonetic symbol [ɸ]),[27] though this may well have been an intermediate stage in its development to the labio-dental.

It may be that a scholarly pronunciation of φ, θ, χ as plosives continued for some time in the schools. A Demotic Egyptian text of the 2 c. A.D. containing some Greek transliterations shows that Greek φ and χ there represented Egyptian *ph* and *kh*, and not the fricatives *f* and *ḫ*; and in the Coptic writing devised in the 3 c. A.D. by Egyptian Christians largely on the basis of the Greek alphabet, φ, θ, χ are used to represent aspirated plosives or a combination of plosive and *h*. Elsewhere, both the Armenian and Georgian alphabets, formed around the 5 c. A.D., use symbols based on Greek χ to represent their aspirated plosive *k'* [kh] and not their fricative *x* [x]; moreover, Greek words borrowed early into Armenian also show *k'* and not *x* for χ (e.g. *k'art* = χάρτης); only after the 10 c. does Armenian *x* or *š* begin to appear for Greek χ. There is even possibly some evidence that the plosive pronunciation continued in the schools up to the time when the Glagolitic alphabet was formed in the 9 c. for the writing of Old Church Slavonic.

However, there is little doubt that generally speaking the fricative pronunciation was well established in the Byzantine period. In such circumstances the earlier grammarians' descriptions of the φ-θ-χ and π-τ-κ series as δασύ and ψιλόν respectively will of course have become meaningless; and the Byzantine commentators make various unconvincing attempts to explain them as applied to fricatives. Perhaps the most ingenious is that of an anonymous treatise Περὶ προσῳδιῶν inserted between two of the prefaces to the scholia on the grammar of Dionysius Thrax in the Codex Vaticanus gr. 14—the editor of which rightly comments, 'multa eius auctor hariolatur'.[28] The term δασύ, this author suggests, is used

---

[27] Such sounds occur in e.g. Japanese (as in *Fuji*, or *firumu* = Eng. *film*); in the Ewe language of Africa they contrast significantly with labio-dental [f]—e.g. [ɸu] 'bone': [fu] 'feather'.

[28] A. Hilgard, *Scholia in Dionysii Thracis artem grammaticam* (= *Grammatici Graeci*, I. iii), p. xxvi.

metaphorically from the 'thicket' (δάσος) of trees on a mountain, since when the gusts of wind blow upon it they produce just such sounds, whereas no such effect is produced in 'unwooded' (ψιλότερος) country! (†*Scholia in Dion. Thr.*, p. 152 H).

In some of the Greek dialects other than Attic the development of the aspirated plosives to fricatives seems to have occurred in quite early times. In the case of φ and χ we can hardly expect literary evidence for this, since an Attic transcription of [f] or [x] could hardly use other than the symbols φ and χ (cf. p. 22). But in the case of θ, the change to a dental fricative [θ] as in modern Greek might be approximately represented in Attic by the alveolar fricative σ; and we do in fact find Laconian speech so represented in Attic writers—e.g. ναὶ τὼ σιώ, παρσένε in Aristophanes, σύματος in Thucydides. In the 4 c. B.C. spellings of this kind appear inscriptionally at Sparta (but the early σιῶν = θεῶν in the text of Alcman may be due to later grammarians). σ for θ is also reported as a Laconian feature by Apollonius Dyscolus (*De Constr.*, p. 54 U). It remains open to question whether the σ in these cases represents a dental [θ] or whether in fact this had already changed in Laconian to the alveolar [s] which seems to be attested in its modern descendant Tsaconian. At an earlier period, however, if the form ϝορϝαια found on a 6 c. ivory relief in the sanctuary of Artemis Orthia at Sparta is not simply an error, it would indicate a value [θ] for θ and [f] for φ.[29]

The places of articulation for the aspirated plosives φ, θ, χ are the same as for the unaspirated π, τ, κ (see p. 16).

Note on φθ, χθ

These combinations call for some comment in view of suggestions that they do not mean what they appear to mean, i.e. a succession of two aspirated plosives. Apart from inherited groups of this type (e.g. in ὀφθαλμός, ἐχθρός), a labial or velar plosive is regularly aspirated by assimilation when it comes to stand before the -θη- suffix of the aorist passive, e.g. in ἐλείφθην (from λείπω), ἐδέρχθην (from δέρκομαι); in inscriptions the

[29] Cf. pp. 23 f. above, and R. Arena, *Glotta*, 44 (1966), pp. 14 ff.

preposition ἐκ is also often assimilated to εχ before an initial aspirated plosive (see p. 17), which gives rise to the additional combination χφ in e.g. εχ φυλεσ and compound εχφο[ρησαντι] (329 B.C.). The reason given for doubting the straightforward interpretation of these groups is that it would be impossible to pronounce an aspirated plosive when followed by another plosive—e.g. 'Combinations like φθόνος...χθών...constitute a physiological impossibility in any actual language'.[30] This *a priori* dogma, frequently repeated in older works and even in some reputable modern ones,[31] has no basis whatever in reality. Any phonetician will confirm and demonstrate the possibility of such sequences, and one can hear them as a normal feature of a number of living languages—as e.g. Armenian *ałotʻkʻ* [aɣothkh] 'prayer', or Georgian *pʻkʻvili* 'flour', *tʻitʻkʻmis* 'almost', or Abaza (N.W. Caucasian) *apʻqʻa* 'in front'. In fact there is a rule in Georgian that if a plosive consonant is followed by another located further back in the mouth, it *must* have the same kind of articulation as the following consonant—thus, if the second is aspirated, so must the first be (otherwise dissimilar groups can occur, as e.g. *tʻbilisi* 'Tiflis' with voiceless aspirated followed by voiced unaspirated plosive);[32] sequences of aspirated followed by unaspirated plosive are also common in modern Indian languages, e.g. in Hindi participial forms such as *likhtā* 'writing', *ūbhtā* 'rising'.

There is thus no phonetic improbability whatever about the first consonant of the groups φθ and χθ being aspirated as well as the second. What has usually been suggested by the objectors to such groups is that the writing with φ and χ was a mere convention for unaspirated π and κ; but it is difficult to see how such a convention could have come about, since in the geminate groups πφ, τθ, κχ (see p. 21), where the first element certainly was unaspirated, the spelling with π, τ, κ is normal;[33]

---

[30] A. N. Jannaris, *Historical Greek Grammar*, p. 58.

[31] E.g. Lejeune, p. 59; Lupaş, pp. 17 f., 31.

[32] Cf. H. Vogt, 'Structure phonémique du géorgien', *NTS*, 18 (1958), pp. 5 ff.

[33] The occasional writing of e.g. Σαφφώ for Σαπφώ is readily explainable as a graphic doubling after the analogy of other (unaspirated) geminated forms. The isolated εχ χαλκιδοσ (445 B.C.) beside usual εκ χ. of the same period could be a simple error, as εχ λεσβου. Eustathius (on *Il.* xii, 208) observes 'ἀνὴρ γὰρ Ἕλλην οὐ διπλάζει τὰ δασέα'.

and even if such a convention were established, we should expect to find numerous misspellings based on the presumed actual pronunciation, whereas in fact there are only an insignificantly few (and non-Attic) examples—e.g. (7 c. Phocis) απθιτον. That an actual change in this direction may have taken place at a later date in Egyptian and Italian Greek is suggested by writings with πθ, κθ in papyri from the end of the 2 c. B.C., and by transcriptions into Latin, Demotic and Coptic. Modern Greek developments, however, suggest that this change was not general. Alternatively it has been suggested (cf. Threatte, p. 571) that the aspirates had 'lenis' (lax) articulation, and that it is this feature rather than the aspiration that is indicated by writing the first element of such groups as φ or χ. The same explanation has been proposed for the pre-Eucleidian writing of φσ, χσ (for later ψ, ξ: see p. 60).[34]

The pronunciation of the aspirated plosives should present no difficulty for English speakers, since models are available in the voiceless plosives of English, when these begin a stressed initial syllable (as in *pot*, *table*, etc.), particularly if they are emphatically pronounced. Some special effort is required in non-initial positions, and here it should be remembered that the aspirated plosive is *one* sound and not two, as may be seen from the fact that the preceding syllable in a word like σοφός is regularly light and not heavy;[35] for the φ belongs entirely to the following syllable (i.e. [so-phos]) and so is quite different from the pronunciation of English words like *saphead*, *fathead*,

[34] But Greek descriptive terminology (see pp. 29 ff.) does not fit in with this suggestion. For π etc. are voiceless and tense; and if φ etc. were voiceless and lax, *these* would be 'intermediate' between π etc. and β etc. (the latter being voiced and lax), as having one feature of each of the other series.

[35] A total of five exceptions from the whole of extant Greek literature (e.g. trochaic ὄφιν once each in Homer and Hipponax) may point to an occasional pronunciation which is of little statistical importance compared with the overwhelming general agreement of the evidence. Ancient authorities vary in their explanation of ὄφιν in *Il.* xii, 208; according to a scholiast on Hephaestion, for example, (p. 291 C) the heavy quantity is due to the aspiration (διὰ τὴν σφοδρότητα τοῦ πνεύματος), and according to Marius Victorinus (*GL*, vi, p. 67 K) is caused by lengthening of the φ; but the author of the treatise Περὶ ἑρμηνείας (255; *Rhet. Gr.*, iii, p. 317 Spengel) suggests that the syllable is in fact light, so that this would be a 'meiuric' line, deliberately used for effect. W. Schulze, *Quaestiones Epicae*, p. 431, comments, 'rem in suspenso relinquere tutissimum est'.

blockhead, where the plosive and the [h] are divided between separate syllables.[36]

However, there is a difficulty which most English speakers are likely to experience—namely, of clearly distinguishing the voiceless *un*aspirated plosives from the aspirated, both in speaking and hearing; and the result of an attempt at the correct pronunciation may thus only be confusion. There is consequently some practical justification, as a pedagogical device, for pronouncing the aspirated plosives, in the Byzantine manner, as fricatives; if this solution is adopted, however, care must be taken to pronounce the χ as a velar *fricative* (i.e. as in *loch*), and not, as often heard, indistinguishably from κ[37] (with consequent confusion between e.g. Κρόνος and χρόνος).

(ii) Voiced* plosives

In his classification of the category of consonants termed ἄφωνα (cf. p. 19) Dionysius Thrax (†*Ars Gramm.*, pp. 12 f. U) describes the series β, δ, γ as 'intermediate' (μέσα) between the aspirated and unaspirated; Dionysius of Halicarnassus (*De Comp.* xiv, pp. 55 f. UR) similarly refers to them variously as μέσα, κοινά, ἐπίκοινα, μέτρια, and μεταξύ. This terminology was continued by the Latin grammarians as *media* (a term still sometimes found, like *tenuis*, in current works: cf. p. 15).

There is no doubt that the sounds represented by β, δ, γ were *voiced*. They do not combine in groups with voiceless sounds (thus e.g. λέγω but λέλεκται), and are regularly rendered by voiced sounds in other languages—e.g. Latin *barbarus*, *draco*, *grammatica*. The question then arises why the Greeks described

---

[36] The fact that in some early forms of the Greek alphabet (as at Thera) φ and χ are represented by πh and κh is of no significance; it is simply a matter of a digraph being used for a single sound, where no special single symbol had been inherited (a single symbol was, however, available for modified use as [th], in the Semitic so-called 'emphatic' dental plosive '*ṭēt*'); one may compare the case of the aspirated plosives in modern Indian languages, where Hindi, for example, (using a Sanskritic script) has single symbols, but Urdu (using a Perso-Arabic script, which has not inherited such symbols) employs the unaspirated consonant-symbols combined with *h*; even the Sanskrit script has to use a conjunct character for the dialectal *ḷh* of Vedic.

[37] There is of course no need to follow modern Greek practice in pronouncing a *palatal* fricative [ç] before front vowels.

them as 'middle'. It has been suggested by Sturtevant (p. 86), following Kretschmer, that they were in fact voiced *aspirates*, rather like the *bh*, *dh*, *gh* of Sanskrit; but there is no evidence whatever for this, and, as Sturtevant has to recognize, transcriptions of Greek names on Indian coins show no such equivalence (Διομήδου, for example, is represented simply as *Diyamedasa* and not *Dhiyamedhasa*).

Whilst accepting that these consonants were normal voiced plosives, the attempt has been made to justify the Greek terminology as meaning that the voiced series was 'indifferent' to the opposition of aspirate/non-aspirate found in the voiceless series[38]—but this is probably to attribute too great a sophistication to Greek phonological theory.[39] More probably the use of such terms as μέσα simply indicates the writers' perplexity when faced with phenomena which were not describable within their favourite binary framework—in H. Ammann's expression,[40] a 'Verlegenheitsausdruck'. The truth is that European phonetics was slow to discover the nature of 'voice', i.e. glottal vibration, as a distinctive feature of consonants— though it had been familiar to the Indians from earliest times;[41] it remained completely unnoticed though the middle ages, and only began to be recognized in the nineteenth century, largely through the impact of Indian teaching. Aristotle does indeed observe (*Hist. An.* iv. 9, 535a) the function of the larynx in distinguishing vowels from consonants, but the matter is taken no further either by him or by later writers.

There seems no reason to doubt that in classical times the value of β, δ, γ was that of voiced plosives, much as the English *b*, *d* and 'hard' *g*, with places of articulation as for the corresponding voiceless sounds (see p. 16).

It is of course well known that in modern Greek these sounds have generally become fricatives, viz. [v], [ð], [ɣ]. But there is no reason to believe that this development had taken place until

---

[38] Thus H. M. Hoenigswald, 'Media, Neutrum und Zirkumflex', in *Festschrift A. Debrunner* (1954), pp. 209 ff.

[39] Cf. N. E. Collinge, 'The Greek use of the term "middle" in linguistic analysis', *Word*, 19 (1963), pp. 232 ff.

[40] *Glotta*, 24 (1935), p. 161. [41] Cf. Allen, pp. 33 ff.

a much later period. None of the philosophers or grammarians classifies β, δ, γ as ἡμίφωνα (cf. p. 19), which they would have done had they been fricatives; and in the *Cratylus* (†427 A) Plato specifically refers to the 'constriction' and 'pressure' of the tongue in pronouncing δ as well as τ. Other evidence is similar to that for the plosive (and against the fricative) pronunciation of the aspirates (see pp. 21 f.). Thus there is no loss of nasal consonants before β, δ, γ as there is before the fricative σ, or as before the modern Greek sounds (e.g. acc. sing. τὸ γάμο); and assimilation is found in inscriptional τεμ βολεν, πληγ γεσ (late 5 c., = τὴν βουλήν, πλὴν γῆς) just as in e.g. τεμ πολιν, τογ κηρυκα. In Attic tragedy and comedy a syllable containing a short vowel before a group consisting of β, δ, or γ plus ρ may be scanned light in the same way as before the groups π, τ, or κ plus ρ—which is also suggestive of a plosive value (see further pp. 106 ff.).

Amongst minor pieces of evidence may be mentioned the presumably alliterative πίνειν καὶ βινεῖν in Aristophanes, *Frogs*, 740[42] (cf. '*w*ine and *w*omen'), which is effectively so only if both initials are of the same, i.e. plosive, type. It seems likely also that Greek β still represented a plosive in the time of Cicero, who (†*Fam.* ix. 22. 3) identifies the pronunciation of βινεῖ with that of the Latin *bini*.

In the Jewish catacombs of Rome, inscriptions of the 2–3 c. A.D. regularly represent the Latin consonantal *u* (which was by then a fricative [v]) by the Greek β (e.g. βιξιτ); this, however, is not necessarily evidence for a fricative value of β, since, even if β were still a plosive in Greek, it was nevertheless the closest Greek sound to the Latin [v].[43]

There is some evidence in non-Attic dialects (Boeotian, Elean, Pamphylian) for a fricative development of these sounds from the 4 c. B.C. In some of these cases (and on Egyptian papyri) we find omission of γ between vowels of which the first is a front vowel (e.g. ολιοσ = ὀλίγος); this is at first sight suggestive of the modern Greek development of γ to [y] (via

---

[42] Cf. *Clouds*, 394: βροντὴ καὶ πορδὴ ὁμοίω.
[43] Cf. H. J. Leon, *TAPA*, 58 (1927), p. 227.

a voiced palatal fricative[44]), but the modern pronunciation applies only to the position *before* front vowels (e.g. ἔφαγε). This particular phenomenon is occasionally found in Attic from the late 4 c. B.C. (e.g. ολιαρχιαι); but it does not seem to have been a standard pronunciation; in fact Herodian (i, p. 141; †ii, p. 926 L) specifically states that Plato Comicus treated it as a barbarism in attributing it to the demagogue Hyperbolus.

When Wulfila established his orthography for Gothic in the 4 c. A.D., he adopted the Greek β, δ, γ to represent Gothic phonemes which in some cases were pronounced as voiced fricatives; but, in the absence of a phonemic contrast between voiced fricatives and plosives in Gothic, this need not indicate a fricative pronunciation for the Greek. Similar considerations apply to the rendering by symbols based on β, δ, γ of Armenian sounds which were probably voiced aspirates.[45] In the 9 c. A.D., however, the Cyrillic alphabet adopted β for the fricative [v], and used a modified letter for the plosive [b] (cf. Russian в, б), which is positive evidence for the fricative value of the Greek letter at that time.

It is not possible to establish with certainty at what precise period the fricative pronunciation of β, δ, γ developed. But certainly it had not done so in classical times.[46]

(iii) Labio-velars

Before leaving the plosive consonants, it may be mentioned that in Proto-Greek, and still preserved in Mycenaean, there was a series of LABIO-VELARS, i.e. velar plosives with simultaneous lip-rounding (as e.g. Latin *qu*: cf. *VL*, pp. 16 ff.). The Mycenaean symbols (which do not distinguish between voiced and

[44] Cf. Armenian *Diožēn* = Διογένης (11 c.) etc.; similarly in some modern Greek dialects.

[45] Cf. Allen, *ArchL.*, 3 (1951), pp. 134 f. Only from *c.* 10 c. A.D. is Greek β sometimes rendered by Armenian *v*: similarly γ by *l* (= voiced velar fricative from *c.* 8 c.); but spellings with *b*, *g* could simply represent learned transcriptions; there are occasional renderings of Greek δ by Arm. fricative *r*.

[46] Evidence from non-literary papyri suggests fricative pronunciations from about the 1 c. A.D., but only in particular environments (especially intervocalic); and here foreign influences may account for the development (cf. F. T. Gignac, 'The pronunciation of Greek stops in the papyri', *TAPA*, 101 (1970), pp. 185 ff.).

voiceless, aspirated and unaspirated) are transcribed with q; in all other dialects the labio-velars have been replaced by labials or (before front vowels) dentals[47]—e.g. Myc. *re-qo-me-no = leiq^{u}omenoi* (cf. λειπόμενοι), *-qe = -q^{u}e* (cf. τε), *-qo-ta = -q^{u}hontās* (cf. -φόντης), *su-qo-ta-o = sug^{u}otāōn* (cf. συβώτης).

(iv) Nasals

Greek has two special symbols for nasal consonants, μ and ν. The values of these are clearly described by Dionysius of Halicarnassus (†*De Comp.* xiv, xxii, pp. 53, 103 UR) as respectively bilabial [m] ('the mouth being firmly closed by the lips') and dental [n] ('the tongue rising to make contact with the edges of the teeth'), the air in both cases being 'partially expelled through the nostrils'. There is a third nasal sound in Greek, namely the velar [ŋ]; but, having no separate symbol, this is generally represented by γ, and is discussed in more detail below.

At the end of a word, before an initial vowel or a pause, only the dental nasal ν occurs. But before initial plosives other than dentals, this is frequently replaced in inscriptions by a nasal of the same class as the initial (i.e. by bilabial μ or velar γ) if the two words are closely connected in sense. Before initial labials, in the case of the preposition ἐν[48] there are rather few exceptions to this practice in the 5 c. B.C. (and indeed up to the Christian era)—e.g. εμ πολει: it is also common in the article (τὸν, τὴν, τῶν), ὅταν, ἐάν, and in other forms before μὲν and πὲρ, particularly from the mid-5 c. to the end of the 4 c. Before initial velars it is principally found in ἐν and the article forms—e.g. εγ κυκλοι, τογ γραμματεα. Examples of its occurrence in looser combinations of words are τετταρομ ποδον, ℎιερογ χρεματον (= τεττάρων ποδῶν, ἱερῶν χρημάτων)—and even στεσαμ προσθε (= στῆσαν π.).[49]

These spellings clearly indicate that, at least in the closer

---

[47] Aeolic, however, generally has labials even before front vowels.

[48] Likewise ξυν/συν, but this is in any case infrequent.

[49] There are rare cases of assimilation across punctuation: thus...οιδ οφειλουσιμ· φιλοδημοσ...(= οἶδ' ὀφείλουσιν· Φ...; late 4 c.).

combinations, the assimilation of μ or γ (= [ŋ]) was normal in speech of the 5 c. The exceptions which write e.g. εν πολει, in the manner of our MSS[50] and texts, are readily explained as analogical spellings (just as in English we invariably write *in* even in e.g. *in between*, where it is commonly pronounced as [im]). The assimilative spelling (i.e. with μ or γ) is of course normal in compounds of συν- and ἐν-, e.g. συμβαίνω, ἐγκλίνω, though even in such cases inscriptions occasionally show the analogical forms.

This assimilation of a final ν seems also to have been normal before other types of initial consonant, the assimilation here being complete; thus inscriptions show e.g. εσ σανιδι, τολ λογον, ερ ρο[δοι (= ἐν 'Ρόδῳ); before initial σ followed by a consonant, the final ν is lost altogether by simplification—hence e.g. ε στελει.[51] A close parallel to this situation survives in modern Greek, where the ν of e.g. τον, την, δεν is assimilated in pronunciation to the class of a following plosive, but is lost altogether before other consonants (or in other words, has been fully assimilated, and the resulting double consonant simplified, as regularly in the modern language: thus e.g. τον λόγον → τολ λόγο(ν) → το λόγο).

We conclude, therefore, that words showing a final ν in our texts, when followed by a word with which they were closely connected in sense, assimilated it in pronunciation to the following initial consonant, either partially or fully, and were pronounced with [n] only when the initial itself was a dental plosive or nasal (i.e. τ, δ, θ, or ν).

It is of course possible that in artificially careful or formal speech the assimilation may have been avoided (rather as some speakers of English use the 'strong' form of the definite article *the* even before consonants). And assimilation will never have been normal between words which were not closely connected; so that Dionysius of Halicarnassus (*De Comp.* xxii, p. 103 UR), discussing a verse of Pindar containing the sequence κλυτὰν πέμπετε, finds it a harsh juxtaposition on account

---

[50] But examples of the assimilative spelling are found on some papyri.
[51] Also rarely the unsimplified form ε]σ στελε[ι (but cf. p. 12, n. 1).

of the difference in class between the final dental ν and the initial bilabial π.

We have already mentioned that, in addition to the dental and bilabial nasals, there was in Greek, as in, for example, English and Latin (*VL*, pp. 27 f.), a velar nasal sound, occurring before velar plosive consonants, where it is represented by γ—e.g. ἄγκυρα, ἔγχος, ἐγγύς. Varro identified this with the sound of the *n* in Latin *angulus* etc., which was clearly a velar nasal (described by Nigidius Figulus as 'inter litteram *n* et *g*' and as not involving contact with the (hard) palate).[52] The use of *n* to indicate this sound, as in Latin, is understandable enough, since the velar pronunciation is automatic before velar plosives; and similar spellings with ν are found in Attic inscriptions (regularly before 5 c., e.g. *c.* 550 ενγυσ).[53] But the normal Greek spelling with γ for [ŋ] is on the face of it remarkable, since it is as though we were to write e.g. English *ink*, *finger* as *igk*, *figger*.[54] There is nothing in the nature of a velar plosive that would account for the nasalization of a preceding plosive; so that the only logical explanation for such spellings would be if γ had this nasal [ŋ] value in some *other* environment where it was phonetically intelligible; from such a context the writing with γ could then have been transferred to other positions (on the principle, familiar also to some modern schools of phonology, that a given sound must always be allotted to the same phoneme).

The most obvious candidate for providing such an environment is the position before a following nasal, that is, if γμ and/or γν were pronounced [ŋm], [ŋn] (like the *ngm*, *ngn* in English *hangman*, *hangnail*), as in the case of Latin *magnus* etc. (*VL*, pp. 23 ff.).

There is in fact a tradition, preserved in Priscian (†*GL*, ii, p. 30 K) as ascribed by Varro to Ion (probably of Chios), that the [ŋ] sound represented by γ in ἄγκυρα etc. had a special name in Greek, and that this name was ἄγμα; since the Greek

[52] Cf. also Marius Victorinus in *GL*, vi, pp. 16, 19 K.

[53] Similarly before labials, e.g. *c.* 550 ολυνπιονικο: cf. Threatte, pp. 588–94.

[54] The Greek practice was adopted by Wulfila for Gothic, but scribes occasionally replace the *g* by *n*.

names of letters are otherwise related to the sounds they represent, such a name makes sense only if it is pronounced [aŋma], that is, if the γ is pronounced [ŋ] in the position before the nasal μ.[55]

This hypothesis further explains certain anomalies in the 1st pers. of the perfect passive; consider, for example, the following forms:

(a) Present	(b) 3rd sing. perf.	(c) 1st sing. perf.
(i) λέγ-ομαι	λέλεκ-ται	λέλεγ-μαι
(ii) φθέγγ-ομαι	ἔφθεγκ-ται	ἔφθεγ-μαι

In the forms of (a) and (b), verb (ii) differs from verb (i) in having a nasal [ŋ], represented by γ, preceding the final consonant of the root; but in (c) both verbs have parallel forms—which, if γ here = [g], would mean that verb (ii) has lost its nasal. This situation would be explained, however, if the γ of γμ were pronounced [ŋ]; for the original form will then have been ἔφθεγγμαι, where γγμ = [ŋŋm], which is phonetically simplified to [ŋm], written γμ: so that the nasality is not then lost. There would be a close parallel to this in the Latin spelling of the combination of con + gnosco as cognosco, etc. (VL, p. 23). The change of [g] to [ŋ] in λέλεγμαι is exactly parallel to that of [b] to [m] in e.g. τέτριμ-μαι from τρίβω.

Such an interpretation of the evidence is not accepted by all scholars. It has been suggested that in e.g. λέλεγμαι the γ could have been pronounced [g], the spellings ἔφθεγμαι (and ἄγμα) etc. representing a purely *graphic* simplification for ἔφθεγγμαι, ἄγγμα (with γγ pronounced as [ŋg]).[56] But it is surprising that the simplified spellings are so consistent, particularly as, on this supposition, they are phonetically ambiguous; and also that such simplification should take place only in the case of this group. Such a hypothesis, of course, simply accepts and fails to explain the [ŋ] value of γ in the sequences γκ, γχ, γγ. On the practical side, its acceptance would involve some difficulty for the modern reader, since it would mean differentiating in pronunciation not only between e.g. λέλεγμαι with γ = [g] and ἔφθεγμαι with γ = [ŋg] (where the latter but not the former has

[55] Cf. B. Einarson, CP, 62 (1967), p. 3 and n. 11. For other possible explanations of the name ἄγμα see Lupaş, pp. 21 f.   [56] Cf. Lejeune, p. 125, n. 5.

a nasal in the present), but also between e.g. εἴληγμαι with [g] and ἐλήλεγμαι with [ŋg], where *both* have a nasal in the present (λαγχάνω, ἐλέγχω).[57] The argument of L. Lupaş (*SC*, 8 (1966), p. 11) that a group [ŋm] is improbable in view of the elimination of [nm] (as in συνμαχία → συμμ., etc.) is irrelevant; a difference of treatment would be entirely in accordance with the much higher frequency of occurrence, and so 'redundancy', of dental over velar in Greek (as in most languages), involving greater phonetic instability: one may compare the case of Sanskrit, where, for example, a junction of the type [n + j] → [ñj], with assimilation of dental to palatal, but [ŋ + j] remains [ŋj].[58]

On the balance of the evidence, as well as on practical grounds, the pronunciation [ŋm] is recommended for γμ in all cases. Surprisingly, however, there is no cogent evidence for γν = [ŋn], so that in this respect the Greek situation appears to be the reverse of the Latin.[59]

As mentioned above (pp. 17 f.), the preposition ἐκ was pronounced as [eg] not only before voiced plosives but also before other voiced consonants; in the case of an initial μ, however, as e.g. εγ μακεδονιασ, it will be apparent from the foregoing discussion that its probable pronunciation was [eŋ] and not [eg].

One cannot of course exclude the possibility mentioned by Sturtevant (p. 65) that some Greeks may have affected a 'spelling pronunciation' for γμ, based on the more general value of γ = [g]; so that the current practice in this country of pronouncing it as [gm] need not be condemned outright. But even for such speakers grammatical analogies are likely to have induced a pronunciation [ŋm] in words like ἔφθεγμαι; and the subsequent development of e.g. πρᾶγμα to colloquial modern Greek πρᾶμα is more readily explained on the basis of a pronunciation with [ŋm].[60]

[57] Being in the one case (ἐλέγχω) an integral part of the root, but in the other an 'infix' characterizing the present.

[58] Cf. Allen, 'A note on "instability"', *MF*, 1960, pp. 27 f.; *Sandhi*, p. 86.

[59] Cf. R. L. Ward, *Language*, 20 (1944), pp. 73 ff. Spellings such as αγγνουσιοσ for Ἀγνούσιος (Threatte, pp. 531, 561) are too isolated to be significant.

[60] In the similar and earlier development of γίγνομαι, γιγνώσκω to γίνομαι etc. (Attic from *c.* 300 B.C.) there may be special considerations connected with the preceding γ (and perhaps ι).

The peculiarity of the Greek convention in rendering [ŋ] before velar plosives by γ leads one to consider its adequacy. According to Varro, the adoption of this convention was also proposed by Accius for Latin (*VL*, pp. 27 f.), which would have involved writing e.g. *aggulus, agcora* for *angulus, ancora*; but it is easy to see that this would have led to phonetic ambiguity, since in Latin both [ŋg] and [gg] occur (e.g. *angeris, aggeris*). Once looks, therefore, for the possibility of similar ambiguity in Greek; and a possible source presents itself. Voiceless plosives in Greek become voiced before other voiced plosives; thus the preposition ἐκ (see above) is inscriptionally written εγ before β and δ, and also, which is relevant to our inquiry, before γ, as e.g. in ἐκ + γονος → εγγονοσ.

This example, meaning 'offspring, descendant', indicates the possible ambiguity of the digraph γγ. For here it has the value [gg]; but in ἐγγενής 'innate, native, kindred' the preposition is not ἐκ but ἐν, and so the pronunciation is [ŋg]. The situation is, however, largely saved by maintaining the spelling ἐκ in the former case; thus, in the 5–4 c. B.C., against 27 Attic inscriptional examples of the spelling εγγονοσ we find 50 examples of εκγονοσ; from *c.* 300 B.C. εγγονος is abandoned, but reappears in the 2 c. A.D. and also occurs as a MS variant with ἔκγονος in literary texts.[61] Similarly ἐκγράφειν is the normal spelling for the word meaning 'to copy' or 'to delete', since a spelling

[61] The situation with regard to ἔγγονος in the special sense of 'grandson' is puzzling. It is sometimes assumed to be the same word, but it appears in literature relatively late (e.g. Dion. Hal., *Ant. Rom.* vi. 37; cf. Plutarch, *Per.* 3) and seems to have been formally distinguished from ἔκγονος = 'offspring'; this is expressly stated by various late sources, e.g. *Etym. Gud.*: ἔγγονα διὰ τῶν δύο γγ σημαίνει τὰ τέκνα τῶν τέκνων· [ὅτε δὲ] διὰ τοῦ κ γράφεται ἔκγονα τὰ ἴδια τέκνα. But as a result of the two possible values of γγ, confusion of the two spellings was evidently common (and is in fact commented upon by Eustathius, 1460, 18); thus in the N.T., whereas the Codex Bezae has ἔγγονα for 'grandchildren' in *I Tim.* 5. 4, other MSS have ἔκγονα; and in an inscription of Ephesus (*c.* 85 B.C.) the same ambiguity probably leads to the writing of εκγεγραμμενουσ for ἐγγ. = ἐν-γ. (cf. G. Dittenberger, *Sylloge Inscr. Gr.*³, no. 742, 29 and note); conversely in Samos (*c.* 305 B.C.) ενγονοισ for ἐγγ. = ἐκ-γ. (Dittenberger, no. 333, 25).

As regards colloquial speech, however, modern Greek εγγονός and εγγόνι (with [ŋg]) suggest that, unless they are based on 'spelling pronunciation', the word for 'grandson' was a compound of ἐν and not ἐκ (cf. W. Schulze, *KZ*, 33 (1895), p. 376; Schwyzer, p. 317), or at least a contamination of ἔκγονος and ἐγγενής, leading in either case to a pronunciation with [ŋg] even in antiquity.

ἐγγράφειν could be interpreted as 'to write in, inscribe'; in an inscription of *c.* 303 B.C. ἐγγραψασθαι is found alongside εκγραψασθαι, both in the sense of 'to copy',[62] and an Arcadian inscription of the 3 c. B.C. has the form εγγραφετω in the sense of 'to delete'.[63] Such forms are, however, rare, although before β and δ (where no ambiguity can arise) εγ is regular in Attic inscriptions until the 1 c. B.C.

The writing of γγ for [gg] also survives in *Il.* xx, 458 κὰγ γόνυ (from κατ(ὰ) γόνυ), though even here some good MSS have κὰκ γόνυ (see note in Leaf's edn.).[64]

A strictly phonemic solution to the spelling of the Greek [ŋ] sound would require a special symbol for it (i.e. its recognition as a distinct phoneme).[65] But it is hardly surprising that the Greeks did not attempt this; for ambiguities were few and avoidable by 'analogical' or 'morphophonemic' writing; and compared with [n] and [m] the occurrences of [ŋ] were limited to a few contexts—it could not, for instance, occur initially or before a vowel. In fact no European languages employing the Greco-Roman alphabet have found it necessary to augment it for this purpose—English, for example, writes *n* for [ŋ] before velars and *ng* elsewhere (with some phonetic ambiguity in e.g. RP *longer, linger, Bangor* beside *banger, hanger,* etc.—apart from the 'soft' pronunciation in *danger* etc.); special symbols are found only in the Old Germanic Runic and Old Celtic Ogham systems of writing.

(v) **Liquids***

This peculiar title is generally applied at the present day to sounds of the [l] and [r] type. It derives from the Latin term

---

[62] Dittenberger, no. 344, 61.

[63] E. Schwyzer, *Dial. gr. exemp. epig. potiora*[3], no. 668, 14.

[64] For further discussions of these matters cf. L. J. D. Richardson, 'Agma, a forgotten Greek letter', in *Hermathena*, 58 (1941), pp. 57 ff., and 'Double gamma as true "double-*g*" in Greek', in *TPS*, 1946, pp. 156 ff.

[65] Cf. B. E. Newton, *Lingua*, 12 (1963), p. 155. It could not be considered as an allophone of the /g/ phoneme since, as we have seen, both [ŋg] and [gg] occur; in most cases it could be treated as an allophone of the /n/ phoneme (viz. before velar consonants), but to do so in the case of the sequence [ŋm] (γμ), though theoretically

liquidus, which in turn is used by the Latin grammarians to translate the Greek ὑγρός.[66] The Greek term is applied by Dionysius Thrax to the four consonants λ, μ, ν, ρ (*Ars Gramm.*, p. 14 U);[67] scholiasts' explanations of the word are various, but the most general opinion seems to be that it means 'fluid', in the sense of 'unstable', with reference to the values of these consonants for quantitative metrical purposes, since many groups consisting of plosive + λ, μ, ν or ρ leave a preceding syllable containing a short vowel of 'doubtful' or 'common' quantity, as in e.g. πατρός, τέκνον (see further pp. 106 ff.)—and this condition of the syllable is also referred to as ὑγρός. In Latin this applies only to *l* and *r*, and since *m* and *n* are in any case classifiable as 'nasals', the term 'liquid' has come to have its more restricted, current meaning; in this sense it remains a useful term, since a class-definition of these sounds in articulatory terms is a somewhat complex matter.[68]

λ There are no useful descriptions of this sound by the grammarians. Dionysius of Halicarnassus simply mentions that it is produced by the tongue and palate, and that, by contrast with ρ, it is soothing to the ear and the sweetest of the continuant sounds (*De Comp.* xiv, pp. 53 f. UR). But from comparison with cognates in other languages, and from its value in modern Greek, we may safely say that it was a lateral* [l] sound; and unlike English or Latin (*VL*, pp. 33 f.), there is no evidence that in Attic it was under any circumstances 'dark' or 'velarized' before consonants; it was thus probably a 'clear' [l] in all contexts, and so more similar to that of French than of English.[69]

possible in the absence of a sequence νμ, would be phonetically perverse, since it would imply that the following *labial* consonant was responsible for the *velar* quality.

[66] Terentianus Maurus, however, translates the Greek word by *udus* or *uuidus* (*GL*, vi, pp. 350, 362 K: cf. Allen, pp. 31 f.).

[67] With an alternative term ἀμετάβολος (explained as not changing when stem-final in noun and verb inflexion). This term is translated as *immutabilis* by Marius Victorinus (*GL*, vi, p. 6 K), but is not generally adopted; it does not appear in the Armenian version of Dionysius.

[68] Cf. R. Jakobson, C. G. M. Fant & M. Halle, *Preliminaries to Speech Analysis*, pp. 19 ff.

[69] Dialectally, however, there is evidence of 'dark' variants in some contexts. Old

ρ Dionysius of Halicarnassus describes this sound as being pronounced by 'the tip of the tongue rising to the palate near the teeth' and 'fanning' or 'beating' out the air (†*De Comp.* xiv, p. 54 UR); the MSS read either ἀπορριπιзούσης or ἀπορραπιзούσης (cf. also p. 56 UR), but it makes little difference to the meaning, and Plato clearly refers to the tongue as being 'least static and most vibrant' in the production of this sound (†*Crat.*, 426 E). What is being described is clearly a trilled, alveolar [r] sound, as e.g. in Italian or some Scottish pronunciations, and not as in southern English, where it is more retracted and less strongly articulated (with single tap, friction, or neither). One may further note the use of the sound in the presumably onomatopoeic ῥάзειν, ῥύзειν, ἀρράзειν for the snarling of dogs (cf. *VL*, p. 32).[70]

Generally speaking [r] is a voiced sound, but in certain environments in classical Attic it seems to have been voiceless. What we are actually told by the grammarians is that ρ was aspirated at the beginning of a word, and that when a double ρρ occurred in the middle of a word the first element was unaspirated and the second aspirated (e.g. †Herodian, i, pp. 546 f. L). These descriptions are followed in the Byzantine practice of writing initial ῥ and medial ῥῥ, and are supported at an earlier period by Latin transcriptions such as *rhetor*, *Pyrrhus*; still earlier occasional evidence is found in inscriptions using *h*, as Corcyra ρhοϝαισι, early Attic [φρ]εαρhιο[(*c.* 500) and on the Themistocles ostraka several examples of φρεα(ρ)ρhιοσ (Threatte, p. 25). But one also finds Boeotian hραφσα[ϝοιδοι (= ῥαψῳδῷ), and the transcription *hṙ* in e.g. Armenian *hṙetor*

Armenian distinguished both a dark *l* and a clear *l*; the former occupies the position of λ in the alphabet, and tends to be used to transcribe λ in Greek words, more particularly in the vicinity of non-front vowels. This may well reflect an Asiatic Greek peculiarity; modern Cappadocian Greek shows developments of a labial or velar nature in such contexts (e.g. ἀβγο < ἀλογο, θογό < θολός), and Hesychius has the perhaps significant gloss κάρυα Ποντικά for both ἄλαρα and αὐαρά; cf. A. Thumb, 'Die griechischen Lehnwörter im Armenischen', *BZ*, 9 (1900), pp. 388 ff.

[70] Armenian distinguishes both a rolled *ṙ* and a fricative *r* (cf. Allen, *TPS*, 1950, pp. 193–7), of which the former occupies the position of ρ in the alphabet (though there is much variation in the rendering of ρ in Greek words).

(similarly in Coptic and Demotic Egyptian). As Sturtevant (p. 62) has suggested, we may probably interpret this variation as meaning that the aspiration neither preceded nor followed the [r], but was simultaneous with it, i.e. that the sound was a 'breathed' or *voiceless* [r] (all aspiration in Greek, unlike Sanskrit, being voiceless). Dialectal support for such a value has been seen in the modern Tsakonian development of [ši-] from Laconian ῥι-,[71] though this also suggests a fricative pronunciation of ρ.[72]

Such a sound is found as a distinct phoneme in e.g. modern Icelandic *hringur* 'ring' (contrasting with voiced [r] in *ringur* 'gust'); but in Greek it was merely a contextual variant, or 'allophone', since initial ρ was regularly voiceless. The only exception of which we are told by Herodian is in the name Ῥᾶρος and its derivatives (loc. cit.; cf. also Choeroboscus, *Schol. in Theod.*, ii, p. 43 H); the reason for this exception may be that the following syllable begins with ρ, but another word ῥάρος is also cited by a scholiast on Dionysius Thrax (p. 143 H) as Aeolic meaning ἔμβρυον or βρέφος, and the non-aspiration is here explained as being due to the dialect (of which 'psilosis' is a characteristic feature). If the reason does lie in the ρ of the second syllable, we should of course also expect to have voiced initial ῥ (and not ῥ) in the rare reduplicated forms of the type ῥερυπωμέμα (*Od.* vi, 59), ῥερῖφθαι (Pindar, *Fr.* 318).[73] In the case of the double ρρ it may be, as the grammatical tradition has it, that only the second element was aspirated, i.e. that the geminate began voiced and ended voiceless; but this rule could be artificial and based on the pattern of e.g. Ἀτθίς, Σαπφώ, Βάκχος (cf. p. 21), which are specifically mentioned in this connection by Choeroboscus (p. 44 H).

[71] Cf. M. Vasmer, *KZ*, 51 (1923), p. 158.

[72] Note also, on e.g. coins of the 'Indo-Scythian' Kušān dynasty (from early 2 c. A.D.), the representation of Iranian (Bactrian) *š*, in a script of Greek origin, by the symbol Ρ, which has been assumed to derive from P with a superscript breathing: cf. R. Göbl in F. Altheim & R. Stiehl, *Finanzgeschichte der Spätantike*, p. 183.

[73] Boeckh does in fact write ῥερίφθαι. This word has a rough breathing, however, in all mss of Choeroboscus (cf. Sommerstein, p. 47, n. 61, where Ῥᾶρος, ῥάρος are also discussed). In fact both this and ῥερυπωμένα are analogical formations, since there are no roots originally beginning with *r* (these are from *wr-* and *sr-* respectively: see further Lejeune (*b*), pp. 122, n., 181, n.).

Apart from initials and geminates, it is also reported that ρ was aspirated (i.e. probably voiceless) after aspirated plosive consonants, i.e. in the groups φρ, θρ, χρ (thus †Choeroboscus, *Schol. in Theod.*, i, p. 257 H; cf. ii, p. 44 H, and *Schol. in Dion. Thr.*, p. 143 H).[74] This peculiarity is further supported by Latin transcriptions such as *Prhygia, Trhepto, Crhysippus*. Conversely it helps to explain the development whereby, for example, τετρ-ίππος becomes τέθριππος and προ-όρα becomes φρουρά, since the ρ in these words will first have become aspirated (devoiced) before an aspirated vowel (which then loses its aspiration in the compound: i.e. ῥί, ῥό → ῥι, ῥο), and this in turn will have required that the preceding plosive be aspirated.

It should be emphasized that the voiceless pronunciation of ρ in certain environments is a purely allophonic matter (cf. p. 9), and no confusion can therefore be caused if ρ is always pronounced with its voiced value, as e.g. in modern Greek.

There is a historical reason for the aspiration of ρ when initial and double in many cases. With few and disputed exceptions, initial ρ in Greek does not correspond to initial *r* in related languages; where the latter have initial *r* (as e.g. English *red*, Sanskrit *rudhiráḥ*, Latin *ruber*), Greek shows a so called 'prothetic' vowel before it (thus ἐρυθρός). When Greek does have an initial ρ, it generally derives from an original consonant-*group*, viz. *sr* or *wr*; thus e.g. ῥέω beside Sanskrit *sravati* (cf. English *stream*), and ῥέζω beside English *work*. Before vowels an original *s* gives Greek [h] ('rough breathing') e.g. ἑπτά beside Latin *septem*; original *sr* may therefore be expected to give ῥ. This argument would not apply to *wr*, since original initial *w* normally gives smooth breathing, e.g. οἶδα beside Sanskrit *veda* (cf. English *wit*); but presumably a contrast between aspirated and unaspirated initial ρ would rarely if ever have been significant,[75] and the aspirated form became standardized.[76]

---

[74] Cf. the voiceless pronunciation of *r* (and *l*) after the aspirated allophones of English voiceless plosives (see p. 28), e.g. in *pray, please*.

[75] A case in point might have been ῥοαί 'streams' and ῥοαί 'pomegranates' (with Herodian's accentuation), if the latter, a borrowing from some unknown language, had originally unaspirated ῥ.

[76] If Grassmann's Law (see pp. 15, 20, 54) ever applied to ῥ, no trace of it survives;

The medial ρρ also derives from these same consonant-groups; but since, after short vowels, a simplification of such groups to single ρ would here alter the quantity of the preceding syllable, the result is a geminate. As in the case of initial ρ, the geminate is aspirated on the model of the original *sr* group (e.g. ἔρρευσα), even when it derives from an original *wr*, as in e.g. ἄρρητος (cf. Latin *verbum*, English *word*). The usual practice in modern texts is to indicate the aspiration of the single initial ρ, but not generally of the medial geminate ρρ; in fact, of course, the indication of the rough breathing on initial ρ is as superfluous as on the geminate, since it is automatic in virtually all cases.

The geminate ρρ also survived to a considerable extent even in initial position after a final short vowel in continuous speech, as is shown by its effect in metre. This is general in the dialogue of Attic tragedy (e.g. Eur., *El.*, 772: τίνι ρρυθμῷ) and comedy (e.g. Ar., *Frogs*, 1059: τὰ ρρήματα), and optional in epic (e.g. *Il.* xii, 159: βέλεα ρρέον; xxiv, 343: εἴλετο δὲ ρράβδον). Texts in such cases generally show single initial ῥ, but spellings with ρρ are occasionally found in inscriptions. In epic gemination is also often extended to initial λ, μ and ν (e.g. *Il.* xiii, 754: ὄρεϊ (ν)νιφόεντι), which in some but by no means all cases derive from an original group (cf. English *snow*).[77]

Conversely, where geminate ρρ would be expected after initial ἐ of the syllabic augment or reduplication, single ρ is occasionally found by analogy with the present-tense forms, e.g. in epic and in tragic lyrics; of ἔρεξε in *Il.* ii, 400, Choeroboscus (*Schol. in Theod.*, ii, p. 44 H) comments that it is 'διὰ τὸ μέτρον'. Inscriptions generally show ρρ in such cases, but practice varies in compounds (e.g. απορ(ρ)αινονται, 431/418 B.C.).[78]

It remains to mention that in some cases Attic ρρ corresponds to ρσ of many other dialects, including Ionic. Attic maintained

thus e.g. I.-E. *swedh-* (cf. Skt. *svadhā́*) → ῾Fέθος → Fέθος → ἔθος, but *srobh-* (cf. Lith. *srebiù*, Lat. *sorbeo*) → ῥοφέω. The situation is thus similar to that of ὑ- (see p. 68, n. 15).

[77] Outside Attic there are a few examples to suggest that the groups *sl* and *s* + nasal gave an aspirated (voiceless) consonant—e.g. Aegina λhαβον = λαβών; but in these cases, unlike ῥ, it was the unaspirated form that became general. On the development of original *sw* see p. 48.

[78] See further Lupaş, pp. 24 f.; Threatte, pp. 519 ff.

ρσ where σ represented the initial of a grammatical element, e.g. ῥήτορ-σι, κάθαρ-σις, ἔσπαρ-σαι; also in some borrowed words (e.g. βύρσα) and proper names (e.g. Περσεύς). But even some words of non-Attic origin showed the Attic change to ρρ— e.g. in inscriptions χερρονεσοσ for Χερσόνησος regularly from 451 B.C.; and the Attic form of Περσεφόνη is Φερρέφαττα. In literature, the Ionic ρσ is general in tragedy and prose up to Thucydides (but even here one finds occasional forms with ρρ, as πόρρω(θεν), δέρρις). Thereafter the ρρ forms become more common, but Koine influence soon tends to restore ρσ; the restoration, however, was never complete, the verb θαρρεῖν, for example, remaining normal alongside the noun θάρσος.[79] This dialectal feature of Attic was perhaps felt to be less provincial than the ττ discussed above (pp. 12 ff.) since it was shared not with Boeotian but sporadically with various other dialects.

(vi) Fricatives*

There was only one fricative phoneme in classical Attic, namely σ (ς). It is fairly clearly described by Dionysius of Halicarnassus as being produced by an elevation of the tongue to the palate, with the air passing between them and producing a whistling or hissing sound (σύριγμα) around the teeth (*De Comp.* xiv, p. 54 UR). This seems to suggest a sibilant sound not unlike that of English alveolar *s*;[80] the description would not in itself entirely exclude a 'hushing' as opposed to a hissing sound (i.e. [š] as English *sh*), but other languages which have both types of sound represent the Greek σ by their [s] and not by their [š]—thus, for example, on Indian coins *Dianisiyasa* = Διονυσίου, and similarly in Coptic.

Whilst σ in most environments was a voiceless [s], there was also a voiced [z] allophone in the position before voiced consonants. For the position before δ this is suggested by the fact that Ἀθήνας + δε is written αθεναζε (= Ἀθήναζε, 445 B.C. etc.),

---

[79] See further Lupaș, pp. 37 f.; Threatte, pp. 534 ff.
[80] The modern Greek sound is rather more retracted.

with the special symbol ȝ = [zd] for σδ (see further pp. 56 ff.).[81] For the position before other voiced consonants direct evidence is not citable before the second half of the 4 c. B.C., when σ before μ is sometimes written as ȝ[82] (which became [z] at this time) or as σȝ (e.g. ενδεσȝμουσ); but since it would not have been possible to indicate a [z] pronunciation earlier, it is entirely possible that σ already had this value in such contexts at an earlier period. The case of σδ makes it virtually certain that the same applied before other voiced plosives, and a reflection of this is perhaps seen in the confusion of the forms Πελασγικόν and Πελαργικόν (inscr. 439 B.C.; cf. also Ar., *Birds*, 832, and the Codex Laurentianus of Thuc., ii. 17);[83] the inscriptional spelling πελαȝγικον appears at Argos in the late 4 c.

At later periods the voiced pronunciation of σ before voiced consonants is attested by transcriptions of Greek words in languages possessing symbols for both [s] and [z], e.g. Gothic *praizbwtairei* = πρεσβυτέριον, Armenian *zmelin* = σμιλίον; and it remains a characteristic of modern Greek. Before vowels, however, and generally at the ends of words, there is no evidence that σ was pronounced other than voiceless [s] in Attic, and care should be taken to avoid the intervocalic and final pronunciation as [z] which is found in English—thus βασιλεύς, μοῦσα, πῶς are *not* to be pronounced like *Basil, muse, pose*;[84] English *cosmic, lesbian*, on the other hand, provide correct models for the pronunciation of σ in κόσμος, Λέσβος.

For fricative developments in late Greek see pp. 22 ff., 30 ff.

On σσ see pp. 12 ff.

---

[81] σδ is retained in transparent compounds such as προσδέχομαι on the analogy of προς etc. and the main word in other environments (cf. e.g. ἐκσώȝω, *not* ἐξ-); note, however, Boeot. διοȝοτοσ = Διόσδοτος. Note also the use of σȝ for (σ)σδ referred to on p. 58.

[82] Ζμ- for Σμ- in the Palatine Anthology is also supported by its alphabetical position (cf. R. Merkelbach, *Glotta*, 45 (1967), pp. 39 f.).

[83] Cf. Threatte, pp. 557 f. The same 'rhotacistic' development in the group [zg] is seen in Latin *mergo* beside Lithuanian *mazgóti*; cf. also Eretrian μιργοσ = Μίσγος. For phonetic discussion cf. M. Grammont, *Traité de Phonétique*[3], pp. 205 f.

[84] As in modern Greek, however, final ς may have been voiced before voiced initial consonants of closely connected words: cf. Argos ϝοιȝ δε (= οῖς δὲ, 6 c.) as modern ο γυιός μου = [o yóz mu] etc.

(vii) Semivowels*

This term is here used in its modern sense, referring to sounds of the type of English *w* and *y*, and not in the sense of the Greek ἡμίφωνα or the Latin *semivocales* (see p. 19 and *VL*, p. 37, n. 1). Although these are not generally reckoned as independent phonemes in classical Attic, some discussion of them is necessary in connection with other features.

[w] (ϝ, 'digamma'). In early Greek this sound existed as an independent phoneme; in the Cyprian and Mycenaean (Linear B) syllabaries there are signs for *wa, we, wi, wo*, and most of the dialects show epigraphic evidence in the form of a special letter, of which the most common shape is of the type ϝ. This was a differentiated form of the Semitic '*waw*', which in the form Y was adopted for the vowel [u]. From the place of ϝ in the Latin alphabet, which is based on a West Greek model, it is evident that it retained its Semitic position (whereas Y, Latin v, was set at the end). This is also shown by Greek alphabets appearing in Etruscan inscriptions, and by a partial alphabet on an early Corinthian votive tablet (? 6 c. B.C.: *IGA*, 20, 13), where it appears between E and Z; and by its later use (normal from late 2 c. B.C.) as a numeral = 6.[85] In this use it develops various forms, e.g. epigraphic Ϲ, Ⱶ and MS ϲ, ϛ, ϥ, ϛ, so ultimately (*c.* 7–8 c. A.D.) coinciding with the cursive ligature for στ

---

[85] An intermediate stage is seen in its use as a paragraph-index in a 5 c. Locrian inscription (*IG*, IX. i. 334), to which Dr Chadwick has drawn my attention. On the earliest uses of alphabetic numerals in Greek see L. W. Daly, *Contributions to a history of alphabetization in antiquity and the Middle Ages* (= Coll. Latomus, 90, 1967), pp. 11 f., with further refs.

The same alphabetical place is occupied by the Georgian letter having the phonetic value [v], which, in the old texts, also has the same numeral value and, in the *xucuri* ('ecclesiastical') script, could well be derived from a Greek form. The place and numeral value are also followed by a derivative in the Cyrillic script of Old Slavonic (but with an arbitrary phonetic value [dz]); and also perhaps in Gothic (with a value [kʷ]). Of the other Greek 'ἐπίσημα' (cf. pp. 17, 60), derivatives of ϙ were taken over with the original position and numeral value by Georgian (but with a phonetic value [ž]), by Cyrillic (with a phonetic value [č], as still Russian ч), and by Gothic (but with no phonetic value); in Armenian the derivative occupies its original alphabetical position, but has a numeral value 900 and a phonetic value [j]. A derivative of ϡ was taken over with its original numeral value by Cyrillic (but with a phonetic value [ẹ]) and by Gothic (but with no phonetic value).

('στίγμα'), with which it is thereafter confused.[86] The original name of the letter in Greek was probably ϝαῦ (like ταῦ after the Semitic 'taw'), though this is attested only by a statement in Cassiodor(i)us that Varro so called it.[87] Later it became known as δίγαμμα, on account of its shape, as described, for example, by Dionysius of Halicarnassus (*Ant. Rom.* i. 20: 'ὥσπερ γάμμα διτταῖς ἐπὶ μίαν ὀρθὴν ἐπιζευγνύμενον ταῖς πλαγίοις').

In Attic, however, [w] was lost as an independent phoneme at an early date (though the fact that Attic has e.g. δέρη, κόρη shows that in some environments it survived for a time in this dialect, since otherwise we should expect Attic ᾱ after ρ; for its preservation cf. Arcadian δερϝα, κορϝα). The sound remained as the second element of diphthongs (cf. p. 5), but was there treated as an allophone of the vowel υ and so written;[88] before vowels the υ in the digraphs αυ, ευ stands for a geminate [ww] (cf. pp. 81 ff.), with the consequence that the syllable is generally heavy; its consonantal value reappears in the modern Greek pronunciation of αυ, ευ as [av, ev] before both consonants and vowels ([af, ef] before voiceless consonants—e.g. αυτός = [aftós]; thence [ap, ep] before σ—e.g. δούλεψα from (ἐ)δούλευσα): cf. p. 80.

In some words initial [w] resulted from an original consonant-group *sw*, and in such cases the expected result would be an aspirated or voiceless [w] (cf. pp. 41 ff.), as in the northern English pronunciation of *wh*. This is attested in Pamphylian ϝhε = ἕ (cf. Sanskrit *sva-*), Boeotian ϝhεκαδαμοε (= Ἑκαδήμῳ). In Attic, the [w] having been lost, only the aspiration ('rough breathing') remains, as e.g. in ἡδύς (cf. Sanskrit *svādúḥ*, English *sweet*).

Though ϝ is only of historical interest so far as Attic is concerned, it should be noted that it plays an important part in the metre of non-Attic poetry. Thus in Homer an original

---

[86] Resulting sometimes even in a majuscule form ΣΤ′.

[87] The 'ϝαϝ' of this source is Ritschl's conjecture for 'ϝα' of the MSS. Nevertheless, the name ϝαϝ is supported by some other sources: cf. A. E. Gordon, *The Letter Names of the Latin Alphabet*, p. 46 and n. 67.

[88] ϝ survives in the spelling of the diphthong αυ in an Attic inscription of *c.* 550, αϝυταρ: cf. Threatte, p. 23.

SEMIVOWELS

ϝ accounts in some 2,300 cases for absence of elision (e.g. *Il.* i, 30: ἐνὶ (ϝ)οίκῳ), in some 400 cases for 'positional' quantity when the preceding word ends in a consonant (e.g. *Il.* i, 108: εἶπας (ϝ)έπος), and in some 160 cases for absence of 'epic correption' (see p. 97) in the second half of the foot (e.g. *Il.* vii, 281: καὶ (ϝ)ίδμεν ἅπαντες). The initial group δϝ also accounts in a number of cases for 'positional' quantity when the preceding word ends in a short vowel (e.g. *Od.* i, 203: οὔ τοι ἔτι δ(ϝ)ηρόν; *Od.* ix, 236: ἡμεῖς δὲ δ(ϝ)είσαντες, cf. Corinthian 6 c. δϝενια = Δεινίου). Even an initial [h] may have the same effect where it derives from an original *sw*, notably in the case of the 3rd pers. pronoun—e.g. ἀπὸ ἕο *Il.* v, 343 etc., and possessive πόσεϊ ᾧ *Il.* v, 71 etc.—but also φίλε ἑκυρέ *Il.* iii, 172 (cf. Sanskrit *śváśuraḥ*, German *Schwäher*); in such cases it stands for a *double* aspirated (voiceless) ϝ (cf. pp. 41 ff.), thus ἀπὸ '(ϝϝ)έο etc.[89]

In many cases later editing has tended to obscure the original presence of a ϝ by emendations of various kinds; thus in *Il.* iii, 103, οἴσετε ἄρν', with hiatus indicating ϝάρν', is preserved only in one papyrus, whereas all the MSS have οἴσετε δ' ἄρν' (for the form cf. Cretan ϝαρεν, and still modern Tsaconian *vanne*). This can be seen also in the alternative devices adopted to maintain quantity in syllables preceding a medial δϝ of the root meaning 'to fear'; thus vowel-lengthening in the reduplicated present δείδιμεν (for δέδϝιμεν) and in the adjective θεουδής (for θεοδϝής), but consonant-doubling in the aorist ἔδδεισα (for ἔδϝεισα) and in the adjective ἀδδεές (for ἀδϝεές).

But there are numerous cases also where the metre does not permit the restoration of an etymologically expected ϝ; as Chantraine comments (i, p. 153), 'Le ϝ est un phonème en train de disparaître au cours de l'histoire de la langue épique' (it may be noted that it is a less viable feature of Ionic than Aeolic); and as a consequence (p. 157), 'il est impossible de restituer systématiquement le ϝ dans l'*Iliade* et dans l'*Odyssée* et les philologues qui pratiquent cette restitution donnent du texte et de la langue une image inexacte'. The relevance of

[89] Note also, with preceding final consonant, *Il.* xxiv, 154 ὅς ἄξει probably standing for ὅς ('ϝ') ἄξει (parallel to ὅς σ' ἄξει in 183): cf. A. Hoekstra, *Homeric Modification of Formulaic Prototypes*, p. 43.

49

'digamma' to Homeric metre was first discussed by Richard Bentley in 1713;[90] but the attempt by Richard Payne Knight a century later to apply the restoration in practice led to ludicrous excesses. Later studies have been based on more scientific principles, but the reader is not advised to attempt any such reconstruction in reciting Homer; in pronouncing the text as it stands he will at least be approximating to its rendering by classical Attic speakers.

The ancients considered the digamma as a peculiarly Aeolic letter, and ϝ is in fact encountered in the texts of the Lesbian poets. It is preserved in an actual book MS only in one instance, viz. initially in the 3rd pers. possessive ϝοισι (= οἶσι) of Sappho, A. 5, 6 (*Oxyrhyncus Papyri*, ed. Grenfell & Hunt, I, vii; Plate II), but it is attested for both this and the pronoun (cf. p. 49) by citations and statements in later authors, notably Apollonius Dyscolus (though copyists tend to read the unfamiliar letter as Ε or Γ). It has also been preserved in the initial group ϝρ with a spelling β (e.g. Sappho, E. 5, 13 βρόδα for ϝρόδα = ῥόδα); and perhaps intervocalically as υ in Alcaeus, D. 12, 12[91] αυάταν (= ἄτην) with light first syllable.

Apart from Aeolic, the grammarians show an awareness of digamma as a feature also of Laconian and Boeotian;[92] and in these cases also there is occasional textual evidence. Initial digamma in both Alcman and Corinna is regularly respected for metrical purposes;[93] one certain example of the letter survives in a book papyrus of Alcman (ϝάνακτα in 1 (1), 6),[94] and it is represented by υ in αυειρομέναι (i (i), 63: light first syllable). This feature of Laconian also survives in the MSS of Aristophanes' *Lysistrata*, where παρευιδών (156) probably = παραϝιδών and γ' ἀδύ (206) probably = ϝἀδύ. For Corinna and other Boeotian fragments of uncertain authorship about a

[90] Cf. R. Pfeiffer, *History of Classical Scholarship from 1300 to 1850*, p. 157.
[91] References for Sappho and Alcaeus are to Lobel & Page, *Poetarum Lesbiorum Fragmenta*.
[92] See D. L. Page, *Alcman, The Partheneion*, p. 110, n.
[93] For further details see Page, *Alcman, The P.*, pp. 104 ff.; *Corinna*, pp. 46 ff.; E. Lobel, *Hermes*, 65 (1930), pp. 360 f., from which works most of the information in this paragraph is derived.
[94] References for Alcman and Corinna are to Page, *Poetae Melici Graeci*.

dozen examples appear in papyri, including two of the aspirated form where it is in fact expected (cf. p. 48), viz. 1 (654), col. iv, 23 ϝᾱ̆δομη[95] (= ἥδομαι): cf. col. iv, 7 ϝᾱ̆δο[.

Finally, in the rare presumed cases of 'synizesis'[96] of the vowel υ in Attic (as Ἐρινύων Eur., *I.T.*, 931 etc.), one may perhaps have an example of a front rounded semivowel (like that in e.g. French *nuit*): cf. pp. 65 ff.

[y]   During the classical Greek period this is not attested as a separate phoneme in any of the dialects. It may just have been in Mycenaean (thus after *w* in *me-wi-jo*, for ? [me(i)wyōs], = μείων; less certainly in initial position),[97] but most of the occurrences of the symbols for [ya, ye, yo] simply indicate an automatic 'glide' following a front vowel (e.g. *i-jo-te* = ἰόντες;[98] cf. Cyprian *we-pi-ja* = ἔπεα, and the Pamphylian spelling διια for δια, etc.).

In Attic, as in other dialects, the sound remained as the second element of diphthongs, but (in parallel with the case of [w]) was there treated as an allophone of the vowel ι and so written. Before vowels the ι of the digraphs αι, οι, and probably ει, generally stands in classical Attic for a geminate [yy] (like the Latin intervocalic *i*: cf. *VL*, p. 39, and pp. 81 ff. below).

A [y] sound may also arise by synizesis of the vowel ι, as Soph., *O.C.*, 1466 οὐρανίᾳ, inscr. (4 c.) πυθιων: cf. also Homer Αἰγυπτίη *Od.* iv, 229 etc., and πότνα probably for πότνιᾳ *Od.* v, 215 etc.[99] A similar synizesis is sometimes assumed for ε in the

---

[95] Reading μ rather than ν with Lobel, op. cit., p. 360, and W. Crönert, *RhM*, 63 (1968), p. 175. A photograph is reproduced in *Berliner Klassikertexte*, v. 2, Tafel vii.

[96] Used here in its modern sense of the reduction of a vowel to a semivowel (but see p. 99).

[97] See further F. W. Householder, 'Early Greek -j-', *Glotta*, 39 (1960/1), pp. 179 ff.

[98] In cases such as gen. si. *-o-jo*, however, the *j* could stand for [yy]: cf. pp. 81 ff.

[99] In epic and inscriptional hexameters such occurrences mostly involve the position between heavy syllables in proper names, which could otherwise not be accommodated. It is noteworthy that the further extension of this practice does not have the effect of rendering a preceding syllable heavy 'by position' (cf. pp. 104 ff.)—with οὐρανίᾳ contrast e.g. Latin *abiete*; cf. also Pind., *Pyth.* iv, 225 γενύων beside Latin *genua* (*VL*, pp. 38, 41, 80). It may be significant that the vast majority of cases involve the groups dental or alveolar +ι (cf. L. Radermacher, *SbAWW*, 170 (1913), ix, 28), and it might be that these could be pronounced as single 'palatalized' consonants (like e.g. Spanish *ñ*). But synizesis in Greek remains no more than a 'Notbehelf' (Radermacher, op. cit., p. 27).

common monosyllabic treatment of ε + vowel or diphthong (e.g. θεός, πόλεως, Hom. τεύχεα, ἡμέας, γνώσεαι); but there are scarcely any examples in any type of verse where such a mono-syllabic ε + short vowel results in a demonstrably light syllable, so that some form of diphthongal contraction rather than synizesis proper could be involved (see further, p. 99); an exceptional example is Pindar, *Pyth.* i, 56 οὕτω δ' Ἱέρωνι θεὸς ὀρθωτὴρ πέλοι (dactylo-epitrite metre), where θεὸς must be light—giving rise to various conjectural emendations.

In no case in classical Greek does consonantal [y] enter into contrast with vocalic [i] in the manner of [w] in some dialects,[100] where phonemic contrast could be established for e.g. (Arc.) disyllabic κόρϝᾱ 'maiden' beside trisyllabic καρύᾱ 'walnut-tree', or (Hom.) monosyllabic 'ϝέ (ἕ) beside disyllabic ὕε.

(viii) The aspirate* [h]

The existence of this phoneme in classical Attic is clearly established. In pre-Eucleidean inscriptions it is represented by a special letter, Η (earlier Β). There are admittedly quite frequent omissions; but some of these are due to the fact that even before 403 B.C. Η was beginning to be used in its Ionic value of [ē] (see p. 73); and the more significant fact is that false writing of Η is rare. After 403 B.C. Η often continues to appear in the word ὅρος, and the phonetic distinction between this and ὄρος is cited as an example by Aristotle (†*Soph. El.*, 177b).[101] In Magna Graecia the sound continues to be indicated in inscriptions by the 'half-Η' sign ⊦, and this was adopted by the Alexandrian grammarians as a superscript diacritic (later '),[102] though originally only to distinguish aspirated from otherwise homophonous words, as ὉΡΟΣ; the complementary ⊣ (later ') was also introduced to indicate non-aspiration.

[100] Unless, of course, one treats the second elements of diphthongs as /y/ and /w/ (see pp. 5, 80, 94, n. 8), thereby producing contrasts of the type αἰσχρός: ἄιστος: cf. L. Lupaş, *SC*, 6 (1964), pp. 99 f.

[101] There is, however, some doubt about this example. It has been suggested that Aristotle wrote not ὅρος but ὀρός ('whey'), which would be distinguished from ὅρος by accent and not by breathing: cf. *AR*, p. 3, n. 2.

[102] It is occasionally found in Attic inscriptions from I c. A.D. and later (Threatte, p. 97).

The fact that Greek words borrowed into Latin are written with *h* (e.g. *historia*) indicates that the aspirate continued to be pronounced in Hellenistic times, and forms in other languages point to its retention up to at least the beginning of the Christian era, e.g. in Coptic and Syriac and in astronomical terms such as *horā* (= ὥρα) in Sanskrit.

Whilst the symbol H in its consonantal value dropped out of general use after the introduction of the Ionic alphabet, the presence of initial aspiration continued to be indicated by the substitution of the aspirated φ, θ, χ for unaspirated final π, τ, κ before words beginning with the aspirate (cf. pp. 19 f.)—e.g. καθ εκαστον (= καθ' ἕκαστον). Even allowing for the conservative spelling of stereotyped phrases, practice in this respect testifies to the retention of initial aspiration until about the 2 c. A.D. The loss of [h] seems in fact to be roughly contemporaneous with the development of the aspirated plosives to fricatives (see pp. 23 ff.), and the two developments could well be connected, since it has been found that 'as a rule, languages possessing the pairs voiced/voiceless, aspirate/non-aspirate, have also a phoneme /h/'.[103] That [h] had been lost, as in modern Greek, by the 4 c. A.D. is indicated by its frequent omission or misplacement in Gothic transcriptions.

As to the precise value of this phoneme in classical Attic, <u>there is no reason to think that it was very different from our own *h*</u>, i.e. a pure voiceless aspirate, or 'glottal fricative', since forms such as καθημέριος based on κατ(ά) ἡμέραν show that it was identified with the aspirate element of the aspirated plosives at an early period, whilst the name πνεῦμα 'breathing' given to it by the grammarians[104] supports the same value for a later period.

Admittedly, when the Greeks adopted the Semitic script, they did not choose the Semitic glottal fricative symbol '*hē*' (E) for the sound, requiring this for vocalic use, but instead

---

[103] R. Jakobson, *Selected Writings*, I, p. 528. R. Hiersche has pointed out, however (*Gnomon*, 44 (1972), p. 760), that this rule does not extend to psilotic dialects of Ionic, which have aspirated plosives but no aspirate.

[104] Cf. also the description in *Schol. in Dion. Thr.*, p. 142 H: 'ἐκ τοῦ θώρακος μετὰ πολλῆς τῆς ὁρμῆς ἐκφερομένου'.

employed the Semitic '*ḥēt*', which represented a more constrictive type of fricative. One of the Indo-European origins of the Greek aspirate, viz. *y* (as in the relative ὅς beside Sanskrit *yaḥ*) could have developed to [h] through the prehistoric stage of a palatal fricative [ç];[105] but already at the time of the operation of Grassmann's Law (see pp. 15, 20) the Greek phoneme must have developed its purely aspirate value.

It is well known that the Greek aspirate, like the Latin *h*, did not prevent elision or crasis, nor have any effect on positional quantity (cf. *VL*, p. 43).[106] This has led some scholars to assume that it must therefore have represented no more than a simultaneous feature of the vowel, that is, probably a voiceless vowel.[107] This, however, does not necessarily follow; the Greek grammarians admittedly classify the aspirate as a προσῳδία, like the accent, rather than as a consonant, but this classification may well reflect its structural function rather than its physical, phonetic nature. The consonantal function of English *h* is indicated by the fact that e.g. *howl* takes the indefinite article *a* like *fowl*, and not *an* like *owl*. But there is nothing to prevent the same type of sound functioning as a consonant in one language and as a 'prosody' in another, particularly when, as here, the sound has no inherent oral articulation but rather conforms to that of the following vowel.[108] Certainly the argument for 'voiceless vowels' in Greek is not so cogent as to recommend the attempt at such sounds in practice.

So far we have considered the aspiration only as a feature of initial position. In compound words, however, one has to consider the possibility of aspiration of the second member, thereby giving rise to medial aspiration, or 'interaspiration' as it is commonly called. When the first member ends in a voiceless plosive, this is of course an established fact (e.g. ἐφορῶ from

[105] But the comparable Armenian change of cl. [y] to mod. [h] in historical times (e.g. *Yoyn* 'Greek' = mod. [hun] etc.) shows no evidence of any such intermediate stage.

[106] C. J. Ruijgh, however (*Études du grec mycénien*, pp. 53 f.), suggests otherwise for Mycenaean.

[107] E.g. A. Thumb, *Untersuchungen über den Spiritus Asper im Griechischen*, p. 68.

[108] Cf. Gimson, p. 186, 'it may be regarded as a strong, voiceless onset of the vowel in question'.

ἐπ(ι) + ὁρῶ), the aspiration having become a feature of the plosive. But the situation is less clear where the first element ends in a vowel or in a consonant which has no aspirated counterpart. In such cases the aspirate does not generally appear in Attic inscriptions which otherwise indicate it, but it is occasionally found—e.g. ευʰορκον, παρʰεδροι, προσʰεκετο (= προσηκέτω). Latin transcriptions show considerable variation, and this may have been a feature of Greek speech itself; the presence of aspiration in such forms could well have depended upon the extent to which the two elements of the compound were still recognized as such by the speaker.[109] Similar considerations may well have applied to the aspirate at the beginning of words in closely connected speech, when preceded by a consonant, and this would further help to explain the phenomena of elision etc. referred to above.[110] Apart from compounds (and exclamations as εὐαῖ), interaspiration is attested for Attic only in the word ταῶς 'peacock', a borrowing of uncertain origin, which is specifically mentioned by Athenaeus (397 E ff., citing Trypho and Seleucus as authorities).

It will be remembered that the aspirated plosives were described as δασύ, and the unaspirated as ψιλόν (p. 15); in discussing the pure aspirate [h] the grammarians adopted the same terminology, calling it not merely πνεῦμα but more specifically and pleonastically πνεῦμα δασύ ('spiritus asper', 'rough breathing'), and then referring to its absence by the self-contradictory πνεῦμα ψιλόν ('spiritus lenis', 'smooth breathing'). This terminology was encouraged by the use of a specific sign for the latter by the Alexandrians as a device for directing attention to the correct reading in forms like ὄρος. It does not, however, justify the assumption sometimes made that the 'smooth breathing' was something more than the absence of the 'rough' breathing, more specifically a glottal stop (as e.g. at the beginning of German words having an initial vowel, or intervocalically in Cockney and some Scottish pronunciations

---

[109] An indication of this perhaps survives in a statement attributed to Herodian (ii, p. 48 L) suggesting that the adjective φίλιππος was pronounced with aspiration, but not the proper name.

[110] Cf. J. Soubiran, L'élision dans la poésie latine, p. 110.

of words like *butter*, *water*). Indeed such an assumption is almost certainly ruled out by the fact that unaspirated initial vowels in Greek permit elision and crasis, which would be highly improbable if they were preceded by a stop articulation.

(ix) Consonant-groups represented by single symbols

(*a*) ζ There is fairly clear evidence that at quite an early period the symbol Ⲓ, later Z, had come to represent the sequence [zd], as is stated by the grammarians (e.g. †Dionysius Thrax, *Ars Gramm.*, p. 14 U; cf. Dion. Hal., *De Comp.* xiv, p. 53 UR), rather than [dz] as it is often pronounced by English classical scholars. Internal indications of this are seen in the following facts: (1) The combinations Ἀθήνας + δε, θύρας + δε (with -δε as in οἴκόνδε) are represented by Ἀθήναζε, θύραζε (cf. pp. 45 f.); (2) In most dialects, including Attic, a nasal is regularly lost before the fricative σ; thus, whereas the ν of συν is preserved before the stop δ in e.g. σύνδεσμος, it is lost in σύστασις. The same loss is regularly found before ζ, e.g. σύζυξ, συζῆν, and πλάζω beside ἔπλαγξα, thus indicating that the sound immediately following the nasal was a fricative and not a stop.

The [zd] value also incidentally adds point to the comic ὦ Βδεῦ δέσποτα cited by Tzetzes, possibly referring to Aristophanes, *Lysistrata*, 940, where the MSS have Ζεῦ.

Prehistorically the combination represented by ζ derives in some cases from an Indo-European *sd* [zd]; thus ὄζος 'branch' is cognate with German *Ast*, deriving from *osdos* (cf. also Hittite *hasd-*); ἵζω is a reduplicated present from an original *si-sd-ō* (from which also derives Latin *sīdo*), related to the root *sed-* in the same way as e.g. μί-μν-ω is related to μένω. But more often ζ derives from an original *dy* or *gy*—e.g. in πεζός from *ped-yos*, ἄζομαι beside ἅγιος; and these original groups must first have developed though an affricate* state, e.g. [dž] (as in *edge*) → [dz] (as in *adze*)[111] (cf. Latin *medius* → Italian *mezzo*); so that the presumed pronunciation of these latter forms with [zd] represents a

---

[111] This is also a probable development for the cases where Greek ζ apparently derives from an original *y*, e.g. ζυγόν = Latin *iugum*.

metathesis of the fricative and stop elements. However, such metatheses are of a particularly common type; R.P. *wasp*, for example, derives from an earlier and still dialectal *waps* (cf. Old Prussian *wobse*); and the particular change in question is closely paralleled e.g. in Old Church Slavonic *mežda* from Indo-European *medhyā*; an intermediate stage must here have been *medža*, which has given Russian *mežá* 'boundary' (Russian *méždu* 'between' is a borrowing from O.C.S., being the locative dual of *mežda*). A sequence [dz] would in any case have been peculiarly isolated in Greek when it possessed neither any other affricates such as [ts] nor an independent /z/ phoneme;[112] in the sequence [zd], on the other hand, the [z] element would be a normal voiced variant of the /s/ phoneme as in, for example, Λέσβος (cf. p. 46).

This having been said, it nevertheless remains probable that at the time when the Semitic alphabet was adopted by Greek the '*zayin*' symbol was at first applied to a still existing affricate type of combination; for it is difficult to see why a sequence [zd] should not have been represented by σδ instead of by a special sign; whereas, since voice-assimilation in Greek is normally regressive rather than progressive,[113] δσ would not be a satisfactory representation of [dz]; it has also been suggested that the affricated combination was at this early period a single phoneme and so preferably represented by a single symbol. Similar considerations apply to the Mycenaean Linear B writing-system, which has a special series of characters corresponding in part to the ʒ of later dialects, and in part representing a voiceless sound derived from *ky* for which an affricate value of some kind is most probable.

The value of ʒ as an affricate may also have survived in some of the Greek dialects; in some early Cretan inscriptions we find it used to represent a voiceless sound (? [ts]) deriving from *ty*; and forms of the letter are used with a probable value [ts]

---

[112] Cf. also Allen, *Lingua*, 7 (1958), p. 121, n. 40 and refs.

[113] I.e. a voiced consonant such as /d/ may account for a voiced allophone of a preceding but not of a following /s/. Note that, for example, in the aorist of a verb such as τρίβω (ἔτριψα) it is the plosive that is assimilated to the following fricative and not vice versa.

in the native Oscan and Umbrian alphabets. A voiced affricate value seems also to have been known to late Latin
speakers if one may judge from such spellings as *baptidiare*
for *baptizare* and conversely *zebus* for *diebus*.[114]

However, the metathesis of [dz] to [zd] must have occurred
at an early date in Attic and most other dialects;[115] and the
continuation of the [zd] value up to the 5th and early 4th
century is indicated by the use of ʒ to represent Iranian *zd* (e.g.
'Ωρομαʒης = *Auramazda* in Plato, 'Αρταοʒος = *Artavazda* in
Xenophon).[116] Later in the 4 c. we begin to find ʒ replacing σ
used for Iranian *z*;[117] and in Greek inscriptions there begin to
be some confusions between ʒ and σ (e.g. αναβαʒμουσ 329 B.C.;
cf. p. 46). This suggests that at some time in the 4 c. the change
to the modern Greek value as [z] was already taking place;
indeed it is probably referred to by Aristotle (†*Met.*, 993 a) when
he says that, whereas some people would analyse ʒ into σ + δ,
others consider it a separate sound which does not comprise
already recognized elements. It has been plausibly suggested
by G. Nagy[118] that this change does not represent a normal
phonetic development but rather a dialectal replacement from
the Koine (just as σσ replaced ττ). Such a [z] would presumably
have arisen from an earlier [dz], and after short vowels at least
the original quantitative pattern is likely to have been preserved
by gemination, i.e. [zz];[119] this is also indicated by its rep-

[114] Cf. also M. Leumann, *Mél. Marouzeau*, pp. 384 ff.

[115] An Attic inscription of *c*. 480 has τοισʒ(ε) for τοῖσδε, where σʒ is a geminated
writing for voiced [zd], parallel to the frequent -σστ- for voiceless [st] in αρισστων for
'Αρίστων etc. Similarly δικασʒοιτο on a 6 c. Argive inscription (Threatte, pp. 527,
546).

[116] Attic inscriptions of the 5 c. show variation between single and double ʒ in the
forms αʒ(ʒ)ειοι, βυʒ(ʒ)αντιοι, κλαʒ(ʒ)ομενιοι—all referring to places in Asia Minor. Just
possibly this is an attempt to represent an affricate of the type [dz]; a spelling δσ would,
by recessive assimilation, be mispronounced as [ts], and ʒ as [zd], whereas a spelling
ʒʒ = [zdzd] would at least include the required sequence [dz].

[117] The evidence is discussed in detail by M. Vasmer, *Izsledovanie v oblasti drevne-
grečeskoj fonetiki* (Moscow, 1914).

[118] *Greek Dialects and the transformation of an Indo-European process*, p. 127.

[119] This appears from its regular prosodic value in later verse, as well as from the
fairly common use of σʒ for intervocalic ʒ in Hellenistic inscriptions (Threatte, p.
547). Gemination will, of course, only have applied to intervocalic position *within*
the word. Cases are found of short quantity before initial (but not medial) ʒ in later
poetry: this applies to all the cases mentioned by Maas, § 123.

resentation as *ss* in the early Latin borrowing *massa* = μάζα (cf. *VL*, p. 46).

The grammarians' statements of the [zd] value are of course of late date and almost certainly reflect a grammatical tradition rather than a continuation of this value in current speech.

It remains to mention that in the texts of Lesbian poetry medial ζ is replaced by σδ (ὔσδος = ὄζος, etc.; initially also according to the grammarians), whereas ζ is used for a result of synizesis in e.g. ζά from [dya] = διά. These spellings almost certainly represent a later editing, based on the then general value of ζ, since they are not found in early Lesbian inscriptions; but they point to the preservation of the pronunciation [zd] in this dialect after it had changed to [z(z)] elsewhere; and to the coexistence with it of some other sound (? [dz] or [z]) of local origin, for which at the editorial date ζ was the most appropriate writing.

(*b*)   ξ and ψ   From grammarians' descriptions of the values of these letters (e.g. †Dionysius Thrax, *Ars Gramm.*, p. 14 U), as well as from the origins of the sounds they represent (e.g. stem φυλακ- + nom. sing. -ς → φύλαξ, stem λειπ- + fut. -σω → λείψω), it is clear that they stand for [ks] and [ps] respectively.[120] The symbol Ξ apparently derives from the Semitic '*samekh*', but the origin of ψ is uncertain; it is in any case surprising that special symbols should have been adopted for these combinations when they could very well have been written as κσ, πσ, and are in fact so written in some early alphabets. They may have been introduced after the analogy of the other combination of plosive + fricative, viz. ζ for [dz], for which, as we have seen, there were special reasons; but it may also be noted that these groups do have a structural peculiarity in that they can occur in both initial and final position, and to this extent are comparable in Greek with single consonants rather than with other groups.[121]

[120] In West Greek alphabets (from which the Latin is derived) [ks] is represented by X, and ψ stands for kh.

[121] Cf. J. Kuryłowicz, *II Fachtagung f. indogermanische u. allgemeine Sprachwissenschaft* (Innsbruck, Oct. 1961), p. 111.

In the pre-Eucleidean Attic alphabet they were written as χσ and φσ respectively (e.g. εδοχσεν, φσεφισμα), i.e. with aspirated first members; and this aspiration survives when, as occasionally, there is metathesis of the sounds (e.g. ε]υσχαμενοσ, σφυχ[ε).[122] It seems unlikely, however, that full aspiration was involved; in forms like γράψω, ἕξω from γραφ-, ἐχ- + -σω the grammarians in fact speak of loss of aspiration; and this is supported by the operation of Grassmann's Law (see p. 15: e.g. original ἔχω → ἔχω, but *not* ἕξω → ἔξω). Certainly there is no contrast between aspirate and non-aspirate in this position,[123] and any degree of aspiration that may have existed here can be ignored by the modern reader without any danger of confusion.

(x) ττ/σσ

It has already been mentioned (pp. 12 ff.) that Attic in a number of words shows ττ where most other dialects have σσ—e.g. μέλιττα, ἐλάττων, τέτταρες. In these forms the double consonants in question derive from original *ty*, *ky* and *tw* respectively, which might have been expected in the first instance to give rise to some kind of affricate stage such as [tš] or [ts] (as in *catch* or *cats*). This stage is probably represented by some early Asiatic Ionic inscriptions which show in such cases a special letter Ͳ (e.g. 6–5 c. B.C. ελαͲονοσ, τεͲαραϘοντα), which may be derived from the Semitic 'tsade' (and perhaps survives in the numeral symbol ϡ = 900,[124] now known by the late Byzantine name of σαμπῖ < ὡς ἂν πῖ);[125] a similar affricate may also be partially preserved in Mycenaean. Such a sound was also evidently a feature of some non-Greek 'Aegean'

[122] They are also generally rendered in Armenian by k'ʻs, p'ʻs.

[123] On e.g. ἐκ-σῴζω, cf. L. Lupaş, *SC*, 8 (1966), p. 9.

[124] If so, it tends to invalidate the derivation of this letter from Semitic; for the numeral value stands at the very end, after ω, and not in the position of the Semitic *tsade*, between *pē* and *qōf* (= Greek π and Ϙ). Earlier shapes (apart from Ͳ) are Τ, Τ and ⋏. For survivals in other alphabets cf. p. 47, n.

[125] Cf. Galen, *Comm. in Hippoc. Epid. III* i. 5 (p. 27 Wenkebach): 'ὁ τοῦ πεῖ γράμματος χαρακτὴρ ἔχων ὀρθίαν μέσην γραμμήν, ὡς ἔνιοι γράφουσι τῶν ἐνακοσίων χαρακτῆρα'. It is called 'παρακύισμα' by *Schol. in Dion. Thr.*, p. 496 H.

languages from which Greek adopted certain nouns and proper names (cf. inscr. αλικαρναΤεων, θαλαΤησ).

These facts have led some scholars[126] to suppose that both the ττ of Attic and the σσ of other dialects represent different attempts to write such an affricate without the use of a special symbol; and that the pronunciation as a double plosive or fricative is a post-classical development, based in part at least on the spelling. But apart from the improbability of spelling influence on colloquial speech in antiquity, it is scarcely credible that the existence of an affricate sound would not have been revealed in any inscriptional spelling outside those mentioned above (e.g. as τσ), nor the tradition of it survive in the account of any grammarian. On the other hand it is perfectly feasible for both [tt] and [ss] to develop from an earlier affricate,[127] and there seems therefore no need whatever to assume that the ττ of Attic or the σσ of other dialects mean anything more than they appear to.

A similar dialectal distribution of initial single τ and σ is seen in a few words, e.g. Attic τήμερον (< *ky-), τεῦτλον (loan-word) beside σήμερον, σεῦτλον of Ionic.

[126] Thus Schwyzer, pp. 318 f.; Grammont, p. 107.

[127] The matter is discussed in more detail in Allen, 'Some problems of palatalization in Greek', *Lingua*, 7 (1958), pp. 113 ff.; *TPS*, 1973, pp. 112 ff.; A. Bartoněk, *Vývoj konsonantického systému v řeckých dialektech* (Prague 1961; English summary, pp. 139 ff.).

CHAPTER 2

VOWELS*

(i) Simple* vowels

Greek, unlike Latin (*VL*, p. 47), shows no evidence of any considerable difference of periphery between the short* and long* vowel-systems—though the fact that the long system has to accommodate more contrasts than the short could mean that its periphery was fractionally larger. Anticipating the presentation of the evidence for the various vowel-qualities, we may approximately represent the classical systems as follows:

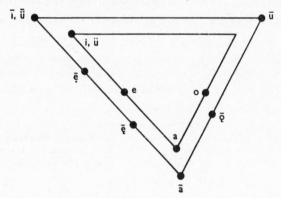

Fig. 2. Classical Attic vowel-systems.

In terms of post-Eucleidean orthography, these sounds are represented in Greek letters as follows:

a, ā	α	ẹ̄	η
e	ε	ē̦	ει
o	o	ǭ	ω
i, ī	ι	ū	ου
ü,ǖ	υ		

α The openness* of the long vowel is expressly mentioned by Dionysius of Halicarnassus (†*De Comp.* xiv, p. 51 UR), but there is no evidence for any marked difference of quality between the long and the short; for both lengths α represents and is represented by Latin *a* in transcriptions. It is therefore most probable that the Greek, like the corresponding Latin, short and long vowels were similar to the first and second vowels respectively in e.g. Italian *amare*. The nearest English approximations are (acoustically) the short [ʌ] in RP *cup*, and the long [ā] in *father*, though the latter is too retracted in quality. For the short vowel the [æ] of RP *cap* is decidedly inaccurate.

In this respect the Greek and Latin short vowels are very different from those of Sanskrit, and of the Indo-Aryan languages up to the present day; for whereas the long *ā* of these languages is a fully open vowel, the Indians themselves have recognized from ancient times that their short *a* has a much closer* quality.[1] One result of this is that the Greek short α may be transcribed by the *long* Indian *ā* (as in the Sanskrit astronomical term *āpoklima-* = ἀπόκλιμα); conversely a short Indian *a* may be represented by a Greek mid* vowel—thus βραμεναι = *brāhmaṇa-*, with ε for *a*, in the Greek translation of an edict of Ashoka recently found at Kandahar.[2] These facts provide a further indication that the Greek short open vowel was not markedly dissimilar in quality from the long.

ε, ο There is no reason to think that the sounds represented by these letters were ever other than short mid vowels, front* and back* respectively, i.e. rather like the vowels of English *pet* and German *Gott*.[3] The view that they were of a specially close mid quality, i.e. [ẹ], [ọ], as in French *gai*, *beau*, is probably mistaken (cf. pp. 72, 89 f.). In modern Greek ε (together with αι) is if anything rather more open than the vowel of English *pet*, being approximately [ę]; and ο (together with ω) is midway between the vowels of English *pot* and *port*, i.e. approximately [ǫ] (though less fully back).

The fact that Greek ε commonly transcribes Latin *ĭ* (κομετιον etc.: *VL*, p. 49) is evidence only that, as known from other sources, the Latin vowel was a peculiarly open one, and so was

---

[1] Cf. Allen, pp. 57 f.   [2] Cf. L. Renou, *JA* 1964, pp. 152 f.
[3] The vowel of English *pot* is decidedly less accurate, being fully open rather than mid.

as near to Greek ε as to ι. Conversely, the representation of Greek ε by Latin ĭ, in, for example, *Philumina* = Φιλουμένη suggests only that the Latin ĭ was about as near as ĕ to the Greek ε; in fact most of such examples involve words in which ε is followed by a nasal (cf. also e.g. *Artimisia* = ᾿Αρτεμισία), and in this environment it is not uncommon for the pronunciation of vowels to be somewhat closer than elsewhere; evidence of this is seen in some Greek dialects, notably Arcadian, in which e.g. -μενος becomes -μινος, ἐν becomes ἰν. Thus the ε in Greek words of this type may, even in Attic, stand for a specially close variety of [e] which would then be particularly near to the Latin ĭ.[4]

In a similar manner, the representation of Greek o by Latin ŭ in e.g. *amurca* = ἀμόργη,[5] inscr. *empurium* = ἐμπόριον (cf. also *VL*, p. 49, n.), suggests only that the Latin ŭ was about as near as ŏ to the Greek o. Many of these cases involve a following *r*, which in some languages has an opening effect on vowels, including short vowels in Latin (*VL*, p. 51); so that the Latin ŭ in such words may stand for a specially open variety, which would be particularly near to the Greek o.[6]

The fact that Greek o often transcribes ŭ of other languages is evidence only that Greek υ had a value other than [u] (see pp. 65 ff.) and so was unsuitable—e.g. Hdt. Μαρδόνιος = Iranian *Marduniya*. On Indo-Greek coins of the 2 c. B.C., conversely, Greek o is represented by *u* OR *a* (e.g. *Heliyu-/ Heliya-kreyasa* = ᾿Ηλιοκλέους), since Indo-Aryan has no short *o* (similarly *Teliphasa* for Τηλέφου in the absence of a short *e*).

---

[4] In Attic inscriptions from late 5 c. to mid-3 c. there are numerous examples of ει being written for ε before other than front vowels: e.g. θειοιν = θεοῖν. The most likely explanation is that the ι here represents a semivocalic glide [y] in the transition from the front vowel to a contrasting vowel (cf. Allen, *Word* 15 (1959), pp. 249 ff.): for other possible explanations see Threatte, pp. 147 ff. Threatte's favoured explanation that ει here = a half-close short vowel [ẹ] seems unlikely unless it is in any case associated with the [y] glide suggested above; for the posited front-closure could not be explained by assimilation to a *non*-front following vowel—but could be explained by assimilation to a [y]; the same will apply to the other dialects mentioned by Threatte (and myself, loc. cit.). See also p. 83.

[5] *c* for γ is in any case abnormal (? Etruscan intermediary).

[6] This argument is, however, somewhat weakened by the fact that a similar opening effect is seen in some *Greek* dialects (e.g. Locrian φάρειν).

64

ι There is no strong evidence that the long and short vowels differed in quality, both being close front unrounded*; and the narrow opening of the long vowel is expressly mentioned by Dionysius of Halicarnassus (†loc. cit.). The short ι of Greek is thus likely to have been of closer quality than the vowel of English *bit*; certainly it was closer than the Latin *ĭ*, and it is this that accounts for the fact that ε rather than ι is used to transcribe the Latin vowel (see above). It was thus similar to unaccented modern Greek ι (or η, υ, ει, οι, etc.), or French [i] as in *vite*.

The long ι of Greek is most nearly represented in English by the vowel of e.g. *bead*; but for most English speakers this is a diphthongal* sound, with a more open starting point: more similar is the accented ι (etc.) of modern Greek, or French [i] as in *vive*. The view that the Greek long vowel was more open than the short (e.g. Sturtevant, p. 31) is probably mistaken; apart from the statement of Dionysius, such a situation would be surprising by comparison with many other languages. There are indeed a number of words in which Greek ῑ is represented by Latin *ē* or Romance *ę*—e.g. inscr. *Chrestus* = Χρῑστός, French *crème* from χρῖσμα, Italian *artetico* from ἀρθρῑτικός; but in many such cases it is to be noted that the vowel is preceded by ρ, and it is possible that in Greek, but not Latin, a long vowel in this position was liable to a rather opener pronunciation than elsewhere (cf. the early differentiation seen in e.g. Attic fem. μικρά beside μεγάλη). In these forms, therefore, the Greek ῑ may well have had a specially open value; but the remaining cases are too few to support the hypothesis that such a pronunciation was normal in other environments.[7]

υ The sounds represented by this letter correspond genetically to the back close rounded* vowels [u] and [ū] of related languages: e.g. Greek ζυγόν = Latin *iugum* = Sanskrit *yugám*; θῦμός = Latin *fūmus* = Sanskrit *dhūmáḥ*; and this was no doubt

---

[7] In *crĕpĭda* from κρηπῖδα the correspondence Lat. *ĭ* = Gr. ῑ is of little significance in view of the anomalous representation of η by *ĕ* (Meillet, *Esquisse d'une histoire de la langue latine*, p. 93, suggests an Etruscan intermediary).

the original Greek value, as is further indicated by the historical retention of this quality in some (non-Attic) dialects (see p. 69). The same symbol continues to be used with the value [u] even in Attic in the diphthongs αυ and ευ (and originally ου: see pp. 75 f.); this quality is also presupposed by the onomatopoeic verbs μῡκάομαι for the lowing of cattle[8] (cf. Latin *mūgire*) and βρῡχάομαι for the roaring of lions (cf. Latin *rūgire*), and by κόκκυξ as the name of the cuckoo (cf. Latin *cucūlus*).[9]

But a change in this value seems to have occurred in Attic-Ionic at quite an early date. For Ionic such a change may possibly be indicated by the occasional inscriptional spellings αο, εο for the diphthongs from the 6 c. B.C. (cf. Bartoněk, p. 113). More certainly, we have already noted that Herodotus found the Ionic υ unsuitable as a rendering of Old Persian *ŭ*, and some indication of its value may be gleaned from the fact that it is used to represent Old Persian *vi* [wi] in Ὑστασπης = *Vištaspa-*. [wi] is a sequence of a back rounded semivowel and a front unrounded vowel; and in the absence of a consonantal symbol for [w] (see pp. 47 ff.), the sequence could well have been approximately rendered by transcribing it with a letter which had the value of a *combination* of rounded and front quality, in fact a *front rounded* vowel, like the French *u* or German *ü*. At a later date the same device is seen in the use of κυ to render the Latin *qui* (e.g. ακυλλιοσ = *Aquilius*, cf. Threatte, pp. 447 f.), where the Latin *ui* probably stands for [ẅi] (with front rounded semivowel: cf. *VL*, p. 17); κυ similarly is sometimes rendered by Latin *qui* (cf. *VL*, p. 52).

When the Boeotians adopted the Attic (Ionic) alphabet and its values around 350 B.C., they found the υ unsuitable for representing the genetically corresponding [u] vowels of their dialect, which they rendered instead by ου: e.g. π]ουθιω = Attic

---

[8] Cf. Dion. Hal., *De Comp.* xvi, p. 62 UR.

[9] See, however, p. 142. Originally onomatopoeic words may of course continue in use after phonetic changes have destroyed their imitative value, as in the case of e.g. English *bleat* since about 1600. It is to be noted that κόκκυ is no longer attested in classical Attic as a simple representation of the cry of the cuckoo. At Arist., *Birds*, 505 it is associated with the noun κόκκυξ and (507) the sense 'Quick!' Similarly γρῦ and (μὺ) μῦ have verbal connexions in γρύζω, μύζω. Cf. also p. 142.

Πυθίου. A more positive indication of the Attic value of υ is suggested from the 3 c. B.C. by the Boeotian use of this letter for the sound corresponding to Attic οι (e.g. τυσ αλλυσ προξενυσ = τοῖς ἄλλοις προξένοις). The development of original [oi] in this dialect is likely to have been first to a close mid front rounded [ǫ̈] (rather as in French *creuse*: cf. p. 81: possibly indicated by the earlier spelling οε), and then to a fully close [ü]; for this would be exactly parallel to an earlier development of the equivalent *un*rounded vowel [ẹ̄] (= Attic ει: cf. p. 70) to Boeotian [ī]—e.g. ἔχι = Attic ἔχει.[10] The value of long υ in Attic is therefore likely to have been [ü] at this time.[11]

On Indo-Greek coins of the 2 c. B.C. υ is represented by *i* (e.g. *Dianisiyasa* = Διονυσίου); but this does not necessarily mean that the Greek [ü] had by then become [i] as in the modern language; it indicates only that Indo-Aryan had no rounded front vowel, and so rendered it by the equivalent unrounded vowel. This conclusion is also supported by the Latin evidence; in early borrowings and transcriptions from Greek, Latin speakers wrote and pronounced *u* (i.e. the equivalent back vowel) for Greek υ, as in e.g. Ennius' '*Burrus*' for Πύρρος (cf. *VL*, p. 52); but with the spread of Greek knowledge, the Greek pronunciation and letter came to be adopted, at least in educated circles—hence e.g. *hymnus, Olympia.* Clearly, whilst the Greek sound was not [u], neither was it [i]; and there are references in Latin writers to its non-existence in native Latin words: thus e.g. Cicero, *Or.* 160 and †Quintilian, xii. 10. 27.

In the 1 c. B.C. a front close rounded value is also roughly suggested by Dionysius of Halicarnassus (†*De Comp.* xiv, p. 52 UR), who refers on the one hand to a 'marked contraction around the lips' and on the other to a sound which is 'stifled and thin'.

[10] In the 5 c. Boeotian varies between ει (or the monograph Ⱶ) and ι, but thereafter ι is regular.

[11] Earlier evidence is provided by the fact that in Attic inscriptions of the earliest period κ rather than ϙ is almost invariably preferred before υ, suggesting that υ was no longer a back vowel (see p. 17). The 'belt-and-braces' spelling κϙυελνιοσ (for κϙυλενιοσ) on an amphora of *c.* 570 may indicate the transitional period. The occasional confusion of υ and ι in semi-literate inscriptions (e.g. αριστονιμο beside αριστονυμο on ostraka of 433/2) suggests that υ was by now a front vowel. Cf. Threatte, pp. 22 f., 261 ff.

A phonetic development in Attic itself suggests that the vowel in question still had a rounded quality in the 2 c. A.D.; for in inscriptions from the end of this century we find cases of υ replaced by ου (= [ū]: see pp. 76 ff.) under certain specific conditions, principally after ρ (e.g. χρουσου for χρυσοῦ).[12] It is true that already from the 4 c. B.C. one finds the spelling ημυσυ for ἥμισυ; but this means only that the unrounded ι [i] was assimilated to the following rounded υ [ü] in this word, and does not indicate a general confusion of the two sounds (it is to be noted that no such change is found when the following syllable has no υ—thus e.g. ημισει). Similarly the substitution (rare in inscriptions) of βιβλίον for βυβλίον simply indicates an assimilation of [ü] to the following [i].[13]

That the pronunciation of υ had still not changed to [i] by the 4 c. A.D. is suggested by the fact that Wulfila found it necessary to adopt the Greek letter in transcribing the υ of Greek words.[14]

We may safely say, then, that in classical times the value of Attic short υ was similar to that of e.g. French *lune*, and of long υ to that of French *ruse*.

It may be noted that, for reasons that are not in all cases clear, initial υ is always aspirated (ὑ).[15]

Confusion of υ with ι is found in Egyptian papyri of the 2–3 c. A.D., or even earlier, but this is probably a regional peculiarity;

[12] Threatte, however (pp. 266–7), doubts the significance of these examples.
[13] The form βύβλος evidently survived (though also replaced analogically by βίβλος), and this may have influenced the maintenance of βυβλίον: see e.g. Plate facing p. 70 below.
[14] In roman transliterations of Gothic it is commonly written as *w*, because in non-Greek words it was used for the semivowel [w]: thus e.g. *swnagoge* = συναγωγή, but Gothic *waurd* 'word'. It is also used to represent the Greek οι, which by this time had evidently the same value as υ (e.g. *in Lwstrws* = ἐν Λύστροις): cf. p. 81. In Armenian, Greek υ and οι are both variously rendered by *iu*, *i* and *u*.
[15] Buck's suggestion ((*a*), p. 134; cf. p. 54 above) that original *u*- first became [yu] ('cf. NE *unit*, etc.') will hardly work; for one thing, the supposed English parallel, involving Middle English [ū] of French origin, has a much more complex history (→ ēu → īu → iu → yū); and for another, the Greek development is not restricted to dialects in which [u] → [ü]. The Boeotian development ιου (e.g. τιουχα = τύχη) indicates only the palatalized quality of preceding dental consonants (cf. Allen, *Lingua*, 7 (1958), p. 117). The generalization of the aspirated initial must be later than the operation of Grassmann's Law (e.g. ὑφαίνω beside Sanskrit *ubhnāti*): cf. p. 43, n. 76.

and the eventual change of [ü] to [i] seems not to be general until around the end of the millennium. The Byzantine naming of the letter as ὒ ψιλόν still suggests a pronunciation [ü]; for ψιλός is commonly used by Byzantine writers as the opposed term to δίφθογγος, and so in this case to distinguish the spelling υ from οι (which had come to have the same phonetic value: cf. p. 79 on ἒ ψιλόν), and not from ι.

Some dialects evidently retained the original *back* [u] quality longer than Attic. We have seen that, when the Boeotians adopted the Attic alphabet, they found the Attic υ unsuitable for representing the corresponding sounds in Boeotian, and instead wrote ου (which in Attic had the value [ū]: see p. 76). The same retention of an [u] value is attested for Laconian by glosses such as (Hesychius) οὐδραίνει· περικαθαίρει (i.e. = ὑδραίνει), Λάκωνες. The modern Tsaconian is also often cited as evidence for the continued retention of [u], in view of forms such as [žuγó] from ζυγόν as against [ziγós] in standard modern Greek (e.g. Buck (*b*), p. 28; Sturtevant, p. 42). But this can hardly be relevant, since Tsaconian also shows [u] for original οι, which makes it more probable that the [u] is a *redevelopment* from earlier [ü]; and this is supported by the occurrence of 'palatalization' before the [u] in these cases (e.g. [šćúlos] = σκύλος, [čumúme] = κοιμοῦμαι), since this can only be caused by a *front* vowel articulation.[16]

η and ει There is little external evidence to establish positive values for these symbols in classical Attic. That they were different is shown by the fact that they later develop differently, the sound represented by ει soon becoming a close long front vowel [ī], whereas the sound of η remains for some time in the

[16] G. P. Shipp ('IOY = Y in Modern Greek', *Glotta*, 43 (1965), pp. 302 ff.) rejects the derivation of Tsak. [u] from [ü], and suggests that a pronunciation ιου [yu] arose (with consequent palatalization of a preceding consonant) as a result of speakers of dialects which allegedly retained the old [u] trying to pronounce words borrowed from other dialects with [ü]. But this will not explain the development of οι. Newton (pp. 19 ff.) assumes [ü] as the general underlying form, but recognizes that there are some words (common to the dialects) which require [u] (e.g. μουστάκι, στουππί). Dialectal details are given by M. Setátos, 'Τὸ πρόβλημα τῆς ἐξέλιξης τοῦ ἀρχαίου ἑλληνικοῦ υ ὡς τὰ νέα ἑλληνικά', ΕΛΛΗΝΙΚΑ, 20 (1967), pp. 338 ff.

mid region. These developments further indicate that the sound of ει was always closer than that of η. This situation is reflected in the transcription of Greek words in Latin, where η is represented by ē until a late date, whereas ει is represented by ī (e.g. sēpia = σηπία, pīrāta = πειρατής, and Aristīdēs = 'Αριστείδης).[17]

The development of ει to [ī] is revealed by occasional confusion between ει and ι from the late 4 c. B.C., becoming common in the 3 c.[18] But there is no such confusion in earlier times, and the mid value of ει is still indicated by Xenophon's rendering as παράδεισος of an Iranian par(i)dēza- 'garden'.[19]

Thus the sounds of both η and ει were long mid vowels in classical Attic, but the former was more open than the latter. Since they had to be accommodated on the front axis between open [ā] and close [ī] (see p. 62), they can hardly have been other than open mid [ę̄] (= η) and close mid [ẹ̄] (= ει)—i.e. approximately the vowels of French tête for η and of German Beet for ει.

There is a frequently cited piece of support for the interpretation of η as [ę̄] in the fact that in some fragments of Attic comedy the bleating of a sheep is represented by βῆ βῆ (note also the gloss in Hesychius, βηβῆν· πρόβατον), and this can hardly stand for close mid [ẹ̄].[20] An onomatopoeic origin is also probable for the verbs μηκάομαι, βληχάομαι, used of the bleating of goats and sheep.[21]

In the pre-Eucleidean alphabet, [ẹ̄] was not distinguished from short [e], both being written as E.[22] In the earlier inscriptions E is also written for some of the cases (a) which later show ει (e.g. νεσθε = νεῖσθε, εναι = εἶναι), but other cases (b) are written

[17] The original form is 'Αριστήδης, but this becomes obsolete by around the mid-4 c. (cf. p. 85): Threatte, pp. 372 f.

[18] The confusion in MSS has led to some words still sometimes being wrongly spelt (as shown by historical, comparative, and inscriptional evidence): thus ει and not ī is correct in e.g. τείσω, ἔτεισα, μείξω, ἔμειξα; and ī, not ει, is correct in e.g. οἰκτίρω.

[19] Cf. H. Jacobsohn, KZ, 54 (1927), pp. 257 ff.

[20] In modern Greek the same imitation is found with the representation μεε.

[21] An earlier value of η was probably [ǣ] (see p. 73); and it is of interest to note that the conventional imitation of sheep's bleating in the modern Thessalian dialect is reported as [bæbæ] (Newton, p. 50): cf. also Allen, 'Varia onomatopoetica', Lingua, 21 (1968), pp. 1 ff. (2 f.).

[22] See e.g. ποτεριον = ποτήριον in Plate opposite.

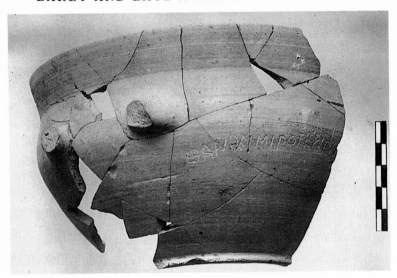

Cup: Athens, *c*. mid-7 c. B.C.
Θαρίο εἰμὶ ποτέριον (see pp. 70 f., 73, 75)

Library notice: Athens, ? early 2 c. A.D.
βυβλίον οὐκ ἐξενεχθήσεται, ἐπεὶ ὠμόσαμεν.
ἀνυγήσεται ἀπὸ ὥρας πρώτης μέχρι ἕκτης.
(See pp. 68, 81 and n. 51)

[Courtesy of the American School of Classical Studies at Athens.]

with EI from earliest times, e.g. τειχοσ = τεῖχος (both classes are exemplified by the form ειπεν = εἰπεῖν). The difference between the two sets of cases is accounted for by the fact that those of class (b) were originally diphthongs (as e.g. in English *eight*), and so were appropriately written with the digraph EI (with τεῖχος, for example, compare the related τοῖχος and Oscan *feíhúss = muros*); those of class (a) on the other hand were the result of 'contraction', or of 'compensatory lengthening' (for the loss of a consonant), of original short [e]—thus the examples cited above derive from original νέεσθε, ἔσναι. Since these cases were not originally diphthongal, it was not at first appropriate to write them with a digraph.[23]

But beginning sporadically as early as the 6 c. B.C., and becoming regular in the 4 c., there is a change of spelling whereby the cases of class (a) also come to be written with EI (for chronology cf. Threatte, pp. 173–90). The only possible interpretation of this is that classes (a) and (b) had come to have the same pronunciation. Theoretically this could mean either that the original monophthongs (simple vowels) of (a) had become diphthongs, or that the original diphthongs of (b) had become monophthongs. But since the tendency of Greek at all periods is to monophthongization rather than diphthongization, only the second supposition is realistic. The fact that the monophthong is in some cases the product of an earlier diphthong [ei], comprising a mid and a close element, is one further indication that the resulting sound was a close mid vowel.

The merging of the two classes of sound had evidently taken place in very early times; the fact that occasional spellings with E for class (a) persist even into the early 4 c. B.C. can well be attributed to orthographic conservatism,[24] and it is virtually

---

[23] The spelling ειμι '*sum*' (< *ἐσμί) is surprising. It appears as early as the 7 c. in graffiti (cf. Plate facing p. 70: subgeometric cup), and is in fact the normal spelling. This suggests that, in spite of its origin, it was pronounced as a diphthong—perhaps by analogy with the second person εῖ (< *ἔσι and so originally diphthongal): cf. Threatte, p. 176. Confusion with εῖμι '*ibo*' is a less likely explanation.

[24] Resulting also in occasional spellings with E for the original diphthong: e.g. τεχο[ποιοι; such spellings are infrequent, but that they occur at all is a further indication that the two classes merged to a monophthong rather than a diphthong: cf. Threatte, pp. 173, 299 ff.

certain that by the 5 c. B.C. all words which are now written with ει had the same sound, i.e. a long close mid vowel [ẹ̄]. The choice of the ΕΙ rather than the Ε spelling is hardly surprising, since it avoids ambiguity with Ε = short [e] (and, in pre-Eucleidean orthography, with Ε = long [ẹ̄]).

Incidentally, the fact that a lengthening of originally short [e] gives rise to a close mid long vowel [ẹ̄], as in class (a), is no indication that the short vowel also was a *close* mid vowel (as assumed e.g. by Sturtevant, p. 34); for it is common for long and short mid vowels to differ in quality.[25]

Since, as we have seen, the ει in some words represents sounds which were not formerly diphthongs, it is in such cases sometimes referred to as a 'spurious diphthong'. This is a peculiar misnomer. For one thing, ει is not a diphthong but a digraph; and for another, in neither class of cases does it represent a diphthong in classical times. The term thus reveals a confusion between speech and writing, and between descriptive and historical statement. 'Shorthand' expressions, at least of the former kind, do no harm (and similar instances may be found in this book) provided they are recognized for what they are; but the case in question has sometimes led to the mistaken assumption of two different *pronunciations* of ει (and ου: cf. p. 76).

To the above account of the value of ει an exception needs to be made in the cases where it is followed by a vowel. With regard to the later correspondence of ει = Latin *ī*, Priscian (*GL*, ii, p. 41 K) specifically observes, '...consonante sequente pro *ei* diphthongo longam *i* ponimus, ut Νεῖλος *Nilus*'. Before vowels, on the other hand, the normal representation is by *ē*, as in *Achilleus, Aeneas, Alexandrea, Alpheus, Augeas, brabeum, Calliopea, chorea, Dareus, Decelea, gynaeceum, Medea, museum, panacea, platea, spondeum*,[26] which suggests that in this context the Greek ει continued until Roman times to have a mid value. Occasional alternative spellings with *ī*, as *Darius*, could represent either a

[25] Cf. Allen, *Word*, 15 (1959), pp. 240 ff.; see also pp. 89 f. below.
[26] Cf. J. Tolkiehn, 'Die Wiedergabe des griechischen -ει- im Lateinischen', *PhW*, 43 (1923), pp. 44 ff. and 68 ff.

yet later Greek pronunciation or a purely graphic transfer of the correspondence ɛɪ = ī from preconsonantal position.[27] Some early loans to Latin show a shortening of ē to ĕ, as bal(i)nĕum and the alternatives chorĕa, platĕa.

This peculiarity agrees with the graphic situation in Greek itself; for whereas before consonants ɛɪ begins to be confused with ɪ in the 3 c. B.C., before vowels it begins about the same period, and continues for some time, to be confused with η rather than ɪ—which is a further indication of its continued mid quality in this context[28] (see also p. 83 below).

We may now return to the other long mid front vowel, [ẹ̄]. In pre-Eucleidean spelling this sound also is represented by E. But with the introduction of the Ionic alphabet, [ẹ̄] was unambiguously represented by the letter H (η), which had earlier stood for [h] (see p. 52), but which, as a result of 'psilosis' ('dropping of h's') in East Ionic, had been left free for vocalic use.[29]

The [ẹ̄] of Attic-Ionic has two origins: one from an original ē, the other from an original ā; thus e.g. μήτηρ [mẹ̄tẹ̄r] from mātēr (cf. Doric μάτηρ). The development of ā to [ẹ̄] probably proceeded via a stage [ǣ] (with the approximate quality of the English vowel in bad), intermediate between [ā] and [ẹ̄]. This stage may perhaps be represented by some Ionic inscriptions of the Cyclades, where H was at first used only to represent the vowel arising from original ā, as e.g. in Ϙορη (from

---

[27] A converse transfer might possibly account for the puzzling instances of ɛɪ = ē before consonants, as in hypotenusa, tenesmos, hypogeson, cyperum, and occasional edyllium, Helotes, Perithous, Polycletus. It seems doubtful whether the comment of F. O. Weise, Die griechischen Wörter im Latein, p. 37, is relevant ('...charakteristisch ist, dass fast durchweg vor oder hinter dem in Frage stehenden Vokale eine Liquida steht'), since one would expect opening to apply only in the case of a preceding ρ (cf. p. 65).

[28] The change to [ī] here is probably datable to the 2 c. A.D., when the writing with η ceases, and Herodian (ii. pp. 415 ff. L) finds it necessary to pronounce on the orthography of words ending in -ιος/-ειος etc.; but an earlier change, due to assimilation, is found in the case of ιει, which develops via [ῑ̆] to simple [ī] (e.g. υγια = ὑγίεια) from the 1 c. B.C.; an even earlier assimilative development of [ẹ̄] to [ī] is seen e.g. in Attic χῑλιοι beside Ionic χείλιοι. For further details cf. Threatte, pp. 166, 190 ff., 202 ff.

[29] The [h] value survived in the West Greek alphabet, whence Latin H. Since the same alphabetical position was maintained for both values, the Latin-derived Gothic h has the same numeral value (8) as the Greek η (and its Old Georgian derivative standing for [ey]).

korwā) = Attic κόρη, whereas E continued to be used for the vowel derived from original *ē*, as e.g. in ανεθεκεν = Attic ἀνέθηκεν (from -*thē*-).[30] But in Attic no such distinction is found, the vowels of both origins being represented by H, so that we must assume a single pronunciation as [ẹ̄].[31]

Boeotian, like Attic, had two mid front long vowels [ẹ̄] and [ę̄]. But the distribution of these did not correspond to that of Attic; for as earlier [ẹ̄] had closed to [ī] in Boeotian (see p. 67), so [ę̄] had closed to [ẹ̄]. Consequently, when the Attic alphabet was adopted for Boeotian, one finds e.g. Boeotian πατειρ corresponding to Attic πατήρ. The [ę̄] of Boeotian was the result of monophthongizing the diphthong [ai], so that Boeotian has κη corresponding to Attic καὶ, etc. It is thus clear from the Boeotian spellings that Attic η still had the value [ę̄] in the first half of the 4 c. B.C.

When, at the end of the 4 c., Attic [ę̄] also began to close to [ī], it is possible that [ę̄] too may have tended to become closer. Its representation by *e* on Indian coins of the 2 c. B.C., however, (as well as in Latin: cf. p. 70) shows that it remained a mid vowel, and had not yet become [ī] as in modern Greek. In the 1 c. B.C. Dionysius of Halicarnassus (†*De Comp.* xiv, pp. 51 f. UR) still distinguishes between η and ι, and the fact that he describes the former as more euphonious suggests that he is referring to their sound and not simply to their graphic form.

Confusion between η and ι in Attic inscriptions begins around 150 A.D.,[32] but some confusion with ε also continues to be found.[33] In some areas the mid value of the Koine η may have

[30] On the Cycladic Ionic practice see further A. L. Eire, *Innovaciones del jónico-ático (vocalismo)* (= *Acta Salmanticensia*, filos. y letras, 60 (1970)), p. 18; and R. Arena, 'La lettera ⊟ nell'uso greco più antico', *RIL*, 102 (1968), pp. 3 ff.

[31] In an article 'On the dual pronunciation of *Eta*' (*TAPA*, 93 (1962), pp. 490 ff.), R. W. Tucker has suggested that, in spite of the spelling, Attic distinguished the two vowels in pronunciation until the 4 c. B.C. But his argument is dubious, being based on the assumption that otherwise, in the choruses of Attic tragedy, the poets would not have known when and when not to substitute the Doric ā for the Attic η. For further discussion see Bartoněk, pp. 104 ff.; Threatte, *TAPA*, 100 (1969), pp. 587 ff.

[32] Startling but quite aberrant is the 5 c. B.C. αθινα αρισ αρτεμισ on the slate of a schoolboy signing himself as διμοσοθενισ (*sic*): cf. *SEG*, 19, no. 37; E. Vanderpool, *AJA*, 63 (1959), pp. 279 f. and Plate 75, fig. 11; Threatte, p. 165.

[33] Even at Athens the [ī] pronunciation may have remained non-standard for some time after 150: cf. Threatte, p. 166.

been preserved even longer, since, whereas the Gothic spelling of Wulfila confuses ει and ῑ as *ei*, η is still represented as *e*. Still later, Old Armenian commonly renders η by *e* or *ē*, whereas ει and ι are rendered by *i*; and the Old Georgian alphabet gives different phonetic values to the letters derived from η and ι ([ey] and [i] respectively).[34] In the Old Slavonic alphabets, however, both Cyrillic and Glagolitic, no phonetic distinction is made between the letters derived from H, η and I, ι, their distribution being purely a matter of orthographic convention.

ω and ου The early development of the sounds represented by these symbols was largely parallel to that of η and ει. That is, at one stage they had the values of a long open mid back [ǭ] and close mid back [ō], to which approximate equivalents are provided by the vowels of English *saw* and French *côte* respectively.

The evidence is derived mainly from the internal structure of the system; the value of ω as an open mid vowel incidentally fits its use in the probably onomatopoeic βρωμᾶσθαι (of donkeys: cf. English (*hee-*)*haw*)[35] and κρώζειν (of crows: cf. English *caw*).[36]

In the pre-Eucleidean alphabet [ǭ] was not distinguished from short [o], both being written as O. In the earlier inscriptions O is also written for *some* of the cases (*a*) which later show ου (e.g. μισθοντα = μισθοῦντα, ελθοσαν = ἐλθοῦσαν),[37] but other cases (*b*) are written with OY from earliest times, e.g. (pr. n.) σπουδιασ (both classes are exemplified in ακολουθοντα = ἀκολουθοῦντα). The difference between the two sets of cases is accounted for by the fact that those of class (*b*) were originally

[34] It is noteworthy that in modern Pontic Greek η is still represented by ε in many categories and contexts (cf. D. E. Oeconomides, *Lautlehre des Pontischen*, pp. 11 ff.).

[35] Cf. the ὤ of Apuleius' Ass (*Met.* iii. 29), which is evidently considered more appropriate than the close mid Latin *ō* (J. L. Heller, *CJ*, 37 (1941–2), pp. 531 ff., and *CJ*, 38 (1942–3), pp. 96 ff.).

[36] Also in μωκᾶσθαι, in its original sense of the roaring of camels; an alternative representation of the element of nasality is seen in the form ὠμάζειν (cf. F. Bancalari, *SIFC*, 1 (1893), p. 93).

[37] See also θαριο = Θαρίου in Plate facing p. 70.

diphthongs (of a type similar to, but more back than, that of English *low*), and hence were appropriately written with the digraph OY (with the above examples compare the cognate σπεύδω, κέλευθος); those of class (*a*) on the other hand were the result of the contraction, or compensatory lengthening, of an original short [o]—thus the cited examples arise from original μισθόοντα, ἐλθόνσαν. Since these latter cases were not originally diphthongal, it was not at first appropriate to write them with a digraph.

But over a period 6–4 c. B.C. there was an increasing tendency, which finally became regular practice, to write the cases of class (*a*) also with OY.[38] The clear interpretation of this is that classes (*a*) and (*b*) had come to have the same pronunciation, and so could be written in the same way; which means (cf. p. 71) that the original diphthong, [ou], comprising a mid and a close element, had come to be a long close mid vowel [ọ̄], identical in quality with the vowel arising from contraction or compensatory lengthening.

The merging of these sounds was certainly complete by the 5 c., though, as in the case of the corresponding front vowel, there are examples of conservative spelling, and occasional spellings with O for the original diphthong (cf. p. 71, n. 24): e.g. σποδιασ.[39] As in the case of ει (see p. 72), the ου representing a vowel of non-diphthongal origin is sometimes referred to as a 'spurious diphthong'.

The fact that the lengthening of an original short [o] gave rise to a close mid long vowel [ọ̄] in class (*a*) is *no* indication that the short vowel also was a *close* mid vowel (cf. p. 72).

We have seen that the Boeotians found the Attic υ unsuitable to represent their own [u] vowels, and used instead the Attic digraph ου. This most probably indicates that by the mid 4 c. the earlier Attic [ọ̄] had become a fully close [ū],[40] as it certainly

[38] For chronology of the change in spelling see Threatte, pp. 238–259, 350 f.

[39] Relatively more frequent than E for original ει, presumably because original ου was less common: cf. Threatte, pp. 350 f.

[40] The proof is not, however, absolute, since even an [ǫ] quality would have been the nearest to Boeotian [u].

had by Roman times (thus e.g. *Thūcȳdides*, and conversely 'Ρουφῖνος). It does not seem possible to determine just how long before 350 B.C. this change took place; it need not have been close to this date (as Sturtevant suggests); the fact that O continued to be written for OY until about this time does not necessarily indicate a continuing mid value, since it may be no more than a conservative spelling. It could be that the change to [ū] took place *during* the classical period; but since the date cannot be fixed, it would clearly be unjustifiable to adopt different pronunciations for different authors! In adopting a single pronunciation for ου, it seems preferable to choose the later [ū] rather than the earlier [ǭ]; for if we are wrong, at least we shall be doing nothing worse than, say, pronouncing Aeschylus as Demosthenes might have done; whereas, if we adopt the other alternative, we may be giving an author a pronunciation which he had never received in antiquity.[41]

Structural considerations make it more probable that the change from [ǭ] to [ū] was quite early. We have already discussed the change of original back [u] to front [ü], for which a period 7–6 c. B.C. has been plausibly suggested (Bartoněk, p. 115). This shift had the effect of reducing the long vowel phonemes on the back axis from four /ā, ǭ, ǫ, ū/ to three /ā, ǭ, ǫ/, which would be in accordance with a general tendency to reduce the number of distinctions on this relatively short axis.[42] Even if we do not go so far as to follow M. S. Ruipérez[43] in envisaging the change of [ū] to [ü] as actually pressured by 'overcrowding' on the back axis, it seems unlikely that, once this change had taken place, the opportunity would long have been resisted of increasing the

---

[41] In favour of the early (6–5 c.) development of [ǭ] to [ū] cf. Schwyzer, p. 233. An argument against a change earlier than about mid-4 c. is suggested by Ruijgh (*Mnem.* 31 (1978), p. 88). Up to that time, as already mentioned, the spelling O could be used for OY: but there are virtually no Attic alternative spellings AO, EO for the diphthongs AY, EY—as might have been expected, in Ruijgh's opinion, if the value of the OY vowel were [ū] (such spellings are common in Ionic: cf. p. 66). This negative evidence, however, is not conclusive, and I tend here to follow the views of other scholars, including Teodorsson (1974, pp. 291 f.).

[42] Cf. A. Martinet, *Économie des changements phonétiques*, pp. 98 f.

[43] *Word*, 12 (1956), pp. 67 ff.

acoustic distance between [ǭ] and [ō̦] by shifting the latter to [ū].[44]

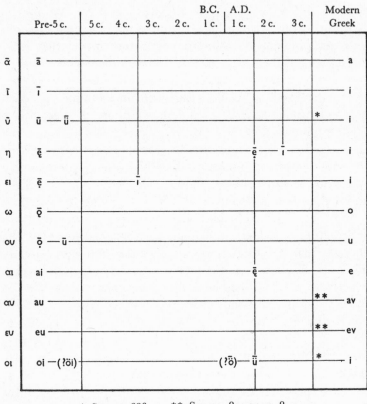

* See pp. 68f.   ** See pp. 8o; 94, n. 8.

Fig. 3. Approximate chronological development of Attic long vowels and 'short' diphthongs (excluding pre-vocalic position).

The clear recommendation, therefore, is to pronounce ου in all cases as a long close back vowel [ū], i.e. as accented ου in modern Greek, or as e.g. in English *pool* or French *rouge*.

[44] See, however, Bartoněk, p. 114. The fact that, whilst short [u] followed its long partner to [ü], short [o] did not shift to [u], would be explained by the fact that in the short vowel-system there was no contrast of open and close mid vowels. [u] in fact remained a gap in the system (see p. 62) until in late Greek the distinction between long and short vowels was abolished (cf. pp. 93 f.).

Whilst it is possible that the open mid vowel [ǭ], relieved of the necessity to avoid confusion with [ọ], may then have moved up into a rather closer position, there is no actual evidence for this, and one is therefore advised to pronounce it as the vowel in RP *saw*.

In pre-Eucleidean spelling [ǭ], like [ọ] and the short [o], had also been represented by O. But with the introduction of the Ionic alphabet, [ǭ] came to be unambiguously represented by the letter Ω (later termed ὦ μέγα as distinguished from ὂ μικρόν).

(ii) Diphthongs*

The diphthongs of classical Attic are represented by the digraphs αι, αυ, ευ, and οι.

αι corresponds to a diphthong [ai] (as in English *high*) in related languages (e.g. αἴθω: Lat. *aedes*), and this value is confirmed up to Roman times by transcriptions into and from Latin (e.g. *palaestra*, Καῖσαρ).

At a later period a monophthongal development took place, giving a quality [ę̄]; this is first revealed by spellings with ε from about 125 A.D., and especially after 150 (cf. Threatte, pp. 294 ff.). The use of ε rather than η in this value is no doubt due to the fact that the value of η had already closed to [ẹ̄], which soon after closed further to [ī] (see p. 74); so that the new [ę̄] vowel could then be approximately represented only by spelling with the short vowel-symbol ε (e.g. κιτε = κεῖται).[45] The monophthongal pronunciation is also confirmed for this period by a specific statement of Sextus Empiricus (*Adv. Gramm.* 116) that the sound of αι, like that of ει, was 'simple and uniform'. In Byzantine times the identical values of αι and ε led to the latter being distinguished as 'ἒ ψιλόν' (cf. p. 69).

αυ similarly corresponds to a diphthong [au] (as in English *how*) in related languages (e.g. αὔξω: Lat. *augeo*), and this value

---

[45] Conversely αι is found for ε, and this is reflected in the Gothic use of *ai* for [e], e.g. *taihun* 'ten'.

79

also is confirmed by transcriptions into and from Latin (e.g. *glaucus*, Κλαυδιος).

ευ There is no evidence that in classical Attic this digraph meant anything but what it appears to, namely a diphthong [eu]. There is no parallel for such a diphthong in English RP, though something like it may be heard in the Cockney pronunciation of *el*(*l*) in words such as *belt*, *bell*. It is to be noted that it is a genuine diphthong, i.e. a glide from [e] towards [u], and not, as is commonly heard from English speakers, a sequence of semivowel and long vowel like the [yū] in English *neuter* (cf. p. 146 and *VL*, p. 63).

In both αυ and ευ the υ preserved its original quality as a back [u], i.e. it was not fronted to [ü] as elsewhere (cf. pp. 66 ff.). Neither of these diphthongs developed to monophthongs;[46] but at a later date, which cannot be certainly determined,[47] the second element (which could alternatively be analysed as a semivowel /w/: cf. p. 5) developed a fricative pronunciation [v]; so that in modern Greek the value of these digraphs is [av] and [ev] (or [af] and [ef]: see p. 48).[48] This development could well be connected with the change of β [b] to [v] (see pp. 30 ff.)—but the date of this also is uncertain.[49]

οι Here also a diphthongal pronunciation is clearly indicated at least until Roman times (e.g. *Phoebus*, *poena*: cf. *VL*, p. 62). The most obvious interpretation would be as [oi] in e.g. English *toy*, *coin*; but in some Greek dialects there is evidence which seems to suggest that, by a process of assimilation, the first element of the diphthong had been fronted, giving something

---

[46] Gothic *au* for [o] is presumably by analogy with *ai* for [e].

[47] The Jewish catacombs at Rome still indicate a diphthongal value in the 2–3 c. A.D.

[48] Similar developments have occurred independently in modern Greek dialects: thus in S. W. Rhodes μάγουλο 'cheek' → *[máulo] → *[máwlo] → [mávlo]; and parallel developments occur even with ι-dipthongs: thus in Zakynthos βόιδι 'ox' → [vóγδi], βοηθάω 'I help' → [voxθáo] (Newton, p. 65).

[49] See further p. 94, n. 8.

of the type [öi],[50] approximately as in French *feuille*. There is no direct evidence for this pronunciation in Attic; it might, however, make rather more plausible the confusion reported by Thucydides (ii. 54) as to whether the oracle had said λοιμός 'plague' or λῑμός 'famine', since [öi], being entirely a front diphthong, would be nearer than the mixed [oi] to the sound [ī].

At a later date οι became confused with υ; thus (*c.* 240 A.D.) ποιανεψιωνα = Πυαν.,[51] indicating a pronunciation [ǖ] for both,[52] following a development attested for Boeotian at a much earlier period (see pp. 66 f.). As in the case of Boeotian also, an intermediate stage in the development was probably [ọ̈] (cf. *VL*, pp. 52, n. 2; 62); the closure of [ọ̈] to [ǖ] would then be parallel to the earlier Attic change of [ē̜] to [ī] (see pp. 67, 70).[53]

'Diphthongs' before vowels

In prevocalic position all the above digraphs are perhaps better considered as representing a sequence of short vowel (/a/, /e/, or /o/) and semivowel (/y/ or /w/), these latter being generally double and so creating heavy quantity in the syllable (cf. *VL*, pp. 38 ff.). The same would apply to υι (prior to its monophthongal development to ū[54]), which in the Attic

---

[50] Cf. Sturtevant, p. 51, n. 48.

[51] Earlier also ανυγησεται = ἀνοιγ. on a notice from the library of Pantainos: cf. *SEG*, 21, no. 500; *Hesperia*, 5 (1936), p. 42, and see Plate facing p. 70 above. The library was dedicated to Trajan (cf. *SEG*, 21, no. 703); such a notice could of course well be later than the foundation, but the graphic style is appropriate to the late 1 c. or early 2 c. A.D. (cf. M. Burzachechi, *Rendic. Lincei*, ser. viii, 18 (1963), pp. 91 f.).

[52] This pronunciation is also probably reflected in late Latin *squinum* for earlier *schoenum* < Gk. σχοῖνος (e.g. Isidore, *Orig.* xvii. 11; cf. Forcellini s.v., and p. 66 above).

[53] For an intermediate development of οι to [ọ̈] as a stage towards the confusion of οι and υ cf. S. G. Kapsomenos, 'Das Griechische in Ägypten', *MH*, 10 (1953), pp. 248 ff. (255 f.). For the confusion in papyri see also F. T. Gignac, 'The language of the non-literary Greek papyri', *Proc. XII Int. Cong. of Papyrology* (= *Amer. St. in Papyrology*, vol. 7, 1970), pp. 139 ff. (141).

[54] Beginning with ὕός for υἱός in the 6 c. B.C. (e.g. hexameter ending ευδικο ηυοσ). Fem. participles in -υῖα were preserved until the 4 c. B.C. This development seems to have been peculiarly Attic, as explicitly stated by Herodian (see Threatte, p. 338), and later υἱός at least was restored.

dialect only occurred before vowels,[55] thus [üyy].[56]

Indications of these values are perhaps given by dialectal spellings such as Arg. αθαναιαι and Cor. ευϝαρχοσ;[57] and they are supported by the fact that in Attic verse the double [yy] semivowel may occasionally be reduced to a single [y], giving light quantity to the syllable—thus e.g. γεραιός, δείλαιος, with light middle syllable in both tragedy (lyric) and comedy, and light initial syllable frequently in ποιῶ, τοιοῦτος. A reduction of [ww] to [w] is also seen in Pindar (*Pyth.* viii, 35) ἰχνεύων with light middle syllable. Similar reductions are found in Homer (e.g. in οἷος *Il.* xiii, 275, etc.; χαμαιεῦναι xvi, 235; υἱός iv, 473); and since a diphthong cannot be shortened in the same sense as a monophthong, the so-called 'epic correption' of a final diphthong before an initial vowel (cf. p. 97) is simply another such instance of short vowel followed by a single semivowel (note the two treatments of οι in *Il.* iii, 172 αἰδοῖός τε μοί ἐσσι). In some cases the reduction led eventually to complete loss of the semivowel, as in the Attic doublet ποεῖν, and πόα, στοά beside Ionic ποίη, Doric στοια.[58] Similar doublets are also found in the text of Homer—e.g. *Od.* vi, 292 νάει beside ix, 222 ναῖον; and alongside the genitive -οιο (= [oyyo]) on the one hand, and the contracted -ου on the other, one must restore -οο (or perhaps [oyo]) in e.g. *Il.* xv, 66; xxii, 313 (MSS Ἰλίου, ἀγρίου).[59]

[55] Preconsonantal υι was generally monophthongized prehistorically to ῡ (e.g. Attic dimin. ἰχθύδιον, Hom. optat. δαινῦτο). Note, however, Hom. πληθυΐ, Lesbian τυΐδε (= τῇδε) etc. (by contraction of υΐ).

[56] Note that υι is *not* to be pronounced as a sequence of semivowel [w] and long vowel [ī] as in English *we* (cf. *VL*, p. 42); such a pronunciation, though often heard, is disproved by the fact of elision before υἱός (as well as by the development to ῠ̆), and by the light first syllable of e.g. ἰδυῖα (where [dw] would create heavy quantity: cf. p. 49).

[57] The inserted ι and ϝ may alternatively be considered simply as automatic glides (which are therefore not normally indicated) following a vocalic element ι, υ (as in e.g. Arg. δαμιιοργοι, Ion. γαρυϝονεσ); but phonetically this makes little difference.

[58] There is also ample inscriptional evidence. αθηναια develops *via* αθηναα to contracted αθηνα, which is regular after 300 B.C. For details of these developments see Threatte, pp. 270–94, 324–33. The vowel-lengthening in Attic ἐλάα, ἀεί, ἀετός, κλάειν etc. (beside e.g. Hom. ἐλαίη) has not been certainly explained.

[59] Failure to recognize this has led to false emendations in e.g. *Il.* v, 21 (ἀδελφειοῦ κταμένοιο, for ἀδελφεοῦ restorable as ἀδελφεο(ι)ο); vi, 34 (κακομηχάνου ὀκρυοέσσης, for -ου κρυ- restorable as -ο(ι)ο κρυ-).

The usual pronunciation of the digraphs αι, αυ, οι, ευ, υι, before vowels was thus probably [ayy], [aww], [oyy], [eww], [üyy], with approximate phonetic parallels for the first three in English phrases such as *high yield*, *bow-wave*, *toy yacht* (and for the 'reduced' forms [ay], [oy] in e.g. *my own*, *coyote*).

We have seen (p. 72) that the long close mid front vowel [ẹ̄] ει was slower to develop to a close [ī] before vowels than before consonants or pause. This could well be the result of a delayed development of prevocalic ει in earlier times; this always derives from a previous 'diphthong' (probably to be interpreted as [eyy]), and it is possible that the monophthongal development was here slower than for preconsonantal [ei]. The earlier value seems to survive in Homer, in view of doublets such as τελέω beside τελείω, χάλκεος beside χάλκειος, which are most readily explained as standing for a reduced variant [ey] beside [eyy], as in the case of e.g. [oy] beside [oyy] (the omission of ι in τελέω, χάλκεος, etc. would be due to the fact that a [y] glide was automatic after a close or mid front vowel; in Attic, with further loss of the single [y], the vowels in these words contracted, giving τελῶ, χαλκοῦς, etc.). The same type of reduction is, however, also attested for Attic from the 5 c. B.C., and becomes particularly common in the 4 c.; it is revealed in inscriptions, as in the text of Homer, by writings without ι, e.g. ιερεα, δωρεα for ἱέρεια, δωρειά; after the 4 c. one or other of the variants tends to be generalized (mostly ει); in the case of πλείων, ει is regular before long vowels, and ε in the neuter πλέον, whilst practice varies before short vowels in other forms of the word.[60]

These developments are most easily understood if one assumes that in the classical period ει before vowels, unlike before consonants (see p. 71), stands for [eyy],[61] in which only later

---

[60] For full details of inscriptional evidence see Threatte, pp. 302–23.

[61] There is a comparable situation in Boeotian, where οι → υ [ǖ] preconsonantally (see p. 67), but rarely prevocalically: thus e.g. βοιωτυσ = Βοιωτοῖς. Sanskrit also provides a parallel, e.g. in the verb meaning 'lie': in the athematic form of the 3 sing. pres. (ending -*te*) this appears as *śete* (= κεῖται), but in the thematic form (ending -*ate*) it appears as *śayate*, with which in turn one may compare the Hom. 3 plur. impf. κείατο ~ κέατο.

does the [ey] portion develop to monophthongal [ẹ̄] (with the second [y] then becoming an automatic glide). An approximate phonetic parallel is provided by an English phrase such as *hay-yield*; the 'reduced' variant, as in πλέον, is approximately represented by e.g. *play on*.[62]

In view of the general parallelism between the development of ει and ου, one might wonder whether a similarly delayed development applied to ου before vowels. Certainly at some early period the value seems to have been [oww], since a reduced form [ow] is found in, for example, Attic ἀκοή[63] beside Hom. ἀκουή; and the Attic ὠτός (gen. sing. of οὖς) beside Hom. οὔατος represents a contraction of ὄατος which in turn presupposes an intermediate stage ὄϝατος. But where prevocalic ου survives, there are no indications that by classical times its pronunciation was other than in preconsonantal position, i.e. [ū].

(iii) 'Long' diphthongs

A particular problem is presented in Greek by a series of diphthongs, commonly known as 'long' diphthongs, which were partly inherited and partly created by contraction, and in which the first element is represented by a long vowel as opposed to the short vowel of the diphthongs so far considered. Where the second element is ι , such 'long' diphthongs are relatively common—thus ᾱι, ηι, ωι; but there are also rarer cases of Attic ᾱυ (e.g. τᾱὐτό), ηυ (e.g. ηὑρέθην), and ωυ (πρωὐδᾶν Ar. *Birds*, 556). Modern texts tend generally to follow Byzantine practice in writing the ι subscript—thus ᾳ, ῃ, ῳ.

In the position before a vowel these might present no difficulty, since they could be considered simply as representing long vowels followed by a semivowel, i.e. [āy] etc.—thus e.g. in ῥᾴων, κλῄω, πατρῷος, or when a final 'long diphthong' is

---

[62] For further details of variations in the 'diphthongs' before vowels see Lupaş, pp. 47 ff.

[63] There was no need to indicate the [w], since this was an automatic glide after a close or mid back vowel.

followed by an initial vowel (e.g. τῇ/τῷ ὄρνιθι).[64] But a problem
does arise where they more certainly represent true diphthongs,
i.e. in the position before a consonant or pause. For diphthongs
in Greek cannot strictly be distinguished as 'short' and 'long';
for accentual purposes they all have the same value of 2 'morae'
(time-units), as for a·long simple vowel. A diphthong consists
of a continuous glide from one vowel quality to another within
the bounds of a syllable, and the only manner in which two
types of diphthong might be distinguished durationally in
Greek is by a different placing of the point of maximal
change—one might, for example, hypothesize that in αι the
glide accelerated at about the $\frac{1}{3}$ stage, whereas in ᾳ it was
delayed until about the $\frac{2}{3}$ stage. Something of this kind seems
to have occurred in Old Indian, where the diphthongs āi, āu
were distinguished from ai, au; but we know that in this case
there was also an important difference in *quality* between the
starting points ā and a (cf. Allen, pp. 62 ff.); and it seems
unlikely that a purely durational distinction would remain
viable for very long in the absence of some such concomitant
factor.

We know of no such qualitative distinction in the case of long
and short Attic α; ῳ may have been more readily distinguished
from οι if, as we have mentioned, the value of the latter was in
fact [öi]; and in historical times η could have been distinguished
from ει by the fact that the latter represented a monophthong
[ẹ̄]. But it seems that the Greeks themselves did not find the
distinctions easy to maintain. The narrowest of the 'long'
ι-diphthongs (i.e. involving the closest similarity of first and
second elements) was η, and in some words this had already
become monophthongal, to coincide with ει, by the early 4 c.
b.c.[65]—thus e.g. κλείς for Old Attic κλής (similarly λειτουργεῖν for
earlier λητ-). The same development occurs, less rapidly, in

[64] Cf. Ion. τη αφροδιτηι (= τῇ ᾿Αφροδίτη) etc., where the prevocalic ι is omitted,
presumably as = [y] and thus automatic after a front vowel (it is maintained before
consonants and in τῷ).

[65] The change could possibly have been earlier, but it would be masked by the
pre-Eucleidean spelling of both ε and η as E.

inflexional endings (e.g. dat. sing. βουλει, 3 sing. subj. ειπει),[66] but is reversed from *c*. 200 B.C. by an analogical restoration of the η from other cases and persons,[67] the levelling being perhaps encouraged by the further change of ει = [ẹ̄] to [ī] (cf. p. 70),[68] producing anomalous paradigms of the type gen. [-ēs] : dat. [-ī].

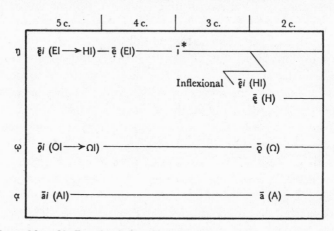

* See p. 86, n. 68. *For values indicated in italic see discussion on pp*. 84 *f*. Epigraphic spellings after the earliest refer to innovations, disregarding conservative retentions.

Fig. 4. Development of the 'long' ι-diphthongs.

But the 'long' diphthongs were evidently no longer viable, and about the same time a new development supervenes whereby they lose their second member, ᾳ η ῳ being replaced by ᾱ η ω; both the diphthongal and monophthongal forms are reflected in the Latin loans *tragoedus, comoedus* from τραγῳδός, κωμῳδός, but later *r(h)apsōdus, melōdus* (hence also the difference in e.g. English *tragedy* and *rhapsody*). In the latter part of the 2 c. B.C. the grammarian Dionysius Thrax (Θρᾷξ!) clearly states that in the verbal forms βοᾷς and βοᾷ the written ι-element was not in fact pronounced (†*Ars Gramm*., p. 58 U); and in the 1 c. A.D. Quintilian implies that in a form such as λῃστῇ the ι

---

[66] Also in augmented syllables (e.g. ειρεθη = ἡρέθη).

[67] Cf. A. S. Henry, *CQ*, N.S. 14 (1964), pp. 240 ff.

[68] I know of no certain confusion between ει < η and ι until Roman times, but it seems improbable that ει < η remained for any appreciable time diphthongal and so failed to share in the change of [ẹ̄] to [ī]: cf. also Threatte, pp. 368 ff.

was in both cases purely orthographic (†i. 7. 17). The various developments are summarized in the table above (Fig. 4).[69]

A similar development in the 'long' υ-diphthongs is shown from the 1 c. B.C. by forms like εατου for ἑᾱυτοῦ.[70]

There remains the practical question of what pronunciation to recommend for the 'long' diphthongs of classical Attic. It would be possible, and perhaps not far from correct, to pronounce ῳ as [oi] in *boy* (cf. the Latin rendering by *oe*)— provided that οι were distinguished as [öi]; and to pronounce ῃ as [ei] in *hay*—provided that ει were distinguished as [ẹ̄], without any diphthongization. But both of these provisos are somewhat doubtful of fulfilment by the average English classical scholar; the above pronunciations of the 'long' diphthongs can therefore hardly be recommended; and there would in any case remain the problem of distinguishing ᾳ from αι.

The simplest solution seems to be one which is in fact quite widely adopted, namely to anticipate developments by two or three centuries and to pronounce ᾳ ῃ ῳ as ᾱ η ω, i.e. without their diphthongal element. This admittedly confuses the 'long' diphthongs and long vowels—but the cases of real ambiguity are relatively few; and the practice has at least some precedent in antiquity.

Since single [y] tended to be lost in Attic (see p. 83), it would also be reasonable to give the same pronunciation to prevocalic ᾳ ῃ ῳ (cf. p. 84).

It should be noted that the ι-element of the 'long' diphthongs is currently written adscript and not subscript in combination with capitals; thus the Αι of Ἅιδης (as currently indicated by the placing of the breathing and accent) is a 'long' diphthong[71]

---

[69] For inscriptional evidence see Threatte, pp. 352–83; and for further discussion Allen, 'Long and short diphthongs', in *Studies offered to Leonard R. Palmer*, pp. 9–16.

[70] The augmented syllable ην-, however, is replaced from the 4 c. B.C. by the 'short' diphthong ευ-, as also ῳ- is replaced by οι- in augmented forms of the verb οἰκοδομεῖν: cf. Threatte, pp. 383–5. The Modern Greek aorist ηὗρα (ηὗρα), pron. [ívra], must therefore be a classicizing formation (the usual form in any case is βρήκα [vríka] < εὕρηκα).

[71] However, though cited by Leumann (*Lat. Laut- u. Formenlehre*, p. 69), the romanized form *Hades* is not citable as evidence, being 'latinate' rather than Latin; the word seems, rather surprisingly, to occur nowhere in any form in Latin literature

(as e.g. in ᾄδει) and, if the above recommendation is adopted, must be pronounced [ā] and *not* [ai] as is commonly heard.

In the case of the 'long' υ-diphthongs, ᾱυ and ηυ may be pronounced as αυ and ευ with little risk of ambiguity, whilst the isolated ωυ may be pronounced very approximately as English *owe*.

(at any rate up to the Renaissance); in English it first appears (with variants such as *Aides*) around 1600 as a direct borrowing from Greek.

In Greek itself αδ[ου occurs beside αιδου on a defixio of ?4 c. B.C., but this may be a graphic error (Threatte, p. 359). In Old Church Slavonic, where ᾰι is rendered by *e*, Ἅιδης appears as *adŭ*.

The accentual marking Ἅιδης (as also Θρᾱιξ, κλῆις, ἥιδεσμαι, τῶιδε, etc. when written with ι-adscript) is in fact anomalous by comparison with e.g. ηὕρημαι: cf. Allen, op. cit. (p. 87, n. 69), p. 11, n. 11.

CHAPTER 3

VOWEL-LENGTH

The orthographic situation in Attic is very different from that of Latin (*VL*, pp. 64 ff.), since the introduction of the Ionic alphabet provided the means of distinguishing between long and short vowels in the mid series. Thus short ε is distinguished from long η [ę̄] and ει [ẹ̄], and short o is distinguished from long ω.

It may be pointed out that there is no good reason for considering the short ε as being specially related to either the long η or ει. It is often assumed that η is the long equivalent of ε, so that the long mid vowel would be more open than the corresponding short (unlike the more common case, as represented in Latin (cf. *VL*, p. 47), where the long vowel is the closer).[1] The assumption of a correspondence ε:η seems to arise from a confusion of descriptive phonology with either historical or graphic considerations. Historically (i.e. going back to 'Proto-Greek' or to Indo-European) ε and η are derivable from an original correspondence ĕ:ē, which is reflected, for example, in grammatical alternations of the type πατέρες:πατήρ, τίθεμεν: τίθημι, or φανέντες:ἐφάνην. Graphically, ει is liable to be excluded from consideration as being a digraph, thus leaving only η; and this factor no doubt explains the statement of Sextus Empiricus (*Adv. Gramm.* 115) that 'both (ε and η) have the same value; η when shortened becomes ε, and ε when lengthened becomes η'.[2] From a purely descriptive standpoint such an assumption is open to contradiction. There are certainly inherited alternations of the type just mentioned, but an ε:ει alternation is seen in e.g. ἐστί:εἰμί, φανέντες:φανείς, resulting from the fact that the Attic compensatory lengthening of [e] produces not [ę̄] η but [ẹ̄] ει. Similarly the temporal augmentation of an

---

[1] Cf. Buck (*a*), p. 92; Heffner, p. 209.
[2] Additionally, of course, ει had by then long had the value [ī], and η was a *close* mid [ę̄] (cf. p. 74).

initial ε admittedly produces η in inherited forms such as Hom. ἦα (cf. Sanskrit *āsam*, < I.-E. *ēsm̥* < *e-es-m̥*) and is extended e.g. to ἤγειρα; but descriptively there are a number of cases of the type ἔχω:εἶχον. Moreover, when the Greeks came to name the letters E and O, on the principle stated by Herodian (ii, p. 403 L) that 'πᾶν ὄνομα μονοσύλλαβον μακροκαταληκτεῖν θέλει', the results in Attic were 'εἶ' and 'οὖ', i.e. '[ẹ̄]' and (originally) '[ǭ]' (e.g. Athenaeus, 453d, quoting Callias, 5 c. B.C.; Plato, *Cratylus*, 426 C, and 4 c. inscriptions; Plutarch, *Mor.* 384 ff.).[3]

There is thus in fact a rather better case for considering ει [ẹ̄] as the long vowel corresponding to ε, and this would seem to reflect the intuitions of native speakers. But phonetically Attic ε [e] probably lies midway between classical η [ę̄] and ει [ẹ̄], and there seems nothing to be gained by setting it in a special relationship with either. On the back vowel axis the situation is rather different, since the change of [ọ̄] ου to [ū] meant that ω came to be the only long mid back vowel, and so might reasonably be considered as corresponding in classical times to the short o.

In the case of [ẹ̄] and [ọ̄], Attic had utilized the fact that original [ei] and [ou] had become monophthongal (see pp. 71 ff., 75 ff.) to provide a means of indicating length by the digraphs ΕΙ and ΟΥ. In the case of [ę̄], East Ionic had utilized its psilosis (see p. 73) to provide a symbol (Η) indicative of length; and even a non-psilotic dialect such as Attic had found it more important to indicate length than the aspirate. In the case of [ǭ] a modification of Ο, viz. Ω (or in some of the islands Θ) was devised to distinguish the long vowel.

But in the case of the open and close vowels [ă], [ĭ], [ŭ] (→ [ü̆]) no such distinctions were inherited or devised, and these vowels are consequently known as δίχρονα, i.e. 'of two lengths'. The Alexandrian grammarians did invent superscript signs ‾ and ‿

---

[3] Herodian (ii, p. 390 L) notes that (as a result of the Attic change [ę̄] → [ī]) the pronunciation of the name of the letter E had by his time become [ī] (we similarly, as a result of the change of Old and Mid. Eng. [ę̄] to modern [ī], now call the corresponding roman letter '[ī]'). Already in classical times the name of Ο will have become [ū].

to indicate long and short, and these are occasionally used in papyri (more particularly of dialect texts, and especially to indicate ᾱ = Attic η), but they never became a normal part of the orthographic system. The reason for this difference of treatment could well be, as suggested by I. Fischer,[4] that the grammatical utilization of the length distinction was much less in the case of these than of the mid vowels, where one finds contrasts of the type ἀληθές, ἀληθής, ἀληθεῖς; τό, τώ, τοῦ, etc. In the case of the open and close vowels such contrasts are rare: e.g. as between present and imperfect in ἱκετεύομεν/ἱκ-, ὑβρίζομεν/ὑβ-. Contrasts of [a]:[ā] which had existed in Proto-Greek were largely destroyed in Attic by the change of [ā] to [ē] η; thus whereas, for example, Arcadian has a contrast ἱστᾱ́ται/ἱστᾶται as between indicative and subjunctive, the corresponding Attic forms are ἵστᾱται/ἱστῆται. Such few contrasts as are found in the case of the open and close vowels are lexical rather than grammatical (e.g. θῡμώδης 'spirited'/ 'thyme-like'), and, particularly if one takes account of differences of accent, are no more numerous than true homonyms (as e.g. τέλος 'end', 'tax', etc.); the context will in any case seldom have left room for ambiguity.

'Hidden quantity'

In open syllables (i.e. ending in a vowel: see p. 104), the length of vowel symbolized by α, ι, or υ can be deduced from the positions occupied by the syllable in verse; for if the syllable is heavy the vowel must be long, and if it is light the vowel must be short. But metre is of no assistance in the case of closed syllables, since they are heavy regardless of vowel-length. For this reason long vowels in such syllables are sometimes said to have 'hidden quantity', and their existence must be discovered by other than metrical evidence.[5]

---

[4] *SC*, 3 (1961), pp. 29 ff.; cf. also Ruipérez, *Word*, 12 (1956), p. 76.

[5] In 'motor' terms, 'hidden quantity' is a feature of syllables which could be described as 'hypercharacterized' (cf. *AR*, pp. 66 f.), since the long vowel permits chest arrest of the syllable, and the following consonant is therefore redundant from the point

In Latin there are a number of more or less general rules about such 'hidden' length (*VL*, pp. 65 ff.); vowels are always long, for example, before *ns* and *nf*; generally also in certain morphological categories (as the -*x*- perfects and -*sco* presents), and by 'Lachmann's Law' (*āctus* etc.). But there are no such rules applicable to Greek; and since the qualities of short and long α ι υ did not greatly differ, the distinction is not reflected in later developments as it was in some cases in the Romance languages. Our knowledge of 'hidden quantity' in Greek is thus somewhat haphazard. It is on the whole uncommon, but some indication may be given of the types of evidence available for its detection.

(*a*) As a result of the change of [ẹ̄] ει to [ī], ει came often to be used in inscriptions (more particularly after about 100 B.C.) and in papyri instead of (long) ι, thereby indicating the length of the latter: thus e.g. ῥειψαι, προσερρειμμενων are found in papyri from Herculaneum (and therefore pre-79 A.D.), indicating a long vowel for the stem of the verb ῥίπτω. But after about 100 A.D. this evidence becomes valueless since ει then begins to appear for short ι also.

(*b*) Under certain circumstances (viz. after ρ, ι, ε) an original long α was preserved or restored in Attic, whereas Ionic showed a development to η. Since, therefore, Attic πράττω, θώραξ, have corresponding forms in Ionic πρήσσω, θώρηξ, we know that the α of the Attic words was long.[6]

(*c*) The internal analysis of a word, or a comparison with cognate forms, may indicate vowel-length. Thus the vowel of ῥίπτω may be inferred as long, on the basis of comparison with ῥῑπή, where, in an open syllable, the length is known from verse; similarly φρίττω on the evidence of e.g. φρῖκί in Homer, and στῦψις on the evidence of ἐνστύφοντι (Nicander, *Alexiph.*, 375).

of view of the ballistic movement, and probably has to be articulated by a controlled action. There is a widespread tendency for such syllables to reduce their -v̄c ending by shortening the vowel (-v̆c), so that the consonant takes over the arresting rôle; thus in Greek (by 'Osthoff's Law') *γνωντες → γνόντες, etc. The various reductions of the 'long diphthongs' (see pp. 84 ff.) represent an aspect of the same tendency: see further *AR*, pp. 222 f.

[6] An awareness of this criterion is already shown by Herodian (ii, p. 932 L).

On the other hand we should expect the ι of πίπτω to be short, since πι- is a reduplicative syllable as in e.g. δίδωμι (but see (e) below).

In (Ion.) ἆσσον a long vowel may be inferred from the fact that it derives from an original ἄγχιον; for a vowel is normally lengthened by compensation for the loss of ν before σ (cf. πᾶσα from παντια).[7]

(d) Accentual evidence may be of value in so far as a circumflex can only occur on a long vowel: thus in the case of e.g. θᾶττον, μᾶλλον; conversely, in a word like κῆρυξ, φοῖνιξ it indicates that the υ and ι are short (in spite of κήρῡκος, φοίνῑκος). But one would normally prefer to have other evidence to confirm the accentual tradition.

(e) Some cases are specifically mentioned by the grammarians—notably in the abstracts of Herodian's work περὶ διχρόνων (ii, pp. 7 ff. L). Thus the long vowels are confirmed for μᾶλλον, θᾶττων (also ἐλάττων). Short vowel is confirmed for κῆρῠξ and long vowel for θώρᾱξ. Since ζ stands for a consonant-group [zd] (see pp. 56 ff.), the preceding syllable is always closed and can therefore conceal vowel-length; long vowel is here expressly mentioned for e.g. κράζω, χαμᾶζε, ἀλαζών.

Long vowel is also confirmed for ῥίπτω; and in one passage (ii, p. 570 L) Herodian confirms our expectations about the reduplicative syllable of πίπτω (ἐπειδὴ οἱ ἀναδιπλασιασμοὶ ἀπὸ βραχείας θέλουσιν ἄρχεσθαι); elsewhere, however, (p. 10 L) he classes it with ῥίπτω as having a long vowel, and this is confirmed by frequent spellings with ει. In fact there could well have existed both forms, πίπτω the original, and πῑπτω an analogical form based on semantic and contextual association with ῥίπτω (cf. e.g. Il. i, 591 ff.; Plato, Rep., 617 E, 619 E).

In modern Greek there are no phonemic distinctions of vowel-length; duration has become merely an allophonic feature, accented vowels being generally longer than unaccented, regardless of their origins. It is not easy to determine just when this loss of the length-distinction came about. We have seen

---

[7] The expected form would be ἆσον; but σσ is probably introduced on the pattern of θᾶσσον.

(p. 79) that the monophthong resulting from αι came often to be written as ε; but this need indicate no more than the *quality* of the monophthong in the absence of any other appropriate symbol (cf. Sturtevant, pp. 39, 103). The appearance of ει for short ι in the 2 c. A.D. need be no more than a graphic reflex of the use of ι (= [ῑ]) for ει. Thus, whilst these phenomena *could* result from a loss of length-distinctions, they need not do so, and cannot therefore be relied upon as evidence. More suggestive is the confusion of ο and ω, which becomes common from the 2 c. A.D. (mainly in private texts: cf. Threatte, p. 387); but since such confusion begins as early as the 4 c. B.C. (Threatte, pp. 223 ff.), it could again indicate a convergence of quality rather than duration, in which the considerations mentioned on p. 90 may be relevant.

It seems probable that the development is linked with the change from a pitch to a stress accent, of which duration became a subsidiary function. Such a role of duration would be favoured by the elimination of diphthongs and the reduction of the long-vowel system to the same dimensions as the short. A movement towards these conditions had begun to accelerate around 100 A.D., and, with the possible exception of the υ-diphthongs (see pp. 79 f.), was complete by about the middle of the 3 c.[8] On other evidence (see pp. 130 f.) the change to a stress accent could be dated to around this period. It seems, therefore, that the loss of distinctive vowel-length may also be placed most probably in the 2–3 c. A.D.[9]

The various apparently unconnected changes which took place in the long-vowel and diphthongal systems during the

[8] Even if the phonetic change of the υ-diphthongs to [av], [ev] had not yet taken place, the other developments mentioned would tend to isolate them and so favour the phonemic structuring of them as /aw/, /ew/ (cf. pp. 5, 80), thereby paving the way for such a change; Gothic and Armenian evidence is difficult to interpret but could reflect an analysis in these terms (cf. Sturtevant, pp. 54 f.; H. Jensen, *Altarmenische Grammatik*, §28).

[9] In non-literary papyri the loss of length distinctions and interchange of vowels in unaccented syllables from the 2 c. B.C. suggests the effects of stress; but this could be a peculiarity of Egyptian speech (cf. Gignac, p. 142 of article cited p. 81, n. 53 above; also C. M. Knight, 'The change from the Ancient to the Modern Greek accent', *JPhil* Cambridge), 35 (1920), pp. 51 ff. (56 ff.)).

preceding centuries could be viewed, according to one theory, as part of a long-term 'conspiracy' aimed at this ultimate revolutionary outcome (cf. Allen, *TPS*, 1978, pp. 103 ff.); or, in terms of an analogy from the field of topology, as an exemplification of 'catastrophe theory', whereby a number of minor, local discontinuities in the relevant manifold build up to a state in which a major, 'catastrophic' change can take place.[10]

A summary of developments involving the Greek long vowels is given on p. 78.[11]

[10] See further Allen, 'The development of the Attic vowel system: conspiracy or catastrophe?' in *Studies in Mycenaean and classical Greek presented to John Chadwick* (= *Minos* xx–xxi, Salamanca, 1987).

[11] The essence of some of the vowel-changes discussed in the preceding pages is neatly incapsulated in an inscription recently observed on a caïque at Ano Kufonisi in the Cyclades: ΠΟΛΙΤΕ (= πωλεῖται, 'For Sale').

CHAPTER 4

VOWEL-JUNCTION

The simplest form of junction between the final vowel of one word and the initial vowel of the next[1] involves the juxtaposition of the vowels in question without any modification of their length, quality, or syllabic function—as e.g. in Hom. ἄνω ὤθεσκε, μὴ ἴομεν, τάχιστα ὑπὲκ, ἀέξετο ἱερόν. Such a pronunciation is generally known by its Latin title of *hiatus* (*VL*, p. 78); corresponding Greek terms (χαίνειν, χασμῳδία) do not occur until the Roman and Byzantine periods; amongst various other descriptive names is σύγκρουσις 'collision'. This juxtaposition does not exclude the possibility, indeed probability, that where the first of the two vowels was of close or mid quality it was followed by a semivocalic [y], [w], or [ẅ] transitional glide (in the case of front, back, and front rounded vowels respectively)— thus e.g. Hom. τί(*y*)ἔκλυες, ὃ(*w*)ἔγνω, σύ(*ẅ*)ἐσσι; similarly in the case of diphthongs, e.g. Hom. ἔμεναι(*y*)ἄγαμος, τίμησόν μοι(*y*)υἱόν (which might equally well be considered as representing [-ayya-] etc.: cf. pp. 81 ff.). In the case of 'long diphthongs' it is simply a matter of the diphthongal element (ι) becoming consonantal [y] (cf. pp. 84 f.)—thus e.g. Hom. ὀπωρινῷ ἐναλίγκιον, σκαιῇ ἔγχος represent [-ọye-], [-ẹye-] respectively.

This type of junction is found commonly in Homer.[2] In Attic verse, however, it is practically confined to interjections, interjectional vocatives as παῖ, and interrogative τί (also, in comedy, περὶ and ὅτι, and the unitary phrases εὖ-οἶδα/-ἴσθι, μηδὲ-/οὐδὲ-εἷς/-ἕν).[3] This limitation is not confined to verse; Maas observes (p. 90) that it applies also to the prose of e.g. Isocrates, 'and dominates great parts of it almost without a

---

[1] Under 'vowels' are included for this purpose diphthongs (unless specifically stated) and aspirated initial vowels and diphthongs (cf. p. 54).

[2] Even when one discounts those cases where it is due to an original ϝ (cf. pp. 48 f.).

[3] Cf. A. C. Moorhouse, *CQ*, N.S. 12 (1962), pp. 239 ff.

break until the late Byzantine period'; Plato shows a progressive tendency to restrict hiatus to 'prepositive' words,[4] and this is a general rule in Demosthenes; it applies also to some of the works of Aristotle. Epigraphic evidence is not very enlightening since, as can be seen from metrical inscriptions, the writing often indicates a hiatus where it was not so pronounced (e.g. 4 c. B.C. π]ατρισδεστιεφεσοσ = πατρὶς δ' ἐστ' Ἔφεσος); in general, however, the more 'official' and less 'popular' the nature of the text, the more does it tend to indicate hiatus, and this could well correspond to a more deliberate style of speech quite apart from graphic convention. For Attic details see Threatte, pp. 418 ff.

The avoidance of hiatus by conscious choice of words or word-order would only have been feasible to a limited extent; and we have now to consider the various other ways in which vowel-junctions were realized.

One such mode involves a shortening of a long vowel at the end of the first word, as e.g. in Hom. πλάγχθη ἐπεί, οὐδέ πω Ἕκτωρ. This is a feature that perhaps goes back to Indo-European, since it is also attested in Vedic;[5] it is commonest in Homer, and is therefore termed 'correptio epica' (more generally the principle is stated as 'vocalis ante vocalem corripitur'); the rarer non-epic instances are in any case largely confined to dactylic/anapaestic rhythms, as e.g. Euripides, Hec., 123 ὄζω Ἀθηνῶν.

Under this category are also generally listed the cases involving a diphthong, giving light quantity in e.g. Hom. καὶ ἀναίτιον, ἄνδρα μοι ἔννεπε, κλῦθί μευ ἀργυρότοξ'. But a diphthong as such cannot be 'shortened' (cf. p. 82), and all that is implied here is the treatment of its second element as a consonant (semivowel) before the following initial vowel: thus, in the above examples, [-aya-], [-oye-], [-ewa-]. It is the same process as is seen in the cases involving 'long diphthongs' (ὀπωρινῷ ἐν. etc.), which, though usually so classified, are not really cases of

[4] 'I.e. article, prepositions, monosyllabic conjunctions, pronouns, etc.' (Maas, p. 84).
[5] Cf. Allen, Sandhi, pp. 35 ff.

hiatus.[6] There are also examples where the [y] element of a 'long diphthong' is lost, and the first element does then undergo the epic shortening: thus e.g. in πειρᾷ ἐμεῖο = [-a,e-], πέτρῃ ἔπι = [-e,e-], οὔτε τῷ ἄλλῳ ἐπεὶ = [-o,a-]...[-o,e-]. Both treatments are seen in *Il*. i, 30 ἡμετέρῳ ἐνὶ οἴκῳ ἐν Ἄργεϊ, with [-ọye-] and [-o,e-].

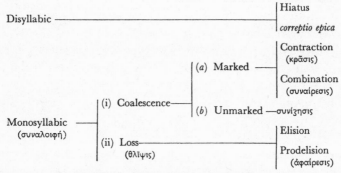

Fig. 5. Types of vowel-junction.

Even these instances of what is sometimes called 'weak hiatus' involve no reduction in the number of syllables. But by far the more common case involves a reduction of the two juxtaposed syllables to one. Such a treatment is termed by the Greek grammarians συναλοιφή, lit. 'blending'. It is traditionally divided into cases where (i) there is a coalescence of the two vowels, and (ii) a loss of one of them. Considering class (i) first, a subdivision is made into cases where the coalescence is (*a*) marked and (*b*) unmarked in writing.

Class (*a*) is then further subdivided under the heads of κρᾶσις and συναίρεσις according to whether a process of vowel-contraction is involved (as e.g. μὴ οὖν → μῶν, τὰ ὅπλα → θὥπλα,

---

[6] Dr Chadwick points out that light quantity is proportionally much more common for final αι, οι than for long vowels in Homer; which could mean that this, rather than an Indo-European inheritance, gave rise to the other cases of 'correptio epica', by a process of analogical extension. Other proponents of this view (which he rejects) are listed by L. E. Rossi, 'La *pronuntiatio plena*: sinalefe in luogo d'elisione', *Omaggio a Eduard Fraenkel*, pp. 229 ff. (234 and n. 13).

καὶ ἐγώ → κἀγώ, μοι ἐστι → μοῦστι)[7] or, more rarely, viz. where the second vowel is ι or υ, simple combination into a diphthong (as e.g. τὸ ἱμάτιον → θοἰμάτιον). In either case coalescences of class (a) are generally marked in the current (originally Alexandrian) system by the κορωνίς 'crook',[8] which is identical in form with the ἀπόστροφος (see p. 100 below).[9]

Class (b) has the traditional title of συνίζησις,[10] and differs from class (a), as we have mentioned, by not being specially marked in writing—thus e.g. μὴ εἰδέναι. In modern terminology 'synizesis' is often used in the sense of a reduction of the first vowel of a sequence to a semivowel (as e.g. [u] → [w] in colloquial English *How do I look?* → trisyllabic [haudwailuk]: cf. p. 51); but this is probably not so in the Greek cases classified under (b). For on the one hand there is no 'lengthening by position' (see p. 104) of a preceding syllable—thus the first syllable of the first word in ἐπεὶ οὐ (*Od.* iv, 353) remains light, whereas one would expect such syllables normally to be heavy in Homer if the junction implied [epyū] (cf. pp. 49; 51, n. 99); and conversely the syllable resulting from the junction is heavy, even if the initial syllable of the second word would normally be light—thus Eur., *Or.*, 599 εἰ μὴ ὁ κελεύσας (cf. p. 52). It is therefore more probable that συνίζησις implies coalescence to a long vowel or a diphthong as in the case of class (a).[11] The separate classification and the absence of any specific indication in writing are presumably due simply to the fact that the result of the coalescence was in these cases a sound or combination of sounds which did not occur in other than junctional contexts— e.g. a 'rising' diphthong [ea] in Ar., *Thesm.*, 476 μὴ ἄλλην (cf.

[7] In Attic especially, however, the normal rules of vowel-contraction are frequently overridden by a tendency (complete in the case of α- except when preceded by ὥ) to maintain the quality of the initial vowel: thus ὁ ἀνήρ → ἀνήρ (beside internal πειθόα → πειθώ; cf. Dor. ὠνήρ), τὸ αὐτό → ταὐτό (cf. Ion. τωὐτό), τὸ ἡρῷον → θἡρῷον (beside internal δηλόητε → δηλῶτε).

[8] Apart from the indication given, in the case of crasis, by the vowel-changes and reductions involved; in inscriptions, however, these indications are uncommon after c. 480 B.C., especially in public texts: cf. Threatte, pp. 427 ff.

[9] It was not, however, originally identical with the 'smooth breathing' (see p. 52).

[10] Also referred to as συνεκφώνησις.

[11] With a possible exception in the rare cases where a final ι is involved, as *Il.* xvii, 324 κήρυκι Ἠπυτίδη (but see Leaf's edn for other explanations); cf. also Maas, p. 73.

p. 5). There is thus no purely phonetic reason for separating class (*b*) from class (*a*); but it must be recognized that in the case of class (*b*) we can do little more than guess at the nature of the resulting combination in the light of general phonetic probability (rather as in the case of similar phenomena in Latin: *VL*, p. 81; cf. Schwyzer, p. 401).

The words involved in junctions of class (i) are mostly in close grammatical connection with one another (notably where the first word is a 'prepositive'), though not exclusively so. Junctions of class (ii), however, are not subject to any such limitation. They are known in Greek by the title of θλῖψις or ἔκθλιψις (occasionally also κουφισμός), and involve the loss of either the first or the second vowel of the sequence. The former loss is by far the more common, and is widely known by the term 'elision' (based ultimately on ἔκθλιψις, which is sometimes restricted to this sense).[12] In literary texts the loss of the vowel at the end of the first word is indicated, apart from its absence, by the sign ἀπόστροφος;[13] in inscriptions, however, the vowel is frequently written even where, as in metrical texts, it is known to have been elided (cf. p. 97). Elision in Greek is restricted basically to short vowels, and even of these υ is never elided, whilst elision of ι is primarily a feature of verbal endings. Apparent elision of a diphthong is seen in e.g. βούλομ' ἐγώ (*Il.* i, 117: primarily in verbal endings of epic, lyric, and comedy); but this most probably represents a loss of [y] from the sequence [-aye-] etc. (as in the case of the 'long diphthongs': see above), with consequent elision of the [-a];[14]

---

[12] The term ἀποκοπή is also used, though this has rather wider connotations. In modern usage '*apocope*' is applied to the special sense of preconsonantal vowel-loss, as e.g. in Hom. κὰπ πέδιον (for κατὰ π.).

[13] I.e. ἡ ἀπόστροφος προσῳδία. The English form *apostrophe* is due to its adoption via French, and its current pronunciation as four syllables is due to a confusion with the rhetorical device ἀποστροφή. The scholia explain the term variously as referring to the 'bent' shape of the sign (like κορωνίς) or to its function as 'averting' hiatus (e.g. *Schol. in Dion. Thr.*, p. 126 H); the latter explanation seems the more probable.

[14] There is a close parallel to this in Old Indian (where coalescence rather than elision is the general rule); for example, a sequence such as *vāi asāu* implies a junction-form *vāyasāu*, from which the *y* (which we know from the ancient authorities to have been weakly pronounced) is then dropped, giving in classical Sanskrit a hiatus-form *vā asāu*; but in the Vedic hymns the words occasionally go on to coalesce, giving a junction-form *vāsāu* (cf. Allen, *Sandhi*, pp. 37 ff.).

the same would apply to the occasional elision of μοι, τοι, σοι.[15]

It is possible that the transition from a consonant to a following vowel was perceptibly different in Greek according to whether the two sounds belonged to the same or different words—as e.g. in the English distinction of *a notion* (with 'internal' transition) and *an ocean* (with 'external' transition).[16] A statement in Herodian regarding the 'attachment' of consonants to vowels (†ii, pp. 407 f. L) seems to refer to writing rather than pronunciation (cf. pp. 105 f.)—but this could well have a phonetic basis, and a scholium on Dionysius Thrax (†p. 156 H) clearly refers to a difference of pronunciation as between e.g. ἔστι Νάξιος and ἔστιν ἄξιος.[17] Herodian's statement continues with a rule which, if phonetically interpreted, would mean that, when a final vowel was elided, a preceding consonant nevertheless retained its original characteristics, so that there was an internal type of transition to the initial vowel of the following word.[18] This may have been a contributory factor in Hegelochus' famous mispronunciation of γαλην' ὁρῶ[19] as γαλῆν ὁρῶ, i.e. with external instead of internal transition, in Eur., *Or.*, 279 (cf. Ar., *Frogs*, 303),[20] particularly as it resulted, according to the scholia, from a shortness of breath on the part of the actor.[21] Further support for a difference in transitions might be claimed from cases (though many are disputed) where

[15] Sommerstein (p. 166, n.) shows that elision of -αι and -οι was not a feature of careful Attic speech.

[16] Cf. D. Jones, 'The Hyphen as a Phonetic Sign', *ZPh*, 9 (1956), pp. 99 ff.; J. D. O'Connor & O. M. Tooley, 'The Perceptibility of Certain Word-boundaries', *In Honour of Daniel Jones*, pp. 171 ff.; P. Delattre, *Comparing the Phonetic Features of English, French, German and Spanish*, pp. 36 ff.

[17] See further Stanford, pp. 145 f. and id., *Ambiguity in Greek Literature*, pp. 42 f.

[18] Unless, of course, there were a natural pause at this point (indicated by punctuation or change of speaker), where elision must have been an artificial extension of normal speech-habits (as also the transfer of aspiration in e.g. Soph., *El.*, 1502: OP. ἀλλ' ἔρφ'. Al. ὑφηγοῦ).

[19] The accentuation of the elided word is uncertain (cf. B. Laum, *Das alexandrinische Akzentuationssystem*, pp. 420 ff.).

[20] Cf. Stanford, op. cit., pp. 51 f.

[21] A simpler explanation of Hegelochus' slip, however, would be as follows. Elision is a characteristic only of continuous speech; if, therefore, a pause were made after the ν, the hearer would interpret this as indicating non-elision—and so not as γαλην(α) but as γαλην (cf. *AR*, p. 227).

a breach of Porson's Law seems to be admitted if an elision is involved,[22] as also from the rather greater toleration of a diaeresis in the middle of a trimeter if it is 'bridged' by an elision.

Where it was desired to avoid both hiatus and elision, the device was available, in the case of -ι and -ε of certain grammatical categories, of adding the so-called ν ἐφελκυστικόν[23] (alias 'paragogic ν'), as e.g. in dat. plur. πᾶσιν, 3 sing. ἔδοξεν. The precise source of this is uncertain, but it seems to be primarily of Attic-Ionic origin (N.B. not in Herodotus) and has presumably spread from forms in which alternants with and without ν were originally inherited (a parallel alternance with ς is seen in e.g. πολλάκις beside Hom. πολλάκι).[24] This use of ν was much extended; the Byzantine rule that it should be used only before a vowel or pause had only a limited basis in practice; in inscriptions it appears almost as often before consonants as before vowels,[25] and in poetry this provides a means of creating heavy quantity (e.g. ἔστιν θάλασσα).

Much rarer than elision is the process of 'prodelision', in which it is the short initial vowel of the second word that is lost after a final long vowel or diphthong—as e.g. in ἦ 'μός. This is more specifically referred to as ἀφαίρεσις (though, like ἀποκοπή, this term in Greek also has wider connotations). The process mainly applies to initial ε of tragedy and comedy. It is not always possible to determine whether a junction involves prodelision or coalescence; for example, MSS vary between μη

[22] Cf. S. I. Sobolevskij, *Eirene*, 2 (1964), p. 50: 'vox elisa tam arte sequenti adhaerebat ut unum cum eo vocabulum faceret'.

[23] This term was originally applied to the final *vowel*, which was described as ἐφελκυστικὸν τοῦ ν, i.e. 'attracting ν'; but the transfer of the epithet to the ν itself is already found in Byzantine sources (e.g. *Schol. in Dion. Thr.*, p. 155 H).

[24] For another suggestion, based on the analogical extension of junctural alternants, see J. Kuryłowicz, 'L'origine de ν ἐφελκυστικόν', *Mélanges...P. Chantraine*, pp. 75 ff. (e.g. plur. ἔλεγον + σ- → ἔλεγο + σ- (cf. pp. 34, 56 above) ∼ ἔλεγον + τ(etc.)-, whence by analogy sing. ἔλεγε + σ- → ἔλεγεν + τ(etc.)-).

[25] Threatte (p. 642) notes that ἔδοξεν always has -ν at all periods; and this is increasingly the case with ἐπεψήφιζεν and ἐγραμμάτευεν (A. S. Henry, 'Notes on the language of the prose inscriptions of Hellenistic Athens', *CQ*, n.s. 17 (1967), pp. 257 ff. (283 f.)).

'ς and the 'crasis' form μῆς—where the point is purely graphic, since the pronunciation will be the same in either case; some phonetic difference is involved, however, as between e.g. χρῆσθαι 'τέρῳ and χρῆσθἀτέρῳ (Ar., *Peace*, 253—Brunck and Bekker respectively), as also between μὴ 'δικεῖν and the 'synizesis' form μὴ ἀδικεῖν (Eur., *Hec.*, 1249; Aesch., *Eum.*, 85). In a case such as λέγω· 'πὶ τοῦτον (Soph., *Phil.*, 591) prodelision is supported by the fact that the junction occurs across a pause, where elision commonly occurs but not coalescence.

For ease of reference, the various types of vowel-junction are classified in Fig. 5 on p. 98, which, from top to bottom, displays the classes in the order in which they have been discussed.

CHAPTER 5

QUANTITY

Quantity and Length

Under the heading of *vowel-length* we have already considered a category which in Greek has intimate connections with *quantity*. But the latter is a property of *syllables* and not of vowels, and a clear distinction must be maintained between the two.

The rules of quantity are readily deduced from metrical usage, and are fully discussed by the Greek grammarians (e.g. Dionysius Thrax, *Ars Gramm.*, pp. 17 ff. U; Hephaestion, *Enchiridion*, pp. 1 ff. C). If a syllable contains a long vowel, it is always '*heavy*', as e.g. the syllables of λήγω or πλῆκτρον. But if it contains a short vowel, its quantity depends upon the nature of the syllable-ending. If it ends with a vowel ('open' syllable), the syllable is '*light*', as e.g. the first syllable of λέ-γω; but if it ends with a consonant ('closed' syllable), the syllable is heavy, as e.g. the first syllable of λεκ-τός.

The Greek grammarians did not distinguish in their terminology between length and quantity, but applied the terms 'long' and 'short' to both vowels and syllables. One consequence of this was an assumption that only a syllable containing a long vowel could be 'naturally' ('φύσει') long (i.e. heavy); but since some syllables containing short vowels also functioned as heavy ('long' in Greek terminology), they were considered as being so only 'θέσει', i.e. 'by convention' or 'by position' (according to one's interpretation of this term). These categories are translated by Latin *naturā* (= φύσει) and *positu/positione* (= θέσει). In the Middle Ages the doctrine became even more confused; for instead of syllables being referred to as 'long by position', the short *vowels* in such syllables were said to be *lengthened* 'by position'.[1] This error continued through the Renaissance, and is still unfortunately encountered in some

[1] Cf. R. Hiersche, 'Herkunft und Sinn des Terminus "positione longa"', *Forschungen und Fortschritte*, 31 (1957), pp. 280 ff.

modern handbooks. It can be minimized by adopting the terminology of the ancient Indian grammarians, who used the terms 'long' and 'short' to apply to vowel-length, but 'heavy' and 'light' to apply to syllabic quantity (though even they were not altogether immune from laxity of expression and consequent confusion).[2] The crucial point is that a closed *syllable* containing a short vowel *is heavy*, and there is no question of the *vowel becoming long*.

Apart from the evidence of metre and grammarians' statements, the quantitative equivalence of 'naturally' and 'positionally' heavy syllables is seen, for example, in the rhythmic patterns of comparative and superlative adjectives; thus a word such as σο-φός, with light first syllable, takes a long vowel (giving heavy second syllable) in the comparative σο-φώ-τερος; but ὠ-μός, with heavy first syllable, takes a short vowel (giving light second syllable) in ὠ-μό-τερος; the relevant point here is that the latter pattern applies also to a word like λεπ-τός, comparative λεπ-τό-τερος, although the vowel of the first syllable is short.

Syllabic division

In order to determine whether a syllable is open or closed, and so whether a syllable containing a short vowel is light or heavy, it is of course necessary to establish the point of division between successive syllables. For this purpose the following rules apply: (i) Of two or more successive consonants, at least the first belongs to the preceding syllable (i.e. this syllable is closed, as in λεκ-τός, πλῆκ-τρον, ἄρκ-τος); this rule also applies to double consonants, e.g. ἄλ-λος, πλήτ-τω. (ii) A single consonant between vowels belongs to the following syllable (i.e. the preceding syllable is open, as in λέ-γω, λή-γω).

The statements of these rules by the grammarians are somewhat misleading, since they tend to confuse speech with writing and to incorporate rules which apply more properly to

[2] Cf. Allen, pp. 85 ff. The terms 'heavy' and 'light' have also sometimes been used by Icelandic grammarians to refer to vowels which in Old Icelandic were respectively long and short.

orthographic word-division (at the ends of lines).[3] In particular they have a rule that any group of consonants which can occur at the beginning of a word (as e.g. κτ in κτῆμα) is allotted *in toto* to the following syllable even when it occurs in the middle of a word—thus e.g. τί-κτω (cf. †Herodian, ii, p. 393 L); but this is quite contrary to the phonetic division in Greek,[4] which is τίκ-τω, giving heavy quantity for the first syllable.[5]

These rules do not necessarily mean that the division between syllables takes place at exactly the points indicated,[6] but they are adequate for the practical purpose of establishing quantitative values.

'Correptio Attica'

In stating the rules of syllable-division, we have so far omitted the special cases where a plosive consonant (πτκ, φθχ, βδγ) is followed by a liquid (ρ, λ) or a nasal (ν, μ). In such cases, with restrictions which we shall discuss, the consonant-group may either be divided, like any other, between preceding and following syllables (thus, for example, πᾰτ-ρός, giving a heavy first syllable), or it may belong as a whole to the following syllable (thus πᾰ-τρός, giving a light first syllable); both types of division are seen in e.g. Soph., *Ant.*, 1240 κεῖται δὲ νεκ-ρὸς περὶ νε-κρῷ.

[3] For details of Attic inscriptional practice see Threatte, pp. 64 ff.

[4] Though it would be generally applicable e.g. to the Slavonic languages.

[5] The Greek rules are taken over by Latin grammarians (e.g. Caesellius Vindex, in Cassiodor(i)us, *De Orthog.*, GL, vii, p. 205 K); but in Latin inscriptions, to a greater degree than in Greek, they tend to be disregarded when they conflict with the pronunciation. The more general principles still provide a framework for the house-rules of modern printers (see e.g. H. Hart, *Rules for Compositors and Readers at the University Press, Oxford*, 36th edn, pp. 64 f.: 'As a rule, divide a word after a vowel, turning over the consonant...Generally, whenever two consonants come together put the hyphen between the consonants'); exceptions such as *divid-ing* are parallel to the common Greek practice of grammatical division as in e.g. προσ-ῆκεν (cf. F. G. Kenyon, *Palaeography of Greek Papyri*, pp. 31 f., and Herodian, ii, p. 407 L).

Whilst the Greek and Latin rules had at least an underlying phonetic basis in these languages, they are often at odds with English pronunciation, and phonetic formulations for English are therefore unwise (as e.g. F. H. Collins, *Authors' and Printers' Dictionary*, 8th rev. edn, under *division of words*: 'avoid separating a group of letters representing a single sound'—a rule which is then followed by the example *des-sert*, where *ss* = [z]!).   [6] Cf. A. Rosetti, *Sur la théorie de la syllable*, pp. 11 ff.

The point is that liquids and nasals involve a degree of occlusion of the air-stream which is intermediate between that of plosives (where it is maximal) and vowels (where it is minimal).[7] A syllable which begins with a single consonant followed by a vowel (as e.g. the second syllable of πά-τος or πά-ρος) involves a diminuendo of occlusion—or, in more positive terms, a crescendo of aperture (and sonority). But there is also a (more gradual) crescendo of aperture in a sequence plosive + liquid-or-nasal + vowel, so that this too may begin a syllable; alternatively it is possible for the plosive to end the preceding syllable, and the liquid or nasal to begin the next, as in the case of other types of group. In 'motor' terms, the group plosive + liquid or nasal can function like a single consonant in assisting the release of the syllable because the pressure built up during the articulation of the plosive can be released during that of the liquid or nasal without interference from the latter (owing to their relatively open aperture).[8]

This situation was duly observed by the Greek grammarians, who accordingly classified the liquids and nasals together as ὑγρά 'fluid, liquid' (see p. 40) as opposed to the ἄφωνα 'mute' i.e. plosives (e.g. †Hephaestion, Ench., p. 5 C), and described the preceding syllable in such cases as κοινή 'common' (Latin anceps 'doubtful'). The optional treatment does not, however, apply where the plosive ends one grammatical element (word, or part of complex word) and the liquid or nasal begins another: thus in e.g. ἐκ μάχης or ἐκλιπών the first syllable can only be ἐκ and therefore closed and heavy[9]—a point that was also noted in antiquity (†Hephaestion, Ench., p. 6 C).

In the earliest period of the Greek language groups of the type

---

[7] From the acoustic standpoint cf. T. Tarnóczy, Word, 4 (1948), p. 71: 'The oscillograms of nasals and of sounds like L and R exhibit many traits similar to those of vowels'; Jakobson, Fant & Halle, Preliminaries to Speech Analysis, p. 19: 'The so-called liquids...have the vocalic as well as the consonantal feature.' From the articulatory point of view, liquids 'combine closure and aperture, either intermittently or by barring the median way and opening a lateral by-pass' (ibid., p. 20); nasals involve, like plosives, complete occlusion of the oral passage, but allow the passage of air through the nose.

[8] For such a treatment in languages other than Greek and Latin (English and Icelandic) cf. AR, pp. 57 f., 69 f.

[9] Cf. VL, p. 90.

QUANTITY

plosive + liquid or nasal were regularly divided between syllables, giving a heavy preceding syllable even though it contained a short vowel; this is seen from the fact that in the formation of comparative and superlative adjectives (cf. p. 105) such syllables have the same rhythmic effect as those of the type λεπτός—i.e. the comparative of πικρός is πικρότερος (as λεπτότερος), and not πικρώτερος (as σοφώτερος).[10] In this respect prehistoric Greek resembles prehistoric Latin,[11] though not the earliest form of literary Latin (*VL*, p. 89 f.). This treatment is still the dominant one in Homer, where a light syllable is found only before the groups plosive + ρ or voiceless plosive + λ, and then almost only *metri gratia*, where a word could not otherwise be accommodated in the metre (as e.g. ἀφροδίτη, ˘ προκείμενα). On the other hand, in the weak position of a foot (cf. pp. 131 ff.), heavy quantity is rarely obtained by a word-final short vowel followed by an initial group of these types; thus here again the grammatical division between words has an effect on the phonetic division.

The more general occurrence of light syllables before plosive + liquid is a characteristic of the spoken metres of Attic tragedy and comedy, and is consequently known as 'correptio Attica'. Since it is particularly common in Aristophanes, this treatment presumably reflects a feature of the spoken language of the time. In Attic, moreover, the treatment is extended to all combinations of plosive + liquid, as well as to the groups voiceless plosive + nasal. But even here the tendency to light quantity is restricted where the group consists of the combination voiced plosive + λ; such groups are accordingly referred to by J. Schade, whose dissertation *De correptione Attica* (Greifswald, 1908) is the basic source of statistics on this matter, as 'coniunctiones graves' (together with voiced plosive + nasal, which never permits light quantity—i.e. βλ, γλ, γν, γμ, δν, δμ).

[10] Cases such as ἐρυθρώτερος, ἐμμετρώτερος, εὐτεκνώτατος are later formations. κενότερος, on the other hand, is due to the earlier form κενϝός with heavy first syllable (cf. Ion. κεινός).

[11] Where the closed nature of such syllables is revealed by the vowel-quality of the middle syllable in a word like *intĕgra*, which follows the pattern of e.g. *infĕc-ta* and not that of *infĭ-cit*.

108

The different tendencies regarding syllabic division displayed by the different groups of consonants both in Homer and in Attic presumably reflect different degrees of crescendo of aperture in the group (see above); it would thus appear that ρ was less occlusive than λ, and λ less occlusive than ν or μ—so that the degree of crescendo is greatest in the groups plosive + ρ and least in the groups plosive + nasal.[12] In addition the distinction between voiced and voiceless plosives is also significant, probably because, as is commonly found, vowels tend to be somewhat longer before voiced than before voiceless sounds (cf. Jones (c), pp. 52 f.; Heffner, pp. 209 f.), and so would tend in Greek to favour heavy quantity (the usually tenser articulation of voiceless plosives might also tend to emphasize the crescendo). In Attic comedy syllables containing a short vowel are seldom heavy before 'light' groups (i.e. other than 'coniunctiones graves'), and never light before medial 'heavy' groups.

On the basis of Schade's figures one may compare comedy with tragedy in regard to their overall treatment of the groups plosive + liquid or nasal. In the trimeters and tetrameters of Aristophanes the following figures are found for non-final syllables containing a short vowel followed by groups of these types:[13]

$$(a) \text{ light syllable:} \qquad 1{,}262$$
$$(b) \text{ heavy syllable:} \qquad 196$$

Approximate ratio a/b: $6\cdot4/1$

In the trimeters of tragedy the following figures are found for Aeschylus, Sophocles, and Euripides respectively:

(a)	214,	438,	1,118
(b)	66,	189,	493
a/b:	3·25,	2·3,	2·25/1

[12] Cf. P. Delattre, 'L'aperture et la syllabation phonétique', *The French Review*, 17. 5 (1944), pp. 281 ff.

[13] (a) includes weak position only, i.e. excludes strong position in resolved feet; (b) includes strong position only, since heavy quantity is indeterminable in weak position.

The much higher ratio a/b in comedy reflects a greater tendency than in tragedy to allot groups of the type plosive + liquid or nasal to the following syllable. The rather surprisingly high ratio for Aeschylus as compared with the other tragedians is probably only apparent; for, as D. L. Page has pointed out,[14] if one excludes the 'heavy groups', the two noun-stems πατρ- and τεκν- account for over half of the examples of heavy quantity in Sophocles; and if these are discounted, Aeschylus and Sophocles show similar ratios.

Before a 'heavy' consonant-group light syllables are found only when the vowel is separated from the group by a grammatical boundary, as e.g. δὲ γλῶσσαν (Aesch., *Ag.*, 1629), ἔβλαστε (Soph., *El.*, 440);[15] before an initial 'light' consonant-group word-final syllables ending in a short vowel are always light in Attic, even in tragedy, as also in most cases is the syllabic augment.[16]

The degrees of incidence of 'correptio Attica' may be summarized (excluding rare exceptions) by the diagram opposite, which takes comedy as its central axis, and displays along different dimensions the roles of the various factors— dialect/genre, voice (of plosives), occlusion/aperture (of liquids and nasals)—on which the incidence depends.

Quantity and duration

Quantity, like vowel-length (see p. 6), should not be considered as a simple matter of duration. As is recognized by Dionysius of Halicarnassus (†*De Comp.* xv, p. 58 UR), the heavy syllable σπλήν is actually of greater duration than ῇ, which, however, is also heavy; similarly the light first syllable of ὁδός is of less duration than that of στρόφος, which, however, is also light. Such variations in duration were discussed by the ancient ῥυθμικοί, who were concerned primarily with their relevance to music, and they adopted the convention of considering a

---

[14] *A new chapter in the history of Greek Tragedy*, pp. 42 f.

[15] An isolated exception is Aesch., *Supp.*, 761 (βύβλου in 2nd foot).

[16] For exceptions see Page, op. cit., p. 24 and n. 25.

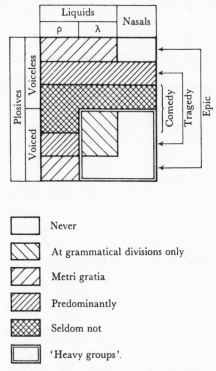

Fig. 6. Incidence of 'correptio Attica'.

consonant as equivalent in duration to half a short vowel; a short vowel was said to occupy a 'primary measure' of time (χρόνος πρῶτος); and a long vowel or diphthong was treated as equivalent to two such measures. On this basis there would be a continuous scale of duration from e.g. the four measures of σπλήν to the one measure of ό, and there would be no reason for drawing a distinction between 'heavy' and 'light' at any particular point in the scale (indeed the 'light' syllable στρο- would have a ½-measure more than the 'heavy' syllable ώ-). But as is noted by Choeroboscus in his commentary on Hephaestion (p. 180 C), the μετρικοί and γραμματικοί used the same term χρόνος πρῶτος to express the quantitative value of a light syllable, a heavy syllable being then considered as equivalent to 2 χ.π. Such a relationship between heavy and light is based on the common metrical equivalence of one heavy and two light syllables. In modern terminology the χ.π. is generally rendered by the Latin '*mora*', a term first so applied by Gottfried Hermann.[17]

Thus quantity is not concerned so much with the duration of a syllable as a whole (though, in general, heavy syllables will have been of greater duration than light), but rather with the nature of the syllabic ending. One might usefully adopt in this connection the terminology of Stetson's 'motor phonetics' (cf. pp. 2, 6), and state simply that the movement of a light syllable is 'unarrested', whereas that of a heavy syllable is 'arrested' (by the chest-muscles in the case of a long-vowel ending, by the oral constriction in the case of a consonant ending, or by a combination of the two in the case of a diphthongal ending, according to Stetson, p. 7, n.). Stetson (p. 46) further points out that a *releasing* consonant 'never adds to the length of the syllable and it actually accelerates the syllable movement'.

Resolution and contraction

Since duration provides an unsatisfactory basis for the definition of quantity, it is also unacceptable as an explanation of the metrical equivalence in Greek of one heavy and two light syllables.

It is essential at this point to distinguish between two quite different types of 'equivalence', which are often confused (cf. *AR*, pp. 60 f.). In one the basic element consists of the two light syllables (as in dactylic hexameters,[18] and in the other the basic element consists of the one heavy syllable (as in iambics and trochaics). It is sometimes convenient to refer to that part of the foot which in its basic form comprises a heavy syllable as the 'strong position', and the other part, which in its basic form

[17] Earlier by Petrus Ramus, *Grammatica Latina*, 3rd edn (Paris, 1560), Lib. 1, Cap. 3, but in the more general sense of a pause, lengthening.

[18] The final foot of a hexameter is basically not a spondee but a trochee (i.e. a catalectic dactyl): for arguments see *AR*, pp. 301 ff. The spondee alternative here arises only by the principle of 'indifference' at end of line.

comprises one or two light syllables, as the 'weak position'. The substitution of two light for a basic heavy syllable (i.e. in the strong position) is generally referred to as 'resolution', and that of a heavy for a basic two light (i.e. in the weak position) as 'contraction'.

Unlike the light syllables in weak position, those arising by resolution in strong position are subject to more or less stringent constraints on the incidence of word-boundaries, and an explanation of the phenomenon involves rather numerous technicalities, which are treated in some detail in *AR*, pp. 316 ff. (cf. p. 137 below). The rationale of metrical contraction (discussed in *AR*, pp. 255 ff.) is also far from obvious, but one possibility, based on an idea proposed by G. Nagy (*Comparative Studies in Greek and Indian Meter*, pp. 49 f.), may be summarized here. It is suggested that the substitution has its origin in the well-known process of vowel-contraction (τιμάετε → τιμᾶτε, etc.). Though this process was carried further in Attic than in other dialects, some vowel-contractions in Homer must go back to an early period, since the metre sometimes precludes their expansion (into the uncontracted forms), even in formulae (cf. Chantraine, pp. 27 ff.). The uncontracted Homeric forms, however, tended to be misunderstood in later times, as may be seen from the phenomenon of 'diectasis' (cf. Chantraine, pp. 75 ff.). The Homeric ὁράω, for example, contracted in Attic to ὁρῶ: but the metre demanded three syllables in Homer, and to meet this requirement Attic reciters (ignorant of any such form as ὁράω) simply 'stretched' the vowel of the contraction to give the ὁρόω of our texts—which is historically non-existent.

The proposed explanation assumes that there was a predecessor of the Homeric hexameter of purely dactylic form; and that later, in certain words of the poems, vowel-contraction produced spondaic sequences. It seems likely that the contracted forms were first admitted in composition to the strong position of the foot *metri gratia*, and then extended in recitation to the weak position. Subsequently, in Nagy's words, this substitution 'extended beyond the original confines of the formulas that generated it' (i.e. to cases *not* arising from vowel-contraction), 'so that new formulas with spondee instead of dactyl are admitted' (loc. cit)—an example of the process whereby metrical patterns develop 'their own dynamics and became regulators of any incoming non-traditional phraseology' (op. cit., p. 145).

If this explanation is correct, then the term 'contraction' for the metrical substitution is also very appropriate from the standpoint of historical phonology.

The question of 'ictus'

We have discussed so far the determinants of quantity in Greek, and have seen that it functions as a rhythmic factor both in the language and in metre. We have, on the other hand, seen that the primary characteristic of quantity is unlikely to have been duration; and since Greek verse is based on quantity, its rhythms also are unlikely to have been based purely on time-ratios. These suppositions are further supported by the fact that in iambics and trochaics a heavy syllable may occur in some of the same positions as a light; and in dactylics and anapaestics may be substituted for two light only in a particular (viz. 'weak') position of the foot (see p. 113 above). For neither the possibility of the former nor the restriction of the latter equivalence seems compatible with a purely durational rhythmic basis.[19] One must therefore seek some other characteristic of quantity which could on the one hand account for a heavy syllable being sometimes rhythmically equivalent to a light; and on the other hand for a spondee, which comprises two elements of the same quantity, to be rhythmically equivalent to either a specifically 'falling' (trochaic or dactylic) foot, or a 'rising' (iambic or anapaestic) foot. One characteristic which seems to meet this requirement is 'stressability'; in other words, it seems possible that heavy syllables were liable to bear stress in the language—but that not all such syllables were stressed; that light syllables tended to be unstressed; and that verse-

---

[19] For the former cf. A. M. Dale, *WSt*, 77 (1964), p. 16: 'long anceps must have been distinguishable from the neighbouring longs, or the clarity of the rhythm would suffer'.

rhythm was based on the alternation of stressed and unstressed syllables, i.e. that an 'ictus' fell on the strong position of the foot, which was normally constituted by a heavy syllable.[20]

This question of stress in classical Greek will be taken up in more detail in another connection (pp. 131 ff.).

[20] On 'resolution' see pp. 112 ff. and 137, with further reference to *AR*.

CHAPTER 6

ACCENT*

It is generally acknowledged that the accent of ancient Greek was basically one of pitch (i.e. 'melodic') rather than of stress. From the time of Plato (e.g. *Crat.*, 399 A) we find two primary categories of accent recognized by the Greeks themselves, to which are generally applied the opposed terms ὀξύς ('sharp, acute') and βαρύς ('heavy, grave'). If ὀξύς in this context meant 'loud', βαρύς would mean 'quiet'—which it does not; indeed, as Sturtevant points out (p. 94), it tends to mean the opposite, being applied to sounds which are both low and loud, as e.g. in βαρυβρεμέτης as an epithet of Zeus; and a passage in the *Phaedrus* (268 D), referring to music, indicates that Plato understood these terms as applying to features of pitch. Similarly from a passage in the *Rhetoric* (1403 b) it is clear that Aristotle considered accentuation as a type of ἁρμονία, whereas loudness is referred to as μέγεθος (with μέγας and μικρός as its two poles). The actual terms used to denote accentuation in Greek are themselves suggestive of its nature: for τάσις or τόνος (lit. 'stretching') may be taken to derive their meaning from the string-tension whereby the pitch of a musical instrument is varied, the 'sharp' accent being commonly associated with ἐπίτασις 'tightening', and the 'heavy' with ἄνεσις 'slackening'— terms which are in fact also applied to stringed instruments (e.g. Plato, *Rep.*, 349 E); and the common term προσῳδία, of which the Latin *accentus* is a literal translation, is a clear reference to the musical nature of the Greek accent (being so called 'quia προσᾴδεται ταῖς συλλαβαῖς', as a Latin grammarian explains).[1]

It may also be significant that the rules relating to the position of the accent in Greek (unlike Latin: cf. *VL*, p. 85) concern primarily the vowel elements, i.e. precisely those elements which are 'singable' in the sense of permitting variations of

[1] Diomedes, *GL*, i, p. 431 K.

pitch; thus, for example, the accentuation of φοῖνιξ (as compared with φαίνω) indicates that in the final syllable only the
short ι vowel is relevant for accentual purposes, and not the
(heavy) quantity of the syllable νιξ as a whole.[2]

A more general indication of the nature of the Greek accent
is given by the phonological studies of the Prague school, which
suggest that stress is normally characteristic of languages in
which the accentual unit is the syllable (as e.g. Latin), but pitch
of languages in which the accentual unit is the 'mora' (as in
ancient Greek: cf. pp. 111 f., 122).[3]

The melodic nature of the Greek accent is further supported
by its close parallelism to that of Vedic, which was unmistakably
described by the Indian phoneticians in terms of 'high' and
'low' pitch,[4] and of 'tense' and 'lax' vocal cords.[5] In spite of
numerous divergences, the Greek and Vedic accentual systems
must be derived from a common Indo-European origin—
witness, for example, their close agreement in part of the
nominal paradigm:

	Greek	Vedic
Nom. sing.	πατήρ	*pitá*
Voc. sing.	πάτερ	*pítar*
Acc. sing.	πατέρα	*pitáram*
Dat. sing.	πατρί	*pitré*
Dat. plur.	πατράσι	(loc.) *pitṣu*

Remnants of this original system are still found in some modern
Baltic and Slavonic languages (notably Lithuanian and Serbo-
Croat);[6] but it is Vedic that preserved it most faithfully, and
J. Kuryłowicz has therefore commented that 'Pour comprendre
l'accent grec il suffit de partir d'un état à peu près védique'.[7]

---

[2] Cf. Choeroboscus, *Schol. in Theod.*, i, pp. 364, 384 f. H.

[3] Cf. Trubetzkoy, p. 179 ('Die Differenzierung der Prosodeme geschieht in sil-
benzählenden Sprachen durch die Intensität, in den morenzählenden durch die
Tonhöhe'); R. Jakobson, *TCLP*, 4 (1931), pp. 166 f. The considerations mentioned
on p. 154 may also be relevant.

[4] For a discussion of the metaphorical use of the terms 'high' and 'low' in relation
to pitch in western antiquity see C. Jan, *Musici scriptores Graeci*, pp. 58 f. and 143 ff.

[5] Cf. Allen, pp. 87 ff.

[6] The melodic accents of certain modern Scandinavian and Indian languages
(Swedish, Norwegian; Panjabi, Lahnda) are of secondary and independent origin.

[7] *L'accentuation des langues indo-européennes*[2], p. 7.

It is the high pitch that is generally considered in antiquity as *the* accent of the word, in the sense of being the 'culminative' feature which occurs in one and only one syllable of the word; all other syllables have the low pitch, which might therefore be considered as a merely negative feature, i.e. absence of high pitch.[8] Thus the high pitch is sometimes referred to as the κύριος τόνος, i.e. 'the pitch proper', and the low pitch as συλλαβικός, i.e. 'inherent in the syllable'.

There seems to be supporting evidence also from some surviving fragments of musical settings of Greek texts. The musical writer Aristoxenus observes that there is a natural melody of speech based on the word-accents (†*Harm.* i. 18, p. 110 M); but in singing, according to Dionysius of Halicarnassus, this melody is subordinate to the requirements of the music. Dionysius mentions the choral lyrics of Euripides as displaying this most clearly, and cites an example from the *Orestes* (140–2: †*De Comp.* xi, pp. 41 f. UR); it so happens that a choral fragment of this play (338–44), with a musical setting that may be the original, has been preserved on papyrus; it is badly mutilated, but it tends to support Dionysius in so far as there is little correlation between the linguistic accents and the music; this, as J. F. Mountford has commented, is not surprising, since 'if the same melody were sung to the strophe and antistrophe of a choral ode, it would frequently happen that the rise and fall of the melody would be contrary to that of the pitch accents of the words; for strophic correspondence did not extend as far as identity of accentuation'.[9]

[8] The ancient Indian authorities refer to the comparable accents in Vedic as *udātta* 'raised' and *anudātta* 'unraised'.

[9] In *New Chapters in Greek Literature* (ed. Powell & Barber), p. 165; cf. also E. K. Borthwick, *CR*, N.S. 12 (1962), p. 160; E. Pöhlmann, *WSt*, 79 (1966), p. 212. It has, however, been suggested by E. Wahlström (*Accentual Responsion in Greek strophic poetry*, *CHL*, 47 (1970), p. 8) that it is 'dangerous to generalize from the compositional practice of a notoriously avant-garde composer like Euripides'; and from an accentual analysis of passages from the lyric poets he seeks to show that there is a tendency to accentual responsion between stanzas, which is particularly marked towards the ends of lines and so suggests that the poet was taking the musical setting into account. But the agreement between stanzas is not complete, and Wahlström recognizes (p. 22) that 'it would have been an inhumanly difficult task to compose large-scale poetry which responded perfectly both accentually and metrically and which in addition was good literature'.

Fig. 7. The epitaph of Sicilus, from the Aidin inscription.

[*Courtesy of Dieterich' sche Verlagsbuchhandlung, Wiesbaden.*]

The case appears to be different, however, with the musical inscriptions from Delphi (probably late 2 c. B.C.); in these there is a tendency to agreement between the music and what we believe to have been the melodic patterns of speech.[10] The same applies to the epitaph of Sicilus, found at Aidin, near Tralles in Asia Minor, in 1883. This inscription (not earlier than 2 c. B.C., and probably 1 C. A.D.) was in better condition than any other musical fragment, and the notation survived intact; the stone was brought to Smyrna, where it disappeared at the time of the fire in 1922 (but was reported in 1957 as having reappeared). The epitaph is reproduced on p. 119 in facsimile and in a modern musical transcription (both after O. Crusius, *Philologus*, 52 (1894), pp. 160 ff.).[11]

So far as the high pitch is concerned, a syllable which would bear the acute accent is nearly always marked in the musical inscriptions to be sung on a higher note than any other syllable in the word (note the treatment of e.g. ὅλως, ὀλίγον, χρόνος in the Aidin inscription).[12] Regarding the range of variation between low and high pitches in speech, there is a well-known statement by Dionysius of Halicarnassus (†*De Comp.* xi, pp. 40 f. UR) to the effect that 'the melody of speech is measured by a single interval, approximately that termed a "fifth", and does not rise to the high pitch by more than three tones and a semitone, nor fall to the low by more than this amount'. This statement is generally understood in its most obvious interpretation, but an alternative suggestion[13] merits notice—namely that the interval of a fifth may refer not to the total range but rather to the variation from a mean.[14] Dionysius does not always express himself clearly, but this interpretation would save the

[10] Cf. Pöhlmann, *Griechische Musikfragmente*, pp. 17 ff.

[11] A photograph appears in *BCH*, 48 (1924), p. 507.

[12] On the apparently contradictory (first word) ὅσον cf. R. P. Winnington-Ingram, *Mode in Ancient Greek Music*, p. 38; it is also possible that ἔστι is intended rather than ἐστί.

[13] J. Carson, *JHS*, 89 (1969), pp. 34 f.

[14] The passage continues by contrasting the melody of music, as employing various intervals up to an octave. This would, however, not necessarily conflict with the above interpretation, provided that one assumed Dionysius here to be referring to variation from the central note of the two-octave 'Greater Perfect System'.

latter part of his statement from tautology; and the total range
then implied need not be excessive, at least if, as it appears, it
is intended as a maximum. Descriptions of the melodic range
of Norwegian, for example, average around a sixth,[15] but these
are generally based on a more or less formal rendering, and 'in
everyday speech the size of the interval can vary greatly, from
nothing to an octave, according to the age, sex, temperament,
and emotional state of the speaker; whether he is speaking
quickly or slowly, with or without strong emphasis and according to the position of the word in the sentence. The length of
the word can also influence the size of the interval.'[16]

It is probable that similar considerations applied to the
melodic range of Greek. It is also certain that the changes of
pitch in speech were more gradual than in singing; one would
expect this from experience of modern languages having a
melodic accent, and it is expressly stated by Aristoxenus
(†*Harm.* i. 8 f., pp. 101 f. M), who distinguishes between continuous change (συνεχής) and interval-change (διαστηματική),
and points out that a speaker who employs the latter type
of intonation is said to be singing rather than speaking.[17] The
graduality of pitch-change in one context at least is confirmed
by the evidence of Old Indian; for we know from the ancient
Indian phoneticians that in Vedic the syllable immediately
following a high pitch did not bear a level low pitch, but a
falling glide, starting at a high pitch and finishing low, to which
they gave the name *svarita* 'intoned'.[18] Since such a glide was
automatic in this context, it is to be considered structurally
(as by the Indians) simply as a variant of the low pitch; the fact,
therefore, that it is not specially indicated in Greek does not rule
out the likelihood of its existence in this language also; and
support for it is also to be seen in certain tendencies of the

[15] See e.g. R. G. Popperwell, *The Pronunciation of Norwegian*, pp. 151 f.; E. Haugen
& M. Joos, 'Tone and intonation in East Norwegian', *Acta Philol. Scand.*, 22 (1952),
pp. 41 ff.
[16] Popperwell, op. cit., p. 169.
[17] Aristides Quintilianus, however, (*De Mus.* i. 4, pp. 5 f. WI) recognizes an
intermediate style for the reading of poetry.
[18] Described by some authorities as a '*pravaṇa*', lit. 'downhill slope' (cf. Allen, p. 88).

musical fragments[19] (e.g. the second syllable of ὅλως in the Aidin inscription).

In Greek, as well as in Vedic, when a syllable contained a long vowel or a diphthong, the high pitch could occur on either the first or the second mora. In the former case the falling glide would occur on the second mora, i.e. the second mora bore a variant of the low pitch. The combination of high and low (falling) pitch in the same syllable was specifically noted by Greek writers, and given such various names as δίτονος, ὀξύβαρυς, σύμπλεκτος, or περισπώμενος (though this last might refer to the accent-*mark* rather than the accent itself). Phonetically the two elements probably fused, so that the 'compound' accent was probably identical with the falling glide which occurred on a long vowel or diphthong in the syllable following a high pitch, and the Indian writers use the same term *svarita* for both (cf. also the musical treatment of λυποῦ, ϳῆν, ἀπαιτεῖ in the Aidin inscription).

In addition to the above categories we also find references in a number of writers (including Aristotle, who does not specifically mention the compound accent) to a μέσος 'middle' accent. There is little agreement as to what was meant by this; it has been variously interpreted by modern scholars as referring to the glide which followed a high pitch (either in the same or in the following syllable), to the compound accent as a whole,[20] to a variant of the high pitch on final syllables marked with a 'grave' (see below), and in more general terms to all levels of pitch intermediate between the lowest and the highest. In this connection we may also consider in some detail the continuation of Dionysius' statement on the melodies of speech:

οὐ μὴν ἅπασα λέξις ἡ καθ᾽ ἓν μόριον λόγου ταττομένη ἐπὶ τῆς αὐτῆς λέγεται τάσεως, ἀλλ᾽ ἡ μὲν ἐπὶ τῆς ὀξείας, ἡ δ᾽ ἐπὶ τῆς βαρείας, ἡ

---

[19] Cf. R. L. Turner, *CR*, 29 (1915), p. 196. There is some musical evidence also for a tendency to rising pitch in the syllable preceding a high pitch; but 'the tendency to fall from the accented syllable is distinctly stronger...than the tendency to rise to it' (R. P. Winnington-Ingram, *Symbolae Osloenses*, 31 (1955), p. 66).

[20] Thus also by a number of Byzantine grammarians, who suggest, however, that the term μέσος is primarily a musical rather than a grammatical term; cf. Pöhlmann, *WSt*, 79, pp. 206 f.

δ᾽ ἐπ᾽ ἀμφοῖν. τῶν δὲ ἀμφοτέρας τὰς τάσεις ἐχουσῶν αἱ μὲν κατὰ μίαν συλλαβὴν συνεφθαρμένον ἔχουσι τῷ ὀξεῖ τὸ βαρύ, ἃς δὴ περισπω-μένας καλοῦμεν· αἱ δὲ ἐν ἑτέρᾳ τε καὶ ἑτέρᾳ χωρὶς ἑκάτερον ἐφ᾽ ἑαυτοῦ τὴν οἰκείαν φυλάττον φύσιν. καὶ ταῖς μὲν δισυλλάβοις οὐδὲν τὸ διὰ μέσου χωρίον βαρύτητός τε καὶ ὀξύτητος· ταῖς δὲ πολυσυλλάβοις, ἡλίκαι ποτ᾽ ἂν ὦσιν, ἡ τὸν ὀξὺν τόνον ἔχουσα μία ἐν πολλαῖς ταῖς ἄλλαις βαρείαις ἔνεστιν.

For this passage the following interpretation is proposed: 'Of course, not every word[21] is spoken with the same pitch-pattern, but one on the high pitch, another on the low, and another on both. Of those which have both, some have the low combined with the high in one syllable, and these we call circumflex; whereas others have each of them on different syllables and maintaining their own quality. In disyllables there is no intermediate position between low and high; but in polysyl-lables, of whatever length, there is a single syllable containing the high pitch amongst a plurality of low pitches.'

Thus for Dionysius, if there is only one low-pitched syllable contrasting with a high, it is simply to be classed as low, even if it has a variant form; but if there is more than one low, all except presumably the lowest occupy τὸ διὰ μέσου χωρίον (and it could be these that some other writers describe by the term μέσος). In other words, in his statement about disyllables Dionysius is speaking structurally, whilst in his statement about polysyllables he is speaking phonetically; but the general picture is consistent with a speech-melody which gradually rises towards the high pitch, whether by steps or glide, and then returns to the low.

Whilst elements preceding the high pitch are generally irrelevant to the location of this pitch, there are (unlike in

[21] The long periphrasis for 'word' is rendered necessary by the fact that Greek has no word which unambiguously means 'word' (cf. e.g. Herodian, ii, p. 407 L: ἐν ἑνὶ μέρει λόγου, ἤγουν ἐν μιᾷ λέξει). λέξις by itself can refer to an utterance of any length, and therefore requires the restriction here made to a single 'part of speech' (clearly based on the definition of Dionysius Thrax, Ars Gramm., p. 22 U: λέξις ἐστὶ μέρος ἐλάχιστον τοῦ κατὰ σύνταξιν λόγου; cf. Priscian, GL, ii, p. 53 K, and the modern definition of the word as a 'minimal free form'—e.g. L. Bloomfield, Language, 2 (1926), p. 156; B. Bloch & G. L. Trager, Outline of Linguistic Analysis, p. 54).

Vedic) restrictions placed upon its location by the elements which follow it. For this purpose the Greek accent may be considered essentially as a 'contonation', comprising the high pitch and the falling pitch which immediately follows it; this contonation may be either monosyllabic (in the case of the compound accent) or disyllabic;[22] but in either case *not more than one vowel-mora* (= short vowel) *may follow the contonation.*[23]

Accentual marking

In inscriptions there is virtually no indication of accent,[24] and we have no reason to think that any system of marking was in general use in classical times. Native speakers naturally knew the position and nature of the accent, since it was part of their everyday speech; there would thus be no more need for them to indicate it in writing than in the case of the Norwegian or Swedish melodic accent, or the English or Russian stress-accent; the relatively few cases of ambiguity would nearly always be resolved by the grammar or sense of the context (e.g. τόμος noun: τομός adj.—cf. English *ímprint* noun: *imprínt* verb; Nor-

[22] This distinction is reminiscent of the Norwegian accents often so named (cf. Haugen & Joos, op. cit.); on 'oxytone' words see below.

[23] For this purpose the final 'diphthongs' αι and οι are generally to be considered as comprising a short vowel and a consonant *y* (see also pp. 81 f., 97); cf. M. Lucidi, *RL*, 1 (1950), p. 74. Lupaş (p. 180) objects to this formulation on the grounds that one would have to consider long vowels other than in final syllables as comprising only one mora (e.g. in a word such as ἄνθρωπος). But this objection assumes that the falling tone necessarily occupied only one mora; and it is clear from p. 121 above that this is not envisaged—and indeed would be phonetically most improbable; the fall is envisaged as occupying the *whole* of the following syllable (just as the *svarita* in Vedic): cf. also *AR*, p. 238.
For other formulations of the rule see *AR*, pp. 236 ff.
On final diphthongs in relation to the rule see further *AR*, p. 238 with n. 2.

[24] Cf. Threatte, p. 97. There is just one clear example from Athens of *c.* 220 A.D., on a fragment of the Sarapion monument, where the word οἷ ('for himself') bears a circumflex (and rough breathing) straddling the digraph, in the medical precept:

Ἔργα τάδ(ε) ἰατρ[οῦ]....πρᾶτον....
καὶ νόον ἰῆσθαι καὶ οἷ πρόπαρ ἢ τῷ ἀ[ρήγην]

(cf. 'Physician, heal *thyself*'). The purpose here could be to disambiguate the poetic form, or for emphasis. Cf. J. H. Oliver (with P. Maas) in *Bull. Hist. Med.* 7 (1939), pp. 315 ff. (drawing on p. 319); a few other cases (including some possible Attic examples) are cited by A. Wilhelm, *SbAWB*, 1933, pp. 845 f.

wegian ´hjelper 'help(s)': ˇhjelper 'helper'). The use of accent-marks in Greek may have arisen partly as a result of a decline in the oral tradition of epic poetry (so that Greek speakers themselves required guidance in the pronunciation of un-familiar forms), and partly from the needs of teaching Greek as a foreign language. The tradition of such marking seems to have started at Alexandria around 200 B.C., and is generally associated with the name of Aristophanes of Byzantium. At first, to judge from papyri, it was used sporadically and mostly to resolve ambiguities.

From the beginning the high pitch on a short vowel was rendered by the acute accent-mark, as in e.g. λέξαι; the same mark was also used when the high pitch occurred on the second mora of a long vowel or diphthong, as in e.g. (optative) λήξαι; but when it occurred on the first mora of a long vowel or diphthong, thereby creating the 'compound' accent (mono-syllabic contonation), this was marked with the circumflex[25] accent-mark, as in e.g. (infinitive) λῆξαι.

In one early system of marking, every low pitch was indicated by the grave accent-mark—e.g. Θὲόδὼρὸς; but such a practice was clearly uneconomical and inelegant,[26] and was later re-placed by the current (Byzantine) system whereby only the high and compound pitches are indicated (by the acute and circumflex symbols). The grave symbol was, however, then substituted for an acute where this occurred on a final mora ('oxytone' words), except in the case of interrogatives (e.g. τίς) or when followed by an enclitic or a pause—thus e.g. ἀγαθός ἐστιν, ἔστιν ἀγαθός·, but ἀγαθὸς ταμίας.[27] There has been much discussion about what this substitution implies from a phonetic point of view, but no clear decision has been reached—e.g. as

---

[25] = περισπώμενος, 'bent round'. There is a Byzantine tradition that this term originally referred to the shape of the mark, having been substituted for the term ὀξύβαρυς by Arist. Byz. upon changing the mark from ˆ (a combination of acute and grave) to ⌒ in order to avoid confusion with the consonant Λ; but there is reason to doubt the authenticity of this story.

[26] Cf. Herodian, i, p. 10 L; Schol. in Dion. Thr., pp. 153 and 294 H.

[27] For early accentual practice see B. Laum, Das alexandrinische Akzentuationssytem; W. Schubart, Das Buch bei den Griechen und Römern[3], pp. 75 f.

to whether it implies a full or partial lowering of the pitch,[28] or is merely a graphic peculiarity.[29]

We have seen that in other types of word a high pitch was probably followed by a falling pitch to complete the contonation. In Vedic, when the high pitch occurred at the end of a word, the falling pitch was carried by the initial syllable of the next word. But, as compared with Old Indian, words in Greek were more autonomous units from a phonetic point of view, and it is likely that such an extension of the contonation across word-boundaries would there have been anomalous. An exception would be understandable in the case of enclitic combinations, since the enclitic lacked any accent of its own, and formed a single phonetic unit with the preceding full word: thus in e.g. ἀγαθός ἐστιν the first syllable of ἐστιν could carry the falling glide; similarly, in combinations such as ἄνθρωποί τινες, δῶρόν ἐστιν, a second contonation is required because otherwise there would be a breach of the rule that a contonation may not be followed by more than one mora. There are, however, restrictions on the extent to which the limiting rule can operate, as e.g. in καλῶς πως, καλοῦ τινος, καλῶν τινων, where the rule is breached but it is impossible to add a secondary accent to the main word; the same applies to e.g. οὕτω πως, since the second syllable of οὕτω carries the falling glide and so cannot receive a secondary accent; and in e.g. οἶκοί τινων the rule is breached on account of the long vowel in the final syllable of the enclitic. In the last case it is usual to say that the length of final vowel in enclitics is irrelevant; but it may simply be a case of an accentual *pis aller*, just as the absence of secondary accentuation in καλῶς πως, οὕτω πως, etc.[30]

---

[28] The grammarians use the term κοιμίζεται, or τρέπουσα εἰς βαρεῖαν (cf. Herodian, i, pp. 10 and 551 L; Apollonius Dyscolus, *Pron.*, p. 36 S).

[29] The fact that the grammarians seem sometimes to assume a high pitch in such cases is not necessarily evidence against a phonetic modification, since they may well be speaking in relative terms, whereby even a lowered variant would still be classified as high. On the 'grave' accent see further *AR*, pp. 244 ff., 269 ff.; Sommerstein, pp. 160 f.

[30] In cases like μεγάλοι τινές (and e.g. παίδοιν τινοῖν) the rather surprising secondary accent on the enclitic may have arisen by a misunderstanding: for further discussion (including also the question of 'proclitics') see *AR*, pp. 241 f., 248 f.; Sommerstein, pp. 162 f; Lupaș, pp. 172 ff.

In non-enclitic contexts, e.g. ἀγαθὸς ταμίας, a high pitch on ἀγαθός could not be followed by a fall, and the contonation would be incomplete. The importance of the fall is further shown by the fact that in enclitic combinations a high pitch may not be *immediately* followed by another high pitch: thus we have e.g. μεγάλοι τινές, *not* μεγάλοί τινες, since the latter accentuation would deprive the full word μεγάλοι of the falling glide, which thus seems to have been an essential adjunct of the high pitch.[31] The system as represented by Vedic, therefore, would have broken down in Greek when an 'oxytone' word was followed by another full word;[32] the anomalous situation might be resolved by some modification of the high pitch—but it must be admitted that the nature of the modification is unknown, and there seems little point in making mere guesses.[33]

Interrogatives and pre-pausal forms are of course inherently special cases, and it may well have been, as the marking and

[31] On the problem of 'synenclisis' (succession of enclitics) see Vendryes, pp. 87 ff.; *AR*, p. 244; Sommerstein, pp. 164 f. The 'Homeric' enclitic accentuation Λάμπέ τε etc. (well attested in papyri and MSS, and by a number of grammarians, but generally 'corrected' by modern editors) is not really an exception, since the first syllable in such cases contains a short vowel followed by a liquid or nasal; such consonants can carry a tonal movement in the same way as vowels (Popperwell, op. cit., §442, comments on them as 'prolonging the vowel glide' in Norwegian); in Indo-European (and still in Lithuanian) such combinations were structurally equivalent to diphthongs; thus the falling tone can occur on the liquid or nasal, so that the accentuation of Λάμπέ τε etc. was originally equivalent to that of e.g. εἶτά τε. The same treatment is, however, further and wrongly extended to heavy syllables in general, e.g. ὄφρά σε (cf. Vendryes, §92).

[32] Oxytones in such cases are referred to as 'enclinomena'.

[33] The foregoing account of the Greek accentual system, and of the implications of the grave accent-mark, is based on Allen, 'A Problem of Greek Accentuation' (*In Memory of J. R. Firth*, pp. 8 ff.); but its essentials are already implicit in C. Lancelot's remarkable *Nouvelle Méthode pour apprendre facilement la langue grecque* (1st edn, Paris, 1655; citations from 9th edn, 1696), p. 22: '...après avoir relevé la voix sur une syllabe, il faut nécessairement qu'elle se rabaisse sur les suivantes;...on ne le figure jamais que dans le discours, sur les mots aigus...qui dans la suite changent leur aigu en grave,...pour montrer qu'il ne faut pas relever la dernière, laquelle autrement porteroit jusques sur le mot suivant, & feroit le mesme effet qu'aux Enclitiques, qui est de les unir avec le mot précédent'; cf. p. 547: '...ils ne l'élèvent pas tout à fait, parce que cet élèvement paroistroit tellement au respect du mot suivant, qu'il sembleroit l'unir a soy, ce qui ne se peut faire qu'aux Enclitiques.' The formulation of the limiting rule as stated on p. 124 above is also foreshadowed by Lancelot, p. 548: '...la dernière syllable qui suit le Circonflexe, ne peut estre longue par nature: parce que cette dernière syllable ayant déjà esté précédée d'un rabaissement, qui est dans le Circonflexe mesme, elle ne peut avoir deux mesures...'

ACCENT

grammarians' statements suggest, that here a final high pitch
would be permitted without a following fall. As Apollonius
Dyscolus comments on τίς, the oxytone accent has not a
distinctive but an interrogatory function (*Pron.*, p. 28 S: οὐ γὰρ
ἕνεκα διαστολῆς τὸ τίς ὀξύνεται ἀλλ' ἕνεκα πεύσεως). The
pre-pausal acute would be a feature of the terminal sentence-
or clause-intonation rather than of the word-contonation; in
Trubetzkoy's terms (p. 215), 'the acute on final syllables was
not an accent in the true sense, but an externally conditioned
raising of the last syllable of a word: this raising occurred before
a pause if the word contained no other high mora'.[34] Though
a rising intonation in non-interrogative sentences is not a
normal feature of English, it may be noted that in Norwegian
'Sentences which contain ordinary, definite, decided statements
end on a rising melody... There is, consequently, a pronounced
rise in pitch within the last word of the sentence. Should the
sentence end in a Tone Group, the rise in pitch can be even
greater.'[35] Interrogative sentences in Norwegian also end on a
rising pitch-pattern, so that 'Norwegian often strikes foreigners
as an unending series of question marks'.[36] The evidence seems
to indicate that the sentence-intonation of ancient Greek was
somewhat similar in effect to that of Norwegian, a language
having a system of melodic accentuation comparable with that
of Greek.

We probably have sufficient knowledge to achieve a rough
approximation to the melodic pattern of isolated Greek words
(including enclitic combinations); but, quite apart from the
particular problem of the 'enclinomena', we know virtually
nothing about 'melodic syntax', i.e. the way in which such

[34] Elsewhere (*Introduction to the principles of phonological description*, p. 38, n. 1)
Trubetzkoy cites the case of Ganda, where the rising pitch occurs 'only in interrogative
verb-forms and this has nothing to do with word phonology, but rather belongs in the
field of sentence phonology'. R. Ultan (*Working Papers in Language Universals* (Stanford),
1 (1969), p. 54) notes in the course of a study of interrogative systems in some 79
languages that, although accentual information is scarce, some 20 of these are known
to have 'fortis stress or sentence stress, high pitch, rising contour, or a combination of
stress and high pitch on the question-word. These languages are evenly distributed.'
For further discussion of interrogatives see *AR*, pp. 251 ff.
[35] Popperwell, op. cit., §454.   [36] Ibid., §455.

patterns interacted with one another and with clause- and sentence-intonations in continuous speech. To judge from what we find in living tonal and melodically accented languages, these interactions may be extensive and complex. Given the melodic patterns of the word-isolates in such languages, it is of course possible to derive the melodic sentence-pattern from them—but the latter is not usually a simple summation of the former.[37] The author has listened to a number of recordings, recent and less recent, of attempted melodic-accentual recitations of ancient Greek, and, whilst some are less objectionable or ridiculous than others, has found none of them convincing; and, as W. G. Clark commented on such efforts over a century ago, the less gifted exponents of this practice 'may fancy that they reproduce it when they do nothing of the kind'.[38]

The carefully considered advice is therefore given, albeit reluctantly, not to strive for a melodic rendering,[39] but rather to concentrate one's efforts on fluency and accuracy in other aspects of the language. For further discussion see App. A2.

These practical difficulties, however, should not be allowed to obscure the fact that the melodic accent was one of the most characteristic phonetic features of ancient Greek; and the accent-marks of our current texts may be generally considered as a faithful indication of the word-melodics;[40] quite apart from the statements of grammarians, and, less reliably, the manuscript traditions, they are supported in principle by the evidence of Vedic and other languages, and in their detailed location by the pronunciation of modern Greek, where, with

[37] As examples of the intricacy of these relations one may consult Haugen & Joos, op. cit. and in particular A. E. Sharp, 'A tonal analysis of the disyllabic noun in the Machame dialect of Chaga', *BSOAS*, 16 (1954), pp. 157 ff.

[38] *Journal of Philology*, i. 2 (1868), p. 108. On the difficulties encountered and the training required for competence in tonal phonetics cf. Pike, *Tone Languages*, pp. 18 ff., and my further comments in *Didaskalos*, 2.3 (1968), pp. 152 ff. (also *AR*, p. 75). On the perceptual side note the wide variation in pitch transcription as revealed by P. Lieberman, 'On the acoustic basis of the perception of intonation by linguists', *Word*, 21 (1965), pp. 40 ff.

[39] Aficionados of the melodic method may however profitably study the recordings by Prof. Stephen Daitz—e.g. *The Pronunciation and Reading of Ancient Greek* (2 cassettes), publ. Jeffrey Norton, Inc., N.Y./London: 2nd edn 1984.

[40] The main doubts concern 'proclitics': see e.g. Vendryes, pp. 63 ff.

explainable exceptions, the marked syllables now bear a stress.[41] It is misleading to speak, as in an address given to the Classical Association,[42] of 'the complex Byzantine rules of Greek accentuation'—the current marking-system is indeed based on an early Byzantine development of Alexandrian principles; but, far from being complex, it is a laudably economical representation of the phonetic facts: and the facts themselves, like the rules which govern them, are as ancient as the other elements of the language.

The change to a stress-accent

The eventual change from a melodic to a stress-accent in Greek cannot be precisely dated. It seems clear that it had taken place by the latter part of the 4 c. A.D., since Gregory Nazianzen composed hymns in metres based on stress-accentuation (as well as in 'quantitative' metres); and there are indications of the transition to a stress-accent in interior elements of an anonymous early 4 c. Christian hymn (*Pap. Amherst*, ed. Grenfell & Hunt, I. ii). In the late 2 c.–early 3 c. there are similar indications in the hymns of Clement of Alexandria. But there is no convincing earlier evidence.[43]

In this connection it is customary to cite certain accentual peculiarities in the choliambics (scazons) of Babrius as indicative of stress (paroxytone accentuation at the end of the line). Babrius' date is uncertain, but probably around the 2 c. A.D.,[44] when the transition could well have been in progress, at least in some areas. But Babrius cannot be used as evidence for this; the argument is based on a misinterpretation of the choliambic rhythm, and the accentual peculiarities can be better explained

[41] The fact that syllables marked with the 'grave' are also stressed need not imply the presence of a high pitch on such syllables in ancient Greek (cf. p. 125), since this could simply represent a generalization from pre-pausal position (a not uncommon process: cf. e.g. Allen, *Sandhi*, p. 27; H. Reichelt, *Awestisches Elementarbuch*, p. 86).

[42] *Proceedings*, 1964, p. 17.

[43] See also p. 94, n. 9 above.

[44] 2nd half of I c. A.D. according to L. Herrmann, *AC*, 18 (1949), pp. 353 ff.; 35 (1966), pp. 433 ff.

in terms of a melodic accent.[45] Similar accentual tendencies in the epic hexameters of Nonnus, however, may legitimately be interpreted as an indication of stress, since the rhythm is quite different; and, since Nonnus is dated around the 5 c. A.D., this explanation of his accentual peculiarities is most probable.

The question of stress in classical Greek

The classical Greek accent was, as we have seen, melodic. It is, however, improbable that Greek words and sentences had no variations of stress. This has often been recognized, but there has been a tendency to assume that any such element of stress must have been connected with the high pitch, since pitch is frequently an important factor in the complex phenomenon of stress-accentuation. But, for one thing, it is not necessarily high pitch that is involved in such cases—in different languages it may be high, low, or changing pitch (cf. *AR*, pp. 74 ff.); and for another, stress is not conversely a necessary feature of melodic accentuation; so that it is possible for a language having a melodic accent to have also a stress-patterning that is quite unconnected with this accent.[46]

Moreover, any connection of stress with high pitch seems to be ruled out by the fact that in classical Greek there is no correlation of the accent with any metrical stress or 'ictus', whereas when later the accent changes to a dynamic type, it does play an increasing and ultimately exclusive rôle. One result of this change is that readings of ancient Greek verse by modern Greek speakers, which commonly stress the accented syllables and make no distinctions of vowel-length, thereby deprive the verse of any element of regular rhythm. For ancient Greek we could postulate a connexion of stress and accent only if we assumed the dynamics of its verse to have been as irregular as those of modern Greek readings, and its 'rhythms' to have been conveyed solely in terms of relative time-ratios. Some difficulties

---

[45] For details cf. Allen, *TPS*, 1966, pp. 138 ff.; *To Honor Roman Jakobson*, i, pp. 58 ff.

[46] For such a situation, in general conditions not unlike those of Greek, see e.g. C. M. Doke, *The Southern Bantu Languages*, pp. 43 f.

inherent in the latter assumption have already been mentioned on pp. 114 f., and modern-language metrical studies tend to underline its improbability.[47] The most likely conclusion, we have suggested, is that the 'strong' positions of the feet, i.e. those which are normally filled by a heavy syllable, tended to bear a metrical stress or 'ictus'.

This, of course, does not mean to say that Greek verse was basically stressed verse, like English for example, with stress as its structural principle. From a structural point of view it was quantitative (i.e. based on alternation between different types of syllable-structure), and certain of its features can only be accounted for in these terms (e.g. the admission of 'anceps' only at one place in the iambic or trochaic metron). We are suggesting only that there was superimposed on this an element of dynamic reinforcement.

Since Greek metrical patterns, unlike those of classical Latin, were, so far as we know, evolved specifically for Greek, it is likely that they represent, in Meillet's terms, 'a stylization or normalization of the natural rhythm of language'. So it is probable that any such patterns of metrical reinforcement would tend to agree rather than conflict with any similar patterns in speech. If this were so, then one might expect that particular syllabic word-patterns would tend to be placed in particular relationships to the strong/weak positions of the verse, even though their purely quantitative structure might qualify them for other placings. And conversely, if one were to discover a strong tendency of this type, it would suggest the presence, in both verse and speech, of some factor additional to quantity—whatever the nature of that factor might be. In spite of the already expressed opinion that classical Greek verse was probably marked by a dynamic ictus, let us avoid prejudging the phonetic issue so far as speech is concerned and for the present refer to the factor simply as 'prominence'.

---

[47] Cf. S. Chatman, *A Theory of Meter*, p. 43: 'I do not deny that time is the medium through which meter flows, or even that length itself is a component of "stress"; what I do deny is that the mind has some elaborate faculty of measuring and identifying time spans and that this is what it does in meter.' The habit of attributing such a faculty to the 'delicate ear of the ancients' is criticized by Stetson, *Bases of Phonology*, p. 71.

For the purpose of investigating any such correlations, the most secure data-base would seem to be that of serious spoken verse (epic hexameters; tragic iambics and trochaics), as against lyric on the one hand, where linguistic patterns may have been affected by musical dynamics, and comedy on the other. It is likely that such non-functional patterns as we are seeking would be phonetically less strongly marked than, say, the accentual stress of a language like Latin or modern Greek. The possibility of an investigation of this kind therefore depends upon our authors having sought to match the regular strong/weak patterns of their verse with such relatively subtle variations of prominence in the spoken language. It is notorious that Greek comic verse does not display the same degree of metrical constraint as tragedy (one may mention the not uncommon neglect of the caesura and of 'Porson's Law', and the frequency of resolved feet, including the admission of anapaests in all but the last, and most significantly of a dactyl in the fifth, with consequent reversal of the rising quantitative pattern even in the cadence of the line): cf. *AR*, pp. 311 f. One cannot therefore agree with B. E. Newton (*Phoenix*, 23, p. 368) that it would be 'exceedingly odd' if our evidence were found in tragedy but not in comedy 'which one would have expected to reproduce as closely as possible the speech rhythms of the market place'. The point is simply that comedy, as exercising less care in the placement of words relatively to the metre, is less likely to produce *regularity* of rhythm; in this repect comedy is indeed more 'natural' and less 'artificial' than tragedy—but for the same reason less valuable as evidence, since it cannot be expected to reveal such regular correlations between metrical and linguistic prominence.

We might further expect constraints of the type we are seeking to be found more particularly in the latter part of the line, the 'coda', where rhythmic regularity is most commonly to be found in the metrics of many languages (note, for example, the attention devoted to agreement of stress-accent and strong position in the last two feet of the Latin hexameter): cf. *AR*, pp. 106, 337.

A study of the relationship between word-placement and strong position in a corpus of Homeric and tragic verse[48] in fact reveals that the preponderant tendencies can be stated in terms of a single formula. The study was based on the portions of the lines following the main caesura (or diaeresis in trochaics), and the category 'word' was extended to include word + appositive combinations, where 'appositive' includes prepositive and post-positive elements in general, not just the traditional 'enclitics' (thus e.g. περὶ πάντων, θνητοῖς γὰρ count as one word each). The resultant formula is as follows, where S = strong positions of feet, $-/\circ$ = heavy/light syllable:

$$(\ldots)\frac{S}{\infty}(\circ)\frac{S}{\circ\ \infty}(\circ)_\circ$$

From this formula may be derived the particular syllabic word-forms and their predominant placement. To derive these forms one works from right of formula (end of word) to left, with optional switching from upper to lower row of syllables and vice versa, but with the proviso that restrictions on sequences of light syllables in verse preclude movement from ($\circ$), indicating an optional syllable, to ∞.

In interpreting the formula it is to be noted that it assumes the application of the traditional 'law of indifference',[49] whereby at the end of a line of verse a heavy syllable in terminal weak position is treated as light, and a light syllable in terminal strong position is treated as heavy. Thus a hexameter may end with a word(-end) $--$ (placed $\underline{S}-$ because it is equivalent to $-\circ$ (= catalectic dactyl), and an iambic trimeter or catalectic trochaic tetrameter may end with a word(-end) $\circ\circ$ (placed $\circ\overset{S}{\circ}$) because it is equivalent to $\circ-$ (cf. AR, pp. 296–303).

What we have so far referred to as 'preponderant tendencies' in fact turn out to approach complete regularity—that is to say, there are very few exceptions to a word of a particular

[48] First discussed in TPS, 1966, pp. 107 ff., and further developed in AR, pp. 274–334 (to which interested readers may refer for detailed analysis of the data).

[49] E.g. Aristides Quintilianus, De Musica i. 21, p. 44 WI (παντὸς μέτρου τὴν τελευταίαν ἀδιάφορον ἀποφαινόμεθα); cf. Hephaestion, Ench., p. 14 C.

quantitative pattern being placed in a particular relationship to the strong positions of the verse coda. It is of course true that many types of word, simply by reason of their quantitative structure, can *only* occur in certain places relatively to the strong and weak positions, and so do not provide positive evidence: this applies to all words where a syllable is flanked (on either or both sides) by one or two light syllables. The crucial evidence is provided, therefore, by words containing heavy syllables only (or a succession of more than·two light syllables in the case of 'resolved' feet). And here the nature of the forms which are *not* derivable from the formula is significant: they include, for example, $\overset{s}{-}-$, $\overset{s}{ooo}$, $\overset{s}{-}oo$, $\overset{s}{oo}-$, $o\overset{s}{-}-$, $oo\overset{s}{-}$, $o\overset{s}{-}-$, $-\overset{s}{-}-$, $oo\overset{s}{-}-$, $\overset{s}{-}ooo$, etc. (as against derivable $-\overset{s}{-}$, $oo\overset{s}{o}$, $-\overset{s}{-}-$, $oo\overset{s}{o}-$, etc.). These non-derivabilities reflect, *inter alia*, the constraints of Porson's Law in iambics and trochaics (cf. *AR*, pp. 304–12), the rules of resolution (see e.g. West, pp. 86 f.), and of 'Naeke's Law' in hexameters. This last law, which is virtually without exception in Callimachus, allows of some exceptions in Homer; but these involve principally the placement of words or combinations of pattern $(o)o\overset{s}{-}-$ ending with the 4th foot, where there is clear evidence of a 'faute de mieux' principle at work (cf. *AR*, pp. 286–91). Another less common exception is the placement $\overset{s}{-}o\overset{s}{oo}$ in iambics, but here there are special contraints on the nature of the final two syllables (cf. *AR*, pp. 323 f.).

If, then, we assume that a very strong preference for placing particular syllables of words in particular relationships to the strong positions indicates that the syllables in question possessed some kind of inherent phonetic 'prominence', we can deduce from the formula certain rules describing the incidence of such prominence in Greek words:

1. Prominence applies to an element constituted by either (*a*) one heavy syllable or (*b*) two light syllables.
2. Words (or word-like sequences) longer than an element have internal contrasts of prominence/non-prominence.
3. If the final syllable of a word is heavy, it is prominent.

4. If the final syllable is light, the next preceding element is prominent.

5. A preceding element separated[50] from the prominent element is also (secondarily) prominent.

It remains to consider what the phonetic parameter of this prominence might be. Of possible candidates, high pitch is already preempted for the accent; length is already preempted as an independent phonemic variable; and the superimposition of either of these on the redundantly prominent syllable would conflict with their existing significant rôles. Of the three common prosodic parameters (cf. *AR*, p. 6) this then leaves only the dynamic, i.e. stress.

This conclusion may be strengthened by an analogy outside Greek.[51] We might consider the patterns of assumed prominence expressed in the Greek formula as a kind of typological 'fingerprint' of that type of prominence. And if it were possible to find a matching fingerprint in a language where the phonetic nature of the prominence was established, we should have quite a strong typological argument for concluding that the prominence in Greek was of the same nature. In *VL*, pp. 124–5 (supplementary note to p. 91) a restatement was proposed for the rule governing the placement of the Latin accent, in terms of 'matrices' comprising either one heavy or two light syllables. The rule may be stated in a formula of the type used above, with the same rules of derivation, where A denotes the location of the accent: thus (for words of three or more syllables):

$$(\ldots)\, \frac{\text{A}}{\text{oo}}\, (\circ)\, \frac{}{\text{o}}$$

where $\frac{\text{A}}{\text{oo}}$ corresponds to the traditional markings ´– and ⌣⌣, as e.g. in *nŏmĭna*, *nōmĭnĭbus*. We could extend this formula to take account of secondary accentuation in longer words, where it is

---

[50] I.e. by a heavy or by one or two light syllables, of which the first and last, though themselves elements, are not separated from the (primarily) prominent element.

[51] The following ideas form the subject of a paper contributed to the *Festschrift for Henry Hoenigswald* (Tübingen, 1987).

likely that the part of the word preceding the main accent was treated as a word for purposes of secondary accentuation (e.g. *indìligéntia, mìsericórdia*: cf. *AR*, p. 190).[52] The extended formula would then be:

$$(\ldots)\,\frac{\mathrm{A}}{\mathrm{oo}}\,(\mathrm{o})\,\frac{}{-}\,\frac{\mathrm{A}}{\mathrm{o}\,\mathrm{oo}}\,(\mathrm{o})\,\frac{}{\mathrm{o}}$$

It will be seen that this Latin A-formula differs from the Greek S-formula only in respect of the final syllable—a fact accounted for by the irrelevance of final quantity in the Latin accentual system.[53] Structurally, therefore, the S-elements of Greek correspond closely to the A-matrices of Latin, and a strong typological probability arises that they were both marked by the same kind of prominence. In the case of Latin it is generally agreed to have been stress, and it would be a rather odd coincidence if the Greek prominence factor were of a quite different kind. The exact correspondence of the disyllabic stress-matrices and disyllabic strong positions may then further suggest a phonetic explanation of the phenomenon of resolution (cf. *AR*, pp. 316 ff.).[54] On the other hand any formula that might be devised for the (melodic) *accentual* rules of Greek would be of a quite different nature.

Other languages with a known stress accent, having similar rules to those of Latin, are Arabic and Indo-Aryan. In the former, and in modern forms of the latter (e.g. Hindi), final syllables also may be accented, but only if they are 'hyper-characterized' (p. 91, n. 5)), i.e. ending in -v̄c or v̆cc[55] (there are a few such cases also in Latin as the result of historical

---

[52] Cf. the statement by D. A. Abdo (*On Stress and Arabic Phonology*, p. 73a) on secondary accentuation in Arabic: 'Starting from the segment immediately preceding the stressed vowel, apply the rule once more to any segments that again meet its structural description. The vowel stressed in the second application receives secondary stress'.

[53] Whether the parallel of the 'indifference' of final quantity in Greek metrical systems is more than fortuitous is probably beyond conjecture.

[54] It is assumed that in a disyllabic matrix the peak occurs on the first syllable and the cadence on the second, thus óò, which corresponds to a monosyllabic matrix △ where both peak and cadence occur within the same syllable. For a full discussion, including parallels in English, see *AR*, pp. 170–7, 191–9, 316 ff.

[55] For fuller discussion cf. Allen, *ICS*, viii.1, pp. 1–10.

sound-changes, such as *nostrás* < **nostrátis*, *illínc* < **illínce*, but no synchronic rule: so *laúdās*, etc.). One result of the accentual rules in both Latin and these other languages is that the place of the accent in a given word is invariable, regardless of context. In this respect the rules for the placement of words in Greek verse differ in an important way. For the quantity, and so the placing, of a Greek final syllable ending in -ῠc will depend on whether the next word begins with a vowel or a consonant: thus, for example, the word νῆας placed νῆᾰς ἐῖσας at *Il.* i. 306 but νηᾰς τε προπᾰσας at ii. 493. This suggests the possibility that in many Greek words the patterns of prominence may have varied with context. This, however, is hardly a matter for surprise. In Greek, unlike the other languages mentioned, we are dealing with redundant, *non-accentual* patterns, and syntagmatic variations in these would be no more peculiar than such variations in the melodic (intonational) patterns of words in a stress-accented language like English.[56] These considerations, together with the probable relative weakness of any such patterns of stress in classical Greek, would explain why they were completely ousted by the strongly stressed word-accentual patterns of the later language.

In the absence of factual evidence for the above conclusions, it is not recommended that they should be applied to the

---

[56] Cf. *AR*, pp. 295 f.: '...the generation of sentences, whether at the grammatical or phonological level, does not take place syllable by syllable, nor even word by word; relatively long stretches of utterance are prepared in advance, and the relationship of the earlier to the later elements in actual phonation is taken account of just as that of the later to the earlier. To take a grammatical example: in Latin the gender concord of an attribute must be determined in advance of the actual utterance of a postponed noun—e.g. "et *hic* quidem Romae, tamquam in tanta multitudine, *habitus* animorum fuit"'; and phonologically 'the principle is clearly demonstrated by the phenomenon of "spoonerism", which presupposes the preparation of the second element of the metathesis before the phonation of the first...There is therefore nothing unreasonable about assuming for Greek a stress-patterning which, in certain types of word, may show a binary variation dependent on context, such context being limited to the immediately following word. It implies simply that the pattern of chest-pulses and arrests is prepared in "blocks" longer than a single word: and whilst in colloquial speech there would no doubt be changes of mind resulting in prosodic "errors" just as in grammatical anacolutha, this is hardly relevant to the types of utterance represented in more formal poetry'.

practical reading of Greek prose (on this see pp. 149 ff.). And as regards the reading of verse, if one follows the common practice of reciting with a stressed verse-ictus, the findings of this study comfortingly suggest that, particularly in the coda of each line, one is also very close to a natural reading, though in the earlier portions one may be introducing various degrees of artificiality, since the exceptions to the S-formula are there considerably more numerous: whether the Greeks themselves preferred nature or artifice to predominate in such cases remains an open question, since we lack the kind of evidence that is available for the similar question in Latin (cf. *VL*, pp. 126 f. (supp. note to p. 94); *AL*, pp. 335 ff.).

Readers wishing to study further the problem of constraints on the metrical placement of words in Greek may well consult the recent work by A. M. Devine & L. D. Stephens, *Language and Metre* (A.P.A., American Classical Studies 12: Chico, Cal., 1984). Though I have reservations about the rhythmic rôle proposed for duration in a language where (as noted above) length is an independent variable—just as they have typological reservations regarding my own proposals—their ingenious approach to an exhaustively generalised theory (including the question of resolution) is of absorbing interest and an important contribution to continuing debate.

APPENDIX A

1. The pronunciation of Greek in England

In 1267 it was remarked by Roger Bacon that there were not five men in Latin Christendom acquainted with Greek grammar. In 1311 the Council of Vienne recommended the appointment of two teachers of Greek in each of the principal cities of Italy; a Greek school was in fact opened in Rome, and money was collected for the founding of a chair at Oxford.[1] In 1325 lectures on Greek were given in the University of Paris, but the language suffered under the suspicion of heresy, and the numerous treatises on Aristotle listed in the 13 and 14 c. catalogues of the Sorbonne show no evidence of acquaintance with the Greek text. In 1360 Petrarch could still count only eight or nine Italians who knew Greek.

The teaching of the language did, however, gradually progress in Italy in the 14 and 15 c., and was accelerated by the increased migration of Byzantine scholars after the destruction of Constantinople in 1453. But the pronunciation used and taught by these scholars was naturally that of their current mother-tongue, i.e. virtually that of modern Greek. Amongst characteristic features of this pronunciation the following may be noted:

β, δ, γ (as well as φ, θ, χ)   pronounced as fricatives;
ʒ   pronounced as a single sound [z];
κ, χ, γ, λ, ν   palatalized before front vowels;
π, τ, κ   voiced after nasals;
υ in αυ, ευ   pronounced as [v] or [f];
αι   pronounced as a monophthong [e];

and, above all, the single value [i] accorded to ι, η, υ, ει, οι, υι. As Roger Ascham was later to complain, though with regret-

---

[1] On the introduction of Greek into England, including some earlier occasional instances, see Ch. 2 of J. C. Collins, *Greek Influence on English Poetry*.

table subjectiveness and exaggeration, 'all sounds in Greek are now exactly the same, reduced, that is to say, to a like thin and slender character, and subjected to the authority of a single letter, the *iota*; so that all one can hear is a feeble piping like that of sparrows, or an unpleasant hissing like that of snakes'.

It was not long before doubts arose in the minds of some scholars as to the validity of the then current pronunciation of ancient Greek. In particular, the values of the vocalic letters and digraphs were seen to conflict with the principle enunciated by Quintilian (i. 7. 30), 'sic scribendum quidquid iudico, quomodo sonat'; on the assumption that the ancients followed this precept, their pronunciation must evidently have been different from that of the Byzantines. The assumption is not altogether valid (Quintilian was in fact careful to add 'nisi quod consuetudo obtinuerit'), and it led to some erroneous conclusions, but it at least provided a starting point for the first essays in reconstruction of the ancient pronunciation.

The earliest suggestions towards a reform date from 1486, in the work of the Spanish humanist Antonio of Lebrixa (Antonius Nebrissensis); and they had as yet, according to his own statement, no support in Spain or elsewhere—indeed he complains that the only effect of his teaching was to turn former friends into enemies when their errors were revealed. In a further treatise of 1503 he argues, *inter alia*, that η was a long vowel corresponding to ε in the same way as ω to ο; that ʒ stood for σδ; and that β, like φ, was not a fricative but a plosive, since β, φ and π were recognized by the ancients as belonging to the same order. He later composed a fuller statement of principles (probably first published in 1516), including a list entitled 'Errores Graecorum', which refers to most of the characteristics mentioned above; his orthographic criteria, however, also misled him into rejecting the monophthongal pronunciation of ου.

The next reformer known to us is the great printer, Aldus Manutius, who in 1508 mentions the erroneous pronunciation of the digraphs, and later refers to a number of other points discussed by Antonio. Like the latter, he assumes ου to

represent a diphthong, and so is content to posit a value [u] for
υ (citing in support Latin cognates and borrowings, as *sus*,
Thule, and conversely ῾Ρωμυλος); but, to his credit, he is the first
to cite the now notorious βῆ βῆ (for the cry of a sheep) as
evidence for a pronunciation '*bē bē*' as against the current '*vi
vi*'.

The monophthongal pronunciation of the digraphs is further
criticized in a statement by Jerome Aleander, probably dating
from about 1512, and he also comments on the confusion of long
and short vowels and the neglect of the rough breathing.

The reforming movement culminated in the publication in
1528 of Erasmus' dialogue *De recta Latini Graecique sermonis
pronuntiatione*, of which the following are amongst the most
important conclusions. The value of η as an open mid vowel [ẹ̄]
('between α and ε') was deduced from the fact that on the one
hand it is represented by the Latin *ē* and on the other hand often
arises from original Greek ᾱ. On the basis of Latin renderings
with *ū*, the value of ου was established as [ū]—though Erasmus
conjectures that, from the evidence of the spelling, it must once
have had a diphthongal value ('Ου vero arbitror priscis fere
sonuisse, quod Batavis sonat *senex, frigidus*', i.e. as Dutch *oud*,
koud). The value of υ is correctly assumed to be [ü], i.e. as the
'*u* Gallicum', though some of the arguments are invalid (e.g.
'idem arguit quod Galli vulgo θύειν dicunt "*tuer*", id est
mactare, usurpata voce Graeca');[2] Leo (the pupil in the
dialogue) ventures to suggest as further evidence against the
current [i] pronunciation the fact that in ancient Greek the
cuckoo was called onomatopoeically κόκκυξ, 'quae in θέσει
cantus non *i* sonat sed *u* Gallicum'—a suggestion that is
dismissed by Ursus, the teacher, with jestingly exaggerated
caution:[3] 'Qui scis an avis haec non eodem modo canat apud
Graecos quo apud nos?' On the basis both of orthography and
of Latin transcriptions the diphthongal values of αυ and ευ
are correctly stated, as also of αι ('Jam αι diphthongum evi-

[2] Actually from Latin *tutare*.
[3] But none the less wise in principle: *Eudynamis honorata*, often referred to as the
'Indian cuckoo', has a call that is well represented by the vernacular name *koïl*.

denter audire licet in lingua Germanorum, quum nominant Caesarem', i.e. *Kaiser*); but ει is also assumed to have had a diphthongal value, 'quam evidenter audis quum nostrate lingua dicis ovum', i.e. as Dutch *ei*.

Some difficulty arises in the case of οι; it is agreed to be a diphthong, but is then compared with the pronunciation of French *oi* ('οι diphthongus Gallis quibusdam est familiarissima, quum vulgari more dicunt *mihi, tibi, sibi*', i.e. *moi, toi, soi*. 'Hic enim audis evidenter utramque vocalem *o* et *i*'). Already in the 12–13 c. French *oi* had come to have the value [wę]; in the 15 c. the modern pronunciation [wa] appeared in vulgar speech,[4] and by specifying 'vulgari more' Erasmus presumably intends to refer to this value. In either case the phonetic comparison is not a good one.

With regard to the consonants, Erasmus recognizes the value of ζ as equivalent to σδ, and rightly criticizes the tendency of Dutch speakers to give a voiced value to σ between vowels (e.g. by pronouncing μοῦσα as [mūza]). β is correctly identified as a plosive, like the Latin *b*, for which the phonetic equation *bini* = βινεῖ is cited (cf. p. 31), but the treatment of the aspirates is erratic; φ is admirably distinguished from the Latin *f* ('primum quia in *f* labium inferius apprimitur superioribus dentibus, deinde quod spiritu leniore profertur, veluti studio vitandi Graecam aspirationem, quae est in φ, cujus sono labiis utrisque diductis spiritus vehementior erumpit...in φ magis stringuntur labia prius quam erumpat spiritus'), but a fricative value seems to be assumed for χ, and is specifically stated for θ ('quam feliciter exprimunt Angli in initio quum sua lingua dicunt *furem*', i.e. as *th* in *thief*).

Erasmus, however, like his predecessor Aleander, did not go so far as himself to adopt a reformed pronunciation. His unreadiness to practise what he preached was also later shared by the humanist Martin Crusius, who wrote in 1596: 'Graeca

---

[4] This pronunciation was, however, still not favoured amongst educated classes in the 16–17 c., and was not fully accepted until after the Revolution (see M. K. Pope, *From Latin to Modern French*, §525). [wę] still survives dialectally and in Canadian and Creole French.

ego vulgari modo, sicut et tota hodie Graecia, pronuntio. Satis mihi est, si auditores moneam de erudita pronuntiatione vetere. Graecia eam hodie non intelligeret' (Crusius had learned modern Greek, but in conversation with Greeks he spoke ancient Greek—with, of course, a modern pronunciation).[5]

The practical application of the principles of reform was due primarily to two young Cambridge scholars, John Cheke and Thomas Smith, who in 1540 were elected Regius Professors respectively of Greek and of Civil Law. The opposition to these reforms, academic, religious, and political, has been described elsewhere in connection with the pronunciation of Latin (*VL*, p. 104), and it was not until Elizabeth's accession that they could proceed unhindered.[6]

The reforms of Cheke and Smith, though not directly derived from Erasmus' dialogue, follow very much on the same lines; Cheke expressly bases his findings on onomatopoeia, cognates and borrowings from Greek to Latin and vice versa, and the statements of ancient authors. In most cases he exemplifies the reconstructed pronunciation by reference to English key-words containing approximately the sound in question; thus the value of η is equated with that of English *ea* in e.g. *bread, meat, great, heat* (in all of which in the 16 c. *ea* = open mid [$\bar{\text{e}}$]); that of ω is equated with the vowels of *moan* or *bone*, i.e. open mid [$\bar{\text{o}}$]. The values of αυ and ευ are correctly identified with those of *aw* and *ew* in English *claw, few*, which were then still diphthongal [au] and [eu] respectively. As evidence for the pronunciation of αυ Cheke incidentally cites Aristophanes' use of αὖ αὖ to represent the barking of a dog, concluding 'ne canes quidem tam crassi sunt ut pro αυ αυ "*af af*" sonent'; Smith, on the other hand, though he arrives at the same conclusion, recognizes that, whereas '*au au*' may be the sound made by Molossian hounds, '*af af*' is heard from Maltese terriers (one is reminded of the

[5] Cf. M. Faust, 'Die Mehrsprachigkeit des Humanisten Martin Crusius', *Homenaje a A. Tovar*, pp. 137 ff.

[6] An astonishing and isolated reaction appeared as recently as 1955 in an article by F. Elliot, 'Greek in our schools' (*Greece & Rome*, 2nd ser., 2, pp. 82 ff.), which asserts the originality of the modern Greek pronunciation!

conventional French '*gnaf gnaf*' as against German '*hau hau*'), and he therefore declines to accept this particular onomatopoeia as evidence.[7]

Like earlier reformers, Cheke interprets ου as a diphthong, and Smith compares it with that of e.g. *gown*, which had the approximate value [öu] or [ʌu]. ει is similarly misinterpreted, and Smith compares it with the sound in *neigh*; but it is doubtful whether by the 16 c. there remained any distinction between this and the diphthong of e.g. *pay*, though there seems to have been considerable variation in pronunciation, with something like [æi] as the mean—in another work, on English spelling, Smith himself admits that there was only a minimal difference and that there was much confusion; alternatively he identifies the value of ει with that of English *pay* as spoken by 'feminae quaedam delicatiores'—i.e. in a 'refayned' pronunciation.

In a number of cases 16th-century English could not provide very close approximations to the ancient Greek vowels and diphthongs. The short and long open vowels of e.g. *man*, *mane* were already tending to a closer value in the region of [æ], and so were not exact renderings of the Greek α. There was indeed a long close [ī] vowel, deriving from Middle English [ē], as in e.g. *green*; but, probably through the influence of spelling, the Greek long ι is identified instead with the *i* of English *bite*, which by the 16 c. had already developed a diphthongal value [əi]—a point about which Thomas Gataker complains in the next century. The Greek υ [ü] had no exact counterpart in English; for the long vowel an approximation was found in the diphthongal [iu] of words such as *duke*, *lute*, *rebuke*; but for the short vowel no such approximation was possible, and it was probably confused with the long.[8] The statements on οι are confusing (as in the case of Erasmus); both Cheke and Smith cite English key-words such as *boy*, *toy*, *coy*, but then proceed to equate these with the French *toi* etc.; it is thus not clear how the Greek οι was in fact pronounced by English speakers in the

[7] Cf. J. L. Heller, *CJ*, 37 (1941–2), pp. 531 f.

[8] An erroneous comparison by Smith with the *u* of e.g. *muddy* (in fact [u]) was evidently not adopted, since this would have resulted in a modern value [ʌ] for the traditional English pronunciation of Greek, which is not the case.

16 c.—there may well have been wide variation, since there is evidence that English words spelt with *oi* or *oy* were at that time variously pronounced with [oi], [ui], and possibly other values.

With all their imperfections, the 16th-century reforms resulted in something like an approximation to what we now believe to have been the classical Attic values, and the practical application of the so-called 'Erasmian' pronunciation soon spread from England to the continent.[9] But, by an irony of linguistic history, the reforms could hardly have come at a less opportune time so far as English speakers were concerned. For in the 16 c. the 'Great English Vowel-shift', which characterizes the development from Middle to Modern English, and which was to transform the values of the long vowels and diphthongs, had only just begun. The English pronunciation of Greek developed as a sub-dialect of English *pari passu* with the changes in the pronunciation of English itself—so that by the 19 c. it bore little relation to the classical values or those of the 16th-century reformers. The same key-words continued in most cases to apply, since English *spelling* remained basically unchanged—but with completely altered values.

On p. 147 these changes are set out chronologically (though the division into centuries must of course be considered as only approximate); where no change is indicated, the value remains unaltered. The following points should be noted in connection with the asterisked items:

* Though probably no distinction was made in practice between long and short υ in the 16–17 c., the change of the diphthong [iu] to a consonant–vowel sequence [yū] in the 18 c. made it possible to distinguish the short vowel by pronouncing it as [yŭ]. The change of [eu] to [iu] in the 17 c. incidently leads Gataker to complain of confusion between ευ and υ.

** The diphthongal pronunciation of English *ai, ay* and *ei, ey* was preserved in careful speech and learned words until the late 17 c., and this was evidently adopted for the pronunciation

[9] The earlier, Byzantine pronunciation is sometimes referred to as 'Reuchlinian', after Johannes Reuchlin (1455–1521), who was largely responsible for the introduction of Greek studies to Germany, and employed the pronunciation he had learned from Greek-speaking teachers in Italy and elsewhere.

	Value in classical Attic	Value in Byz. and Mod. Gk	Classical value according to 16 c. reformers	Key-words cited by English reformers	16 c. English value in key-words	17 c.	18 c.	Present-day English value
α	a	a	a	MAN	æ	*(often ə when unstressed)*		
ᾱ	ā		ā	MANE	ǣ	ę̄	ē̆	ei
ι	ĭ	i	i	BIT	i			
ῑ	ī		ī	BITE	ai			ai
υ	ü̆		ü̆	—	*		yū*	
ῡ	ǖ		ǖ	DUKE	iu			
ε	e	e	e	MEN	e			
η	ę̄		ę̄	MEAT	ę̄	ię̄	ī	
ο	o	o	o	HOP	o			
ω	ǭ		ǭ	BONE	ǭ	ǭ	ō	ou
αι	ai	e	ai	PAY	æi	**	(ai)	ai)
ει	ę̄i		ei	NEIGH	æi *etc.*	***		
οι	oi		oi	BOY	au	ǭ	oi	oi
αυ	au	av	au	CLAW	eu	iu	yū	
ευ	eu	ev	eu	FEW	ǭu or au	ǽu		au
ου	ū	u	ou, ū	GOWN				

On asterisked items see pp. 146, 148.

Fig. 8. Development of the traditional English pronunciation of Greek vowels and diphthongs.

147

of Greek αι and ει. Various renderings were probably current, but it is unlikely that the two diphthongs were effectively distinguished from one another; and once the diphthongal pronunciation had been abandoned for English itself, a model no longer existed for the Greek, which thereafter became confused with the only other English *i*-diphthong, viz, the [əi] of English *bite*, resulting in an identical pronunciation of ī, αι and ει. In English itself the normal development of 16 c. [æi] etc. was to 17 c. [ę̄], 18 c. [ę̄], present-day [ei].

*** In the 18 c. the pronunciation of English *oi*, *oy* was generally standardized as [oi], the spelling being no doubt a contributory factor;[10] at least from this period, therefore, the [oi] pronunciation was probably normal for Greek οι, replacing whatever variants had previously been in use.

The strange pronunciation of Greek resulting from the Great Vowel-shift was in general use in English schools and universities until quite recent years, and is still often heard from those who (like the author) were brought up in this tradition.[11] As regards the consonants, φ and θ were, not unreasonably (see p. 29), pronounced as fricatives, but χ was generally pronounced as a plosive [k] and so confused with κ, since southern English

[10] The 16 c. variant [ui] developed via [ʌi] to present-day [ai], as preserved e.g. in dialectal pronunciations of *boil*.

[11] It also survives, for example, in the borrowed *nous* (17 c.), and in 19 c. learned derivates and constructions, as *seismic, deictic, pleistocene, kaleidoscope*. *Acoustic* is generally now pronounced with the middle syllable as '*coo*' and not '*cow*'—correctly (and, at least in part, independently of the 'new' pronunciation of Greek) since it is a 16–17 c. borrowing via French *acoustique*, and its Early Modern English rendering with [ū] would normally remain unchanged, as in the case of other French loans such as (17 c.) *soup, group*. The '*cow*' pronunciation of this word could be due either to display of 'learning', or to more ordinary ignorance (on the analogy of e.g. *house, mouse*, where *ou* = Middle English [ū], which is diphthongized in Modern English); the diphthongal pronunciation of a French loan such as *couch* is due to its having been borrowed in the Middle English period (similarly in *rout*, and the military pronunciation of the originally identical *route*; the more normal pronunciation of the latter is due to a later re-borrowing). The title of the philosophical journal *Nous* is, however, generally pronounced as 'noose'. Something of an oddity is the pronunciation of the Kantian *noumenon* = νοούμενον. English dictionaries prescribe '*nowm-*' (though nowadays most philosophers say '*noom-*'), but German dictionaries '*no-ūm-*'. When Kant borrowed the term he presumably intended the *u* to represent the Greek ου (as in German *akustisch* beside English *acoustic*), and this has been misunderstood by English lexicographers (and many philosophers).

On the value of English *ou*, *ow*, and their developments cf. C. A. Reinhold, *Neuenglisch ou (ow) und seine Geschichte* (= Palaestra, 189).

provides no model for a fricative [x]. Though Erasmus, following the statements of ancient authorities, had correctly established the classical value of ζ as [zd], this was misinterpreted (as commonly on the continent) as [dz] in medial position; in initial position this unfamiliar combination was generally replaced in England by simple [z].

Thus, by the 19 c., a new set of reforms was needed if the English pronunciation of Greek were to approximate once more to that of the classical original. The first systematic programme of reform was sponsored by the University of Wales, in a pamphlet on 'The restored pronunciation of Greek and Latin', by E. V. Arnold and R. S. Conway, published by the Cambridge University Press in 1895; a 4th revised edition appeared in 1908, with minor changes to conform with the recommendations of a committee of the Classical Association (of which Conway was also a member). This was on the whole an accurate reconstruction, and approximations were given by means of keywords in English, Welsh, and French. For practical reasons a fricative pronunciation was recommended for φ, θ, χ. For no evident reason a value [dz] was recommended for ζ, in spite of the fact that, as the authors themselves recognized, 'in the 5 c. B.C. ζ had a sound like English *zd*'—and this pronunciation is still often persisted in even by those who know better.[12]

It is basically the recommendations of this pamphlet which are generally followed in English schools and universities at the present day.

2. The oral accentuation of Greek[13]

An important characteristic of Byzantine and modern Greek is the replacement of the original melodic accent by a stress on the same syllable; the distinctions of vowel-length are lost, and duration becomes simply a concomitant feature of the accent. Erasmus clearly recognizes the confusion to which this may lead

[12] *The Teaching of Classics* (Cambridge, 1961) correctly recommends 'As *zd*, not as *dz*; ancient grammarians make this very plain' (p. 221).
[13] This section is based on an article under the same title published in *Didaskalos*, 2.2 (1967), pp. 90 ff.; cf. also *TPS*, 1966, pp. 108 ff.

in pronouncing ancient Greek; and he points out that a raising of pitch need not induce lengthening—'vel ab asinis licebat hoc discrimen discere, qui rudentes corripiunt acutam vocem, imam producunt'; but he nowhere makes a clear distinction between pitch and stress, and there is little doubt that, if he had actually used his reformed pronunciation, he would himself have continued to replace the melodic accent by the stress familiar from most modern European languages—though, misled by the Latin grammarians (cf. *VL*, pp. 83 ff.), he may well have imagined it to be melodic.[14] So far as the English reformers are concerned, there is no reason to believe that their recommendations included any change in regard to accentuation. There is no mention of it in the extensive correspondence between Cheke and Smith on the one hand and the Chancellor on the other, nor in the Chancellor's edict of 1542; Cheke does indeed point out that we should adhere in all respects to the pronunciation of the ancients, and mentions the *position* of the accent as a case in point—but no criticism is made of the *nature* of the accent in current practice. It is highly improbable, therefore, that the 'Erasmian' pronunciation of Greek made any change in the existing Byzantine system of stressing the accentually marked syllables.

The subsequent history of oral practice in this respect is independent of other factors in pronunciation, and is therefore discussed as a separate issue.

The Byzantine system of stressed accentuation, which respected the original position of the accent, has continued in use in most countries up to the present day. But in 1673 there was published at Oxford an anonymous treatise *De poematum cantu et viribus rhythmi*, identifiable as the work of the Dutch scholar Isaac Vossius, formerly tutor in Greek to Queen Christina of Sweden, who had received an honorary degree at Oxford in 1670 and a canonry of Windsor in 1673. He was evidently a man of eccentric ideas, and Charles II was once moved to observe, 'He is a strange man for a divine; there is

---

[14] He does in fact follow the Latin writers in attributing the same kind of accent to Greek and to Latin.

nothing he will not believe if only it is not in the Bible'. In his Oxford treatise Vossius argued that the accent-marks of Greek had nothing whatever to do with the original pronunciation; and this doctrine paved the way for a well-named *Dissertatio Paradoxa* some eleven years later by one Heinrich Christian Henning (self-Latinized as 'Henninius'), a doctor of medicine from Utrecht.[15] Accepting Vossius' rejection of the traditional accents, Henning went on to claim that in view of the close relationship of Greek and Latin, and particularly of their metrical structures, the Greek accentual system must have been the same as that of Latin—'ergo ut Latine pronunciamus ita et Graece erit pronunciandum'. The Latin system is, as we know, governed by the so-called 'penultimate' rule (cf. *VL*, p. 83), whereby a stress-accent falls on the penultimate syllable if it is of 'heavy' structure, and on the antepenultimate if the penultimate is 'light'; according to Henning, therefore, Greek also was to be pronounced in conformity with this rule, i.e. as if it were Latin.[16]

Henning's remarkable doctrine found acceptance both in Holland and in England, where it seems to have been well established by the early 18 c.[17] (though the older system survived in some quarters until about the middle of the century),[18] and the 'Henninian' pronunciation is now general

[15] ΕΛΛΗΝΙΣΜΟΣ ΟΡΘΩΙΔΟΣ *seu Graecam Linguam non esse Pronunciandam secundum Accentus, Dissertatio Paradoxa: qua Legitima et Antiqua Linguae Graecae Pronunciatio et Modulatio demonstratur.*

[16] Henning classifies accentual systems as 'rational' or 'conventional' according to whether or not they follow this rule; to the former category are assigned Latin, Ancient Greek, and Arabic; all modern European languages are classified as 'conventional', though Spanish and Italian are singled out as being more 'rational' than the others, and English as being particularly 'irrational'.

[17] In the case of Greek proper names and loans some independent encouragement may have come from their occurrence in Latin (but note e.g. Shakespeare's *Andrónicus*). For an apparent adoption of this practice by some English scholars long before the time of Henning see *AR*, p. 273.

[18] *Metamórphosis* is still heard, though generally replaced by the latinized *metamorphósis*. Mr Christopher Logue has drawn my attention to the occurrence of the two competing pronunciations of this word in successive lines of Pope's *Sandys's Ghost* (*c.* 1716): the penultimate verse ends, 'A strange *Metamorphósis*', and the final verse begins, 'A *Metamórphosis* more strange'.

The normally unlatin accentuation of *idéa* is also probably due to Greek (the word is expressly recognized as Greek from its first appearance in the early 16 c., and the pronunciation is frequently reinforced by a latinate spelling *idaea*).

both in the Netherlands and South Africa and in Great Britain and the Commonwealth. Elsewhere Henning's conclusions, after some considerable initial successes, were sooner or later rejected as resting upon false premisses, and the Byzantine system consequently prevails, for example, in Germany, Italy, the Slavonic countries, Scandinavia, and Hungary. The Henninian system survived in the U.S.A. until the early 19 c., but later succumbed to the German influence in classical studies there.[19]

Thus the words λανθάνει, ἄνθρωπος, τελαμών, for example, are pronounced by English and Dutch scholars with stress on respectively the initial, middle, and initial syllables, but by German and American scholars with stress on respectively the middle, initial, and final syllables. It is interesting to note that, even in countries where the native language has a melodic system of accentuation (as e.g. in Yugoslavia and Norway), the Greek accent is nevertheless rendered by stress; in Norwegian, moreover, stress tends to correlate with low pitch, so that the result is a reversal of the ancient Greek melodics. Most French speakers follow neither the Byzantine nor the Henninian system, but pronounce Greek, like French, with a weak final stress.

One result of accepting the views of Vossius and Henning was that the original accents came to be omitted from a number of Greek texts printed in England in the 18 c.—'as if a gale from the Netherlands had stripped the letters of a superfluous foliage';[20] support was lent to this practice by the attack upon accents in Richard Dawes' *Miscellanea Critica*, first published in 1745; and in 1759 it was adopted as the official policy of the Oxford University Press. The practice was, however, deplored by many scholars, including John Foster, fellow of King's

[19] I am particularly grateful to the following scholars for assisting me in a survey of current European practice: Dr A. Bartoněk (Univ. of Brno); Prof. Simon Dik (Univ. of Amsterdam); Prof. I. Fischer (Univ. of Bucharest); Dr P. Ilievski (Univ. of Skopje); Prof. J. Kuryłowicz (Univ. of Krakow); Prof. M. Lejeune (Centre nat. de la recherche scientifique, Paris); Prof. G. Lepschy (Dept. of Italian Studies, Univ. of Reading); Prof. E. Liénard (Univ. Libre de Bruxelles); Prof. Hans Vogt (Univ. of Oslo).

[20] I. Errandonea, *Emerita*, 13 (1945), p. 90.

College, Cambridge, whose admirable essay *On the different nature of Accent and Quantity* was first published in 1762. Later, in his edition of the *Medea* (1801), Porson also insisted upon the importance of accentuation, and urged the reader to persist in its study 'scurrarum dicacitate et stultorum irrisione immotus'; the influence of so great a scholar was probably decisive in ensuring that the Greek accents were thereafter respected in English printed texts.

Most English scholars at the present day would recognize the inaccuracy of the Henninian, 'latinizing' pronunciation as a rendering of the original Greek; but many are prepared to defend it against its rival on practical, pedagogical grounds. Two main arguments are generally adduced in its defence, both dating from the times of Vossius and Henning.

First, it is said, the type of pronunciation used for Greek prose in most other countries in any case requires the adoption of a different system, based on quantity, in reading Greek verse; whereas the latinizing accent, being already, as they say, 'according to quantity', is immediately suited to this purpose. But just how true is this? A hundred lines of Greek iambics, for example, chosen at random, showed the following figures of agreement between the verse-ictus and the marked accent in each of the six feet:

41.   50.   55.   36.   31.   31.

The agreement admittedly averages well below 50%. For the latinizing accentuation of the same passage, figures of agreement with the verse-ictus are as follows:

35.   72.   84.   37.   31.   2.

Certainly there are some notable differences in the distribution of these figures amongst the various feet—but the overall difference is insignificant. A sample of epic hexameters proved rather more favourable to the latinizing accent, but even so agreement averaged only around 60%.[21] In fact, as G. J.

[21] For further discussion cf. *AR*, pp. 280 ff.

Pennington had already noted in 1844,[22] 'the Latin can no more claim to be read according to quantity than the Greek'— indeed a sample from the *Aeneid* averaged no more than 55%. The most, then, that can be said for the Henninian pronunciation in this connection is that it is based upon the same general principles as the verse-ictus, i.e. that its location is regulated primarily by syllabic quantity.

The second argument concerns the distinctions of vowel-length. In Byzantine and modern Greek the effect of the stress accent has been to suppress the independent distinction between long and short vowels, all stressed vowels being of rather longer duration than unstressed, regardless of their original values. A similar effect is commonly encountered in current pronunciations of ancient Greek by Russian and Italian speakers, for example, in whose native languages there is a similar linkage of stress and duration; and one of the objections made by the Henninian 'reformers' against the traditional accentuation in England was that it tended to lengthen accented short vowels and, more particularly, to shorten unaccented long vowels.

As a matter of general linguistic typology,[23] it is probably true that if a language has a free stress-accent (which is consequently capable of distinctive function—as e.g. modern Greek *pinó* 'I am hungry': *píno* 'I drink'), it tends to eschew phonemic distinctions of vowel-length. This does not apply, however, to languages with a fixed stress-accent; Finnish, Hungarian, and Czech, for instance, which generally have a primary stress-accent on the initial syllable, nevertheless maintain distinctions of length even in polysyllabic words—e.g. Hungarian *felszabadítás* 'liberation' (the acutes in Hungarian indicate length, not stress).[24] And indeed present-day RP English, in spite of its 'free' stress-accent, provides numerous models for the pronun-

[22] *An Essay on the Pronunciation of the Greek Language*, p. 183.
[23] Cf. Jakobson, *Selected Writings*, i, p. 624; *TCLP*, 4 (1931), p. 182; Trubetzkoy, *Scritti in onore di A. Trombetti*, p. 160.
[24] Modern Icelandic, which also has an initial stress-accent, has lost its former phonemic distinctions of vowel-length (replacing these by qualitative differences), but there are clear phonetic differences in the duration of vowels and diphthongs according to syllabic structure.

ciation of stressed short vowels and unstressed long vowels[25] (the latter more particularly in complex and compound words). As early as 1804, W. Mitford (*An Inquiry into the principles of Harmony in Language*, p. 279) had pointed this out in connection with the pronunciation of Greek, citing as examples of an unstressed long [ī] such words as *íncrease* (noun), *cólleague*, *thírteen*, etc., and the compounds *héartsease*, *swéetmeat*; and in 1852 J. S. Blackie (*The Pronunciation of Greek; Accent and Quantity*, pp. 56 f.) observes that English speakers show no tendency to lengthen the first vowel in *vísible* or to shorten the [ī] of *hóusekeeper*; those who claimed that such changes were a necessary corollary of stress in English, says Blackie, 'had got their ears confounded by the traditional jargon of teachers inculcating from dead books a doctrine of which they had no living apprehension'. No doubt there were English speakers of Greek who did exhibit some of the tendencies complained of by the Henninians, but their performance must have been due to carelessness or perversity[26] rather than to any irresistible constraints of the English language. The effort required to maintain the correct values is certainly no greater than is called for in avoiding neutral vowels or in pronouncing double consonants in words like θάλασσα, or Latin *corōlla*.

As English (RP) models for unstressed long vowels, both pre- and post-accentual (and often combined with stressed short vowels), we may add a few other examples to those cited by earlier writers, which readers will be able further to augment for themselves:[27]

[25] The typological rule can be saved (as by Jakobson; cf. also Jakobson & Halle, *In Honour of Daniel Jones*, pp. 96 ff.) by treating English (cf. p. 6) as having primarily distinctions of tenseness rather than length.

[26] It seems to have been deliberately taught in the Westminster School pronunciation introduced by Richard Busby (headmaster 1638–95), whose pupil Dryden even writes εὕρεκα (*Religio Laici*, 43). That it still survived there in the next century is shown by a letter from W. Cowper to Wm Unwin in 1785, to which Professor E. J. Kenney has drawn my attention: 'They that read Greek with the accents, would pronounce the ε in φιλέω as an η. But I do not hold with that practice, though educated in it. I should therefore utter it just as I do the Latin word *filio*, taking the quantity for my guide'. In other words, he was brought up to stress and lengthen the accented vowel of φιλέω, but rejects this in favour of the Latinizing stress on the first syllable: he will of course have pronounced *filio* (wrongly, in the traditional manner) with a short first vowel (cf. *VL*, p. 105).   [27] Cf. also Gimson, p. 141.

(for ω):   *audítion, morónic, récord, lándlord, óutlaw, báckwater, móuth-organ.*

(for ᾱ):   *carbólic, partisán, plácard, bróadcasting, télegraph* (note also the distinction maintained between short [ə] in *laggard* [lǽgəd] and long [ā] in *blackguard* [blǽgād]).

(for ου):   *rheumátic, slíde-rule, bús-route, péa-shooter.*

(for η, approximately):   *wáyfarer.*

Unstressed diphthongs, of course, provide no problem, since there is no possibility of confusion—for Greek αι, αυ compare English *mídnight, súndowner,* etc. (most English speakers will also tend to diphthongize ει, in which case models are provided by e.g. *sándpaper, óperate*).

The pattern of stress on short vowels in English, even before single consonants (e.g. *bátter, bétter, bítter, blótter, bútter, búllet*), is so common that no one can take seriously the objection that in speaking Greek it must lead to a lengthening of the vowels in question. It is, on the other hand, true that long vowels and diphthongs in English more commonly occur in stressed than in unstressed position; in the terminology proposed by G. F. Arnold,[28] they belong to the class of '*fortes*', in the sense of being '*normally* rhythmically strong'. But, as we have seen, departures from the norm are far from rare,[29] and the unstressed

[28] 'Stress in English Words', *Lingua*, 6 (1957), pp. 221 ff. and 397 ff.

[29] Stress in English is a very complex phenomenon, and in such cases the syllables in question are probably best considered, as by Arnold, as bearing '*non-tonic* strong' rather than weak stress, i.e. as being contrasted with the accented syllable not so much by their weaker force of articulation as by their bearing a non-prominent (non-nuclear) pitch (Arnold, op. cit., pp. 224 f.). This does not of course affect our argument, but it may provide an additional explanation of *how* English speakers are able to maintain vowel-length in 'unstressed' position (cf. p. 155, n. 25 above). It has been noted by J. Ondráčková (*Linguistics*, 83 (1972), p. 62) that in Czech also pitch-contrasts are most strikingly utilized in cases of the less common pattern of stress/length relationship.

For a discussion of the possible physiological basis of the tendency for stress to correlate with length (and conversely) see *AR*, pp. 80 f., 169 f., 185, 191 ff.

The less common pattern, with stress on a light syllable followed by an unstressed long vowel, might be compared with the so-called 'Scotch snap' in music, whereby the accented notes are shortened and the unaccented lengthened. It is perhaps of interest to note that this is also a characteristic feature of Bohemian and Magyar folk-music—and that both the Czech and Hungarian languages (cf. p. 154) frequently display this less common pattern (e.g. Cz. *kabát*, Hung. *barát*, with initial stress but long second vowel).

pronunciation of these vowels in Greek involves little more than a greater frequency of occurrence.

A further point may also be made with regard to the objection that this practice must lead to the replacement of unstressed long vowels by the corresponding short. The English vowels most similar to ε, ο, ᾰ, viz. [e], [o], [ʌ], are *also* '*fortes*' in Arnold's sense, and so, when they occur in unstressed position, also involve a deviation from the 'normal' pattern, thereby requiring some degree of attention in speaking Greek; and they are therefore in any case not natural substitutes for unstressed η, ω, ᾱ. (It is interesting to note that no one has ever objected to the unstressed pronunciation of ε, ο, ᾰ, occurring in the second syllables of e.g. ἄνεμος, ὄνομα, θάνατος, although, as we have just seen, these are also deviant from the 'normal' English pattern in the same way as the unstressed long vowels—the reason being, one suspects, that most English speakers tend to replace them by the more familiar '*lenes*'[30] [i] and [ə]!) Short [i] in English is admittedly a *lenis*, but most English speakers will make a considerable difference of *quality* between this and long [ī], so that any tendency to shortening of the latter in unstressed position is unlikely to lead to confusion of Greek ī and ĭ. There is a tendency to shorten pre-tonic English [ū], as e.g. in *rheumátic*, but, since there is no short [u] in Greek, no confusion can arise here either.

There is thus no real problem for English speakers in pronouncing words like ἄνθρωπος or ἡλίκος with a stress on the accented syllable and correct vowel-length. Moreover, if the arguments of the objectors to this practice were valid, they would equally apply to words like καλῶς, πρώταρχος, where the Henninian pronunciation should, according to them, produce changes in vowel-length which the non-Henninian, Byzantine rendering avoids. In fact the only considerable difficulty arises in words like παιδίον, since English does not provide models for short stressed vowels in hiatus—but ambiguity in such cases is exceedingly rare, and in any case the Henninian pronunciation

---

[30] I.e. '*normally* rhythmically weak'.

can hardly claim an advantage, since in addition it precludes the making of any distinction between e.g. δῖος and Διός, or between πίων 'fat' and πιών 'having drunk'.

The prevailing English habits in regard to Greek accentuation led Blackie (op. cit., pp. 50 f.) to comment in the following terms:

'They neglect the written accents which lie before their nose, and read according to those accents which they have borrowed from Latin!...And, as if to place the top-stone on the pyramid of absurdities which they pile...they set seriously to cram their brain-chambers with rules how Greek accents should be placed, and exercise their memory and their eye, with a most villanous abuse of function, in doing that work which should have been done from the beginning by the ear! If consistency could have been looked for from men involved in such a labyrinth of bungling, there would have been something heroic in throwing away the marks altogether from their books and from their brains, as well as from their tongue; certainly this procedure would have saved many a peeping editor a great deal of trouble, and many a brisk young gentleman riding up in a Cambridge "coach" right into the possession of a snug tutorship in Trinity, would have travelled on a smoother road.'

In fact the Committee on Greek Accentuation set up by the Classical Association in 1926, having resolved by a majority of 8:3 that they 'cannot recommend any general attempt in teaching to give an oral value either by pitch or stress to the traditional signs of Greek accent', proceeded, by a smaller majority of 6:5, to recommend that 'where no oral value is given to the signs of accent the use of these signs in writing Greek be not insisted on in Schools or Universities' (*Proc.*, 26 (1929), p. 46).

So long as we pronounce Greek as we do, it would be hard to deny the logic of these conclusions. But it remains none the less deplorable that our students and future scholars should remain in ignorance of one of the most characteristic features of Greek (and deprived of a valuable aid to the learning of its modern form), for no better reason than that we persist in an oral rendering of the language which does not reflect its native structure at any time in its history. What then is one to recommend? We have already rejected as impracticable any general attempt at a melodic rendering, enthusiasm for which in some cases tends to be in inverse proportion to phonetic experience. It will by now have become apparent that the author favours a return to the pre-Henninian, Byzantine system, thereby abandoning the Dutch alliance and conforming to the more general practice of the scholarly world, secure moreover in the knowledge that our native speech-habits afford us an advantage over most other countries in the ability to combine a free stress-accent with a proper regard for vowel-length.[31] It has to be admitted that such a pronunciation still does not help in determining when to write an acute and when a circumflex accent; but once the *position* of the accent is known, the rules which govern this choice can be very simply and briefly stated, and the exceptions are not intolerably numerous.

We have already mentioned what is often claimed as a pedagogical advantage of the Henninian system—namely that it is based primarily on quantity, and so does not require the separate learning of this concept in order to 'scan' verse, i.e. to read it with a metrical rhythm. But most students will already be familiar with the general concept of quantity from Latin, so that its application to Greek prose[32] (where in any case, as we

---

[31] It is interesting to find that Lancelot, writing at a time when Vossian views had considerable support in France, saw no particular difficulty even for French speakers in the type of pronunciation recommended: thus (op. cit., p. 549), '...quelques-uns ont cru qu'il seroit peut-estre utile, au moins pour un temps, de ne plus marquer aucun accent, puisqu'ils ne servent qu'à nous accoutumer à une fausse prononciation, et à nous faire prendre souvent pour long ce qui est bref, ou pour bref ce qui est long. Je croy néanmoins qu'on se peut relever de cet inconvénient sans en venir à cette extrémité, pourvu qu'on suive la véritable prononciation que j'ay marquée au I. Livre, qui est d'autant plus facile que je l'ay toute rapellé à celle de nostre langue..., qui n'est ni rude, ni difficile, mais qui enferme...une utilité qui se fera bien-tost sentir à ceux qui prendront quelque soin de s'y appliquer.'

[32] In fact most English scholars, in their Henninian pronunciation of Greek prose, ignore the Attic rules of quantity where they are different from those of Latin, stressing a word such as ἄτεχνος, for instance, on its middle syllable—i.e. treating it as heavy instead of light (cf. pp. 106 ff. above and *TPS*, 1966, p. 134, n. 3), as was actually done by Lucilius (cf. A. Gellius, xviii. 7. 2).

have seen, the rhythmical patterns are very different even on a Henninian basis). And even if this limited advantage were as real as it is imagined to be, the author at any rate would feel that to treat it as decisive would be to let the metrical tail wag the linguistic dog.

It would be unrealistic not to acknowledge the *external* difficulties inherent in any change, since the Henninian system is at present, and has long been, almost universal in this country. But the prevalence and antiquity of a bad habit is no argument for its continuance; the reform involved is considerably simpler than was required by the 'new' pronunciation of vowels and diphthongs—with the reservation that we should then have to learn the accent as the Greeks themselves did, and as we have to when learning a modern language like Russian, as an integral part of each word.

Select bibliography for Appendix A

Bywater, I. *The Erasmian Pronunciation of Greek and its Precursors* (O.U.P. 1908).

Clarke, M. L. *Greek Studies in England 1700–1830* (C.U.P. 1945), Appendix II.

Dobson, E. J. *English Pronunciation 1500–1700* (2 vols, O.U.P. 1957).

Drerup, E. *Die Schulaussprache des Griechischen von der Renaissance bis zur Gegenwart* (St. z. Gesch. u. Kultur des Altertums, Ergänzungsb. 6, 7: Paderborn, 1930, 1932).

Errandonea, I. '¿Erasmo o Nebrija?', *Emerita*, 13 (1945), pp. 65 ff.

Hesseling, D.-C. & Pernot, H. 'Érasme et les origines de la prononciation érasmienne', *REG*, 32 (1919), pp. 278 ff.

Kukenheim, L. *Contributions à l'histoire de la grammaire grecque, latine et hébraïque à l'époque de la Renaissance* (Leyden, 1951).

Postgate, J. P. *A short guide to the accentuation of Ancient Greek* (London, 1924), Ch. IV.

Sandys, J. E. *A History of Classical Scholarship* (3 vols, C.U.P. 1903–8).

Stoll, H. A. 'Erasmisches und Reuchlinisches Griechisch?' (*Renaissance und Humanismus in Mittel- und Osteuropa*, ed. J. Irmscher = *DAWB*, Schr. d Sektion f. Altertumswissenschaft, 32 (1962), i, pp. 89 ff.).

The relevant writings of Erasmus, Cheke and Smith are collected in S. Havercamp, *Sylloge altera scriptorum qui de Linguae Graecae vera et recta*

Pronunciatione commentarios reliquerunt (Leyden, 1740). The writings of Erasmus and Cheke are now available in Scolar facsimile reprints (*European Linguistics 1480–1700*, ed. R. C. Alston, nos. 1 (1971) and 2 (1968) respectively); and there is a critical edition of the former by M. Cytowska (= *Opera Omnia Desiderii Erasmi*, 1. 4: Amsterdam, 1973).

APPENDIX B

1. Selected quotations from ancient grammarians and other writers

(*Editions of grammatical and technical works are referred to by editors' initials only; for further details see abbreviations on pp.* xviii *f.*).

Ps.-Aristotle, `De Audibilibus`, 804b (see p. 15). ψιλαὶ δ' εἰσὶ...ὅσαι γίγνονται χωρὶς τῆς τοῦ πνεύματος ἐκβολῆς.

Aristides Quintilianus, `De Musica` ii. 11, p. 76 WI; i. 20, p. 41 WI (see p. 15). τούτων δὲ τὰ μὲν ἠρεμαίως προάγοντα τὸν ἀέρα...κέκληται ψιλά—τῶν μέντοι γε ἀφώνων τὰ μὲν ἐπιπολῆς κινοῦντα τὸ πνεῦμα ψιλά.

Dionysius of Halicarnassus, `De Compositione Verborum` xiv, p. 56 UR (see p. 16). ...ἀπὸ τῶν χειλῶν ἄκρων, ὅταν τοῦ στόματος πιεσθέντος τότε προβαλλόμενον ἐκ τῆς ἀρτηρίας τὸ πνεῦμα λύσῃ τὸν δεσμὸν αὐτοῦ—τῆς γλώττης ἄκρῳ τῷ στόματι προσερειδομένης κατὰ τοὺς μετεώρους ὀδόντας, ἔπειθ' ὑπὸ τοῦ πνεύματος ἀπορριπιζομένης καὶ τὴν διέξοδον αὐτῷ κάτω περὶ τοὺς ὀδόντας ἀποδιδούσης—τῆς γλώττης ἀνισταμένης πρὸς τὸν οὐρανὸν ἐγγὺς τοῦ φάρυγγος καὶ τῆς ἀρτηρίας ὑπηχούσης τῷ πνεύματι.

Quintilian, i. 4. 14 (see p. 23). nam contra Graeci aspirare F ut φ solent, ut pro Fundanio Cicero testem, qui primam eius litteram dicere non possit, irridet.

Plato, `Cratylus`, 427 A (see p. 23). ...ὥσπερ γε διὰ τοῦ φῖ καὶ τοῦ ψῖ καὶ τοῦ σῖγμα καὶ τοῦ ζῆτα, ὅτι πνευματώδη τὰ γράμματα, πάντα τὰ τοιαῦτα μεμίμηται αὐτοῖς ὀνομάζων, οἷον τὸ ψυχρὸν καὶ τὸ ζέον καὶ τὸ σείεσθαι καὶ ὅλως σεισμόν. καὶ ὅταν που τὸ φυσῶδες μιμῆται, πανταχοῦ ἐνταῦθα ὡς τὸ πολὺ τὰ τοιαῦτα γράμματα ἐπιφέρειν φαίνεται ὁ τὰ ὀνόματα τιθέμενος.

Scholia in Dion. Thr., p. 152 H (see p. 26). Ἔλαβε δὲ ταῦτα τὰ ὀνόματα ἐκ μεταφορᾶς τῶν ἀνεμαίων πνευμάτων, ἃ πνέοντα ἐν τοῖς ὄρεσι δάσει μὲν ὕλης προσκρούοντα μέγαν ἦχον ἀποτελοῦσιν, ὑποψιθυρίζουσι δὲ ἐν τοῖς ψιλοτέροις ὄρεσιν ἤγουν ἀδένδροις ἢ ὀλιγοδένδροις.

Dionysius Thrax, *Ars Grammatica*, pp. 12 f. U (see p. 29). μέσα δὲ τούτων τρία, β γ δ. μέσα δὲ εἴρηται, ὅτι τῶν μὲν ψιλῶν ἐστι δασύτερα, τῶν δὲ δασέων ψιλότερα.

Plato, *Cratylus*, 427 A (see p. 31). τῆς δ' αὖ τοῦ δέλτα συμπιέσεως καὶ τοῦ ταῦ καὶ ἀπερείσεως τῆς γλώττης τὴν δύναμιν χρήσιμον φαίνεται ἡγήσασθαι πρὸς τὴν μίμησιν τοῦ δεσμοῦ καὶ τῆς στάσεως.

Cicero, *Fam.* ix. 22. 3 (see p. 31). Cum loquimur *terni*, nihil flagiti dicimus, at cum *bini*, obscenum est. Graecis, quidem, inquies. nihil est ergo in uerbo; quando et ego Graece scio, et tamen tibi dico, *bini*; idque tu facis, quasi ego Graece, non Latine dixerim.

Herodian, ii, p. 926 L (see p. 32). Πλάτων μέντοι ἐν Ὑπερβόλῳ διέπαιξε τὴν ἄνευ τοῦ γ χρῆσιν ὡς βάρβαρον, λέγων οὕτως·

ὁ δ' οὐ γὰρ ἡττίκιζεν, ὦ Μοῖραι φίλαι,
ἀλλ' ὁπότε μὲν χρείη διητώμην λέγειν,
ἔφασκε δητώμην, ὁπότε δ' εἰπεῖν δέοι
ὀλίγον ὀλίον.

Dion. Hal., *De Comp.* xiv, p. 53 UR; xxii, p. 103 UR (see p. 33). τὸ δὲ μ τοῦ μὲν στόματος τοῖς χείλεσι πιεσθέντος, τοῦ δὲ πνεύματος διὰ τῶν ῥωθώνων μεριζομένου—τοῦ μὲν γὰρ ν περὶ τὸν οὐρανὸν γίνεται ὁ ἦχος καὶ τῆς γλώττης ἄκροις τοῖς ὀδοῦσι προσανισταμένης καὶ τοῦ πνεύματος διὰ τῶν ῥωθώνων μεριζομένου.

Priscian, *GL*, ii, p. 30 K (see p. 35). ...quod ostendit Varro in primo *De Origine Linguae Latinae* his uerbis: 'ut Ion scribit, quinta uicesima est litera, quam uocant "*agma*", cuius forma nulla est et uox communis est Graecis et Latinis, ut his uerbis: *aggulus, aggens, agguila, iggerunt.* in euismodi Graeci et Accius noster bina *g* scribunt, alii *n* et *g*, quod in hoc ueritatem uidere facile non est. similiter *agceps, agcora.*'

Dion Hal., *De Comp.* xiv, p. 54 UR (see p. 41). τὸ δὲ ρ τῆς γλώττης ἄκρας ἀπορριπιζούσης τὸ πνεῦμα καὶ πρὸς τὸν οὐρανὸν ἐγγὺς τῶν ὀδόντων ἀνισταμένης.

Plato, *Cratylus*, 426 E (see p. 41). ἑώρα γάρ, οἶμαι, τὴν γλῶτταν ἐν τούτῳ ἥκιστα μένουσαν, μάλιστα δὲ σειομένην.

Herodian, i, pp. 546 f. L (see p. 41). Τὸ ρ ἀρχόμενον λέξεως δασύνεσθαι θέλει, ῥά, ῥανίς, ῥάξ, χωρὶς τοῦ 'Ῥᾶρος (ἔστι δὲ ὄνομα κύριον) καὶ χωρὶς τῶν ἐξ αὐτοῦ—Τὸ ρ, ἐὰν δισσὸν γένηται ἐν μέσῃ λέξει, τὸ μὲν πρῶτον ψιλοῦται, τὸ δὲ δεύτερον δασύνεται οἷον συρράπτω.

Choeroboscus, *Scholia in Theodosii Canones*, i, p. 257 H (see p. 43). Κανὼν γάρ ἐστιν ὁ λέγων ὅτι τὸ ρ μετὰ τῶν δασέων δασύ ἐστι καὶ μετὰ τῶν ψιλῶν ψιλόν ἐστιν.

Aristotle, *Soph. El.*, 177 b (see p. 52). ...εἴπερ μὴ καὶ τὸ ὄρος καὶ ὅρος τῇ προσῳδίᾳ λεχθὲν σημαίνει ἕτερον. ἀλλ' ἐν μὲν τοῖς γεγραμμένοις τὸ αὐτὸ τὸ ὄνομα, ὅταν ἐκ τῶν αὐτῶν στοιχείων γεγραμμένον ᾖ καὶ ὡσαύτως (κἀκεῖ δ' ἤδη παράσημα ποιοῦνται), τὰ δὲ φθεγγόμενα οὐ ταὐτά.

Dion. Thr., *Ars Gramm.*, p. 14 U (see pp. 56, 59). Ἔτι δὲ τῶν συμφώνων διπλᾶ μέν ἐστι τρία· ζ ξ ψ. διπλᾶ δὲ εἴρηται, ὅτι ἓν ἕκαστον αὐτῶν ἐκ δύο συμφώνων σύγκειται, τὸ μὲν ζ ἐκ τοῦ σ καὶ δ, τὸ δὲ ξ ἐκ τοῦ κ καὶ σ, τὸ δὲ ψ ἐκ τοῦ π καὶ σ.

Aristotle, *Met.*, 993 a (see p. 58). οἱ μὲν γὰρ το ζα* ἐκ τοῦ σ καὶ δ* καὶ α φασὶν εἶναι, οἱ δέ τινες ἕτερον φθόγγον φασὶν εἶναι καὶ οὐθένα τῶν γνωρίμων.

* Restored after the commentary of Alexander Aphrodisiensis (MSS σμα, μ).

Dion. Hal., *De Comp*. xiv, pp. 51 f. UR (see pp. 62, 65, 67, 74). αὐτῶν δὲ τῶν μακρῶν πάλιν εὐφωνότατον μὲν τὸ α, ὅταν ἐκτείνηται· λέγεται γὰρ ἀνοιγομένου τε τοῦ στόματος ἐπὶ πλεῖστον καὶ τοῦ πνεύματος ἄνω φερομένου πρὸς τὸν οὐρανόν. δεύτερον δὲ τὸ η, διότι κάτω τε περὶ τὴν βάσιν τῆς γλώττης ἐρείδει τὸν ἦχον ἀλλ᾽ οὐκ ἄνω, καὶ μετρίως ἀνοιγομένου τοῦ στόματος. τρίτον δὲ τὸ ω—ἔτι δ᾽ ἧττον τούτου τὸ υ· περὶ γὰρ αὐτὰ τὰ χείλη συστολῆς γινομένης ἀξιολόγου πνίγεται καὶ στένος ἐκπίπτει ὁ ἦχος. ἔσχατον δὲ πάντων τὸ ι· περὶ τοὺς ὀδόντας τε γὰρ ἡ κροῦσις τοῦ πνεύματος γίνεται μικρὸν ἀνοιγομένου τοῦ στόματος καὶ οὐκ ἐπιλαμπρυνόντων τῶν χειλῶν τὸν ἦχον.

Quintilian, xii. 10. 27 (see p. 67). ...iucundissimas ex Graecis litteras non habemus, uocalem alteram, alteram consonantem...quas mutuari solemus quotiens illorum nominibus utimur...ut in *Zephyris*...

Dion. Thr., *Ars Gramm*., p. 58 U (see p. 86). ...διὰ τῆς ᾳ διφθόγγου, προσγραφομένου τοῦ ι, μὴ συνεκφωνουμένου δέ, οἷον βοῶ βοᾷς βοᾷ.

Quintilian, i. 7. 17 (see p. 87). Idque iis praecipue qui ad lectionem instituentur, etiam impedimento erit; sicut in Graecis accidit adiectione *i* litterae, quam non solum datiuis casibus in parte ultima adscribunt sed quibusdam etiam interponunt, ut in ΛΗΙΣΤΗΙ, quia etymologia (*sc.* < ληΐζω) ex diuisione in tris syllabas facta desideret eam litteram.

Herodian, ii, pp. 407 f. L (see p. 101). (Περὶ ὀρθογραφίας) Πᾶν σύμφωνον μεταξὺ δύο φωνηέντων ἐν ἑνὶ μέρει λόγου ἤγουν ἐν μιᾷ λέξει τῷ ἐπιφερομένῳ φωνήεντι συνάπτεται—ἐὰν εὑρεθῶσι δύο μέρη λόγου ἤγον δύο λέξεις, οὐ συνάπτεται τὸ σύμφωνον τῷ ἐπιφερομένῳ φωνήεντι, ἀλλὰ χωρὶς εὑρίσκεται τὸ σύμφωνον τῆς προηγουμένης λέξεως καὶ χωρὶς τὸ φωνῆεν τῆς ἐπιφερομένης, οἷον ὑπὲρ Ἀπολλωνίου—δεῖ προσθεῖναι χωρὶς τῶν ἐχόντων ἔκθλιψιν· ἐπὶ τούτων γὰρ τὸ σύμφωνον τῷ ἐπιφερομένῳ φωνήεντι συνάπτεται, οἷον κατ᾽ Ἀπολλωνίου.

APPENDIX B

Scholia in Dion. Thr., **p. 156 H** (see p. 101).   Ὑποδιαστολὴ δ᾿
ἐστιν ἡ προσῳδία ἡ τιθεμένη ὑπὸ τὴν διαστολήν, οἷον ἔστιν, ἄξιος,
ἵνα μὴ συνημμένως ἀναγνοὺς ἀμφιβολίαν τῷ ἀκούοντι ἐμποιήσῃ, τοῦ
ν πῇ μὲν δοκοῦντος τέλος εἶναι τοῦ ἔστιν, πῇ δὲ ὑπολαμβομένου ἀρχὴ
τοῦ Νάξιος. Εἰ δέ τις εἴποι ὅτι ἀρκεῖ τὸ πνεῦμα τοῦ φωνήεντος εἰς
διάγνωσιν τοῦ ἔστιν ἄξιος, ἀκούσεται ὅτι ἀρκεῖ μέν, ἀλλὰ πρὸς τὸν
ἀναγινώσκοντα, οὐ μέντοι γε δὴ συμβάλλεται τῷ ἀκούοντι· ὁ γὰρ
ἀκούων οὐχ ὁρᾷ τὸ πνεῦμα τοῦ ἄξιος.

Herodian, ii, p. 393 L (see p. 106).   Τὰ σύμφωνα τὰ ἐν ἀρχῇ
λέξεως εὑρισκόμενα, καὶ ἐν τῷ μέσῳ ἐὰν εὑρεθῶσιν, ἐν συλλήψει
εὑρίσκονται, οἷον ἐν τῷ κτῆμα τὸ κτ ἐν ἀρχῇ λέξεως ἐστίν, ἀλλὰ καὶ
ἐν τῷ ἔτικτον εὑρεθέντα ἐν τῷ μέσῳ τὸ κ καὶ τὸ τ ὁμοῦ ἐστιν.

Hephaestion, *Enchiridion*, p. 5 C (see p. 107).   (Περὶ κοινῆς)
Δεύτερος δέ ἐστι τρόπος, ὅταν βραχεῖ ἢ βραχυνομένῳ φωνήεντι
ἐπιφέρηται ἐν τῇ ἑξῆς συλλαβῇ σύμφωνα δύο, ὧν τὸ μὲν πρῶτον
ἄφωνόν ἐστι, τὸ δὲ δεύτερον ὑγρόν, οἷον ὅπλον, ἄκρον.

Hephaestion, *Ench.*, p. 6 C (see p. 107).   Ἐὰν μέντοι ἐν τῇ
προτέρᾳ συλλαβῇ τελικὸν ᾖ τὸ ἄφωνον, τῆς δὲ δευτέρας ἀρκτικὸν τὸ
ὑγρόν, οὐκέτι γίνεται κοινὴ συλλαβή, ἀλλὰ ἄντικρυς μακρά, ὡς παρὰ
Ἀλκαίῳ, «ἐκ μ᾿ ἐλάσας ἀλγέων».

Dion. Hal., *De Comp.* xv, p. 58 UR (see p. 110).   ὁμολογεῖται
δὴ βραχεῖα εἶναι συλλαβή, ἣν ποιεῖ φωνῆεν γράμμα βραχὺ
τὸ ο, ὡς λέγεται ὁδός—τρίτον ἔτι γράμμα τῇ αὐτῇ συλλαβῇ
προστεθήτω...καὶ γενέσθω στρόφος· τρισὶν αὕτη προσθήκαις
ἀκουσταῖς μακροτέρα γενήσεται τῆς βραχυτάτης μένουσα ἔτι
βραχεῖα—ὁ δ᾿ αὐτὸς λόγος καὶ ἐπὶ τῆς μακρᾶς. ἡ γὰρ ἐκ τοῦ η
γινομένη συλλαβὴ μακρὰ τὴν φύσιν οὖσα τεττάρων γραμμάτων
προσθήκαις παραυξηθεῖσα τριῶν μὲν προταττομένων, ἑνὸς δὲ ὑπο-
ταττομένου, καθ᾿ ἣν λέγεται σπλήν, μείζων ἂν δήπου λέγοιτο εἶναι
τῆς προτέρας ἐκείνης τῆς μονογραμμάτου.

Aristoxenus, *Harmonics* i. 18, p. 110 M (see p. 118).
λέγεται γὰρ δὴ καὶ λογῶδές τι μέλος, τὸ συγκείμενον ἐκ τῶν

προσῳδιῶν τῶν ἐν τοῖς ὀνόμασιν· φυσικὸν γὰρ τὸ ἐπιτείνειν καὶ ἀνιέναι ἐν τῷ διαλέγεσθαι.

Dion. Hal., *De Comp*. xi, pp. 41 f. UR (see p. 118). τάς τε λέξεις τοῖς μέλεσιν ὑποτάττειν ἀξιοῖ καὶ οὐ τὰ μέλη ταῖς λέξεσιν, ὡς ἐξ ἄλλων τε πολλῶν δῆλον καὶ μάλιστα ἐκ τῶν Εὐριπίδου μελῶν, ἃ πεποίηκεν τὴν Ἠλέκτραν λέγουσαν ἐν Ὀρέστῃ πρὸς τὸν χορόν·

> σῖγα σῖγα, λευκὸν ἴχνος ἀρβύλης
> τίθετε, μὴ κτυπεῖτ᾽·
> ἀποπρὸ βᾶτ᾽ ἐκεῖσ᾽, ἀποπρό μοι κοίτας.

ἐν γὰρ δὴ τούτοις τὸ «σῖγα σῖγα λευκὸν» ἐφ᾽ ἑνὸς φθόγγου μελῳδεῖται, καίτοι τῶν τριῶν λέξεων ἑκάστη βαρείας τε τάσεις ἔχει καὶ ὀξείας—etc.—καὶ τοῦ «τίθετε» βαρυτέρα μὲν ἡ πρώτη γίνεται, δύο δ᾽ αἱ μετ᾽ αὐτὴν ὀξύτονοί τε καὶ ὁμόφωνοι—etc.

Dion. Hal., *De Comp*. xi, pp. 40 f. UR (see p. 120). διαλέκτου μὲν οὖν μέλος ἑνὶ μετρεῖται διαστήματι τῷ λεγομένῳ διὰ πέντε ὡς ἔγγιστα, καὶ οὔτε ἐπιτείνεται πέρα τῶν τριῶν τόνων καὶ ἡμιτονίου ἐπὶ τὸ ὀξὺ οὔτ᾽ ἀνίεται τοῦ χωρίου τούτου πλέον ἐπὶ τὸ βαρύ.

Aristoxenus, *Harm*. i. 8 f., pp. 101 f. M (see p. 121). δύο τινές εἰσιν ἰδέαι κινήσεως, ἥ τε συνεχὴς καὶ ἡ διαστηματική—Τὴν μὲν οὖν συνεχῆ λογικὴν εἶναί φαμεν, διαλεγομένων γὰρ ἡμῶν οὕτως ἡ φωνὴ κινεῖται κατὰ τόπον ὥστε μηδαμοῦ δοκεῖν ἵστασθαι. Κατὰ δὲ τὴν ἑτέραν ἣν ὀνομάζομεν διαστηματικὴν ἐναντίως πέφυκε γίγνεσθαι· ἀλλὰ γὰρ ἵστασθαί τε δοκεῖ καὶ πάντες τὸν τοῦτο φαινόμενον ποιεῖν οὐκέτι λέγειν φασὶν ἀλλ᾽ ᾄδειν.

2. Chronology of sources

Aelius Dionysius	fl. *c.* 117 A.D.
Apollonius Dyscolus	1st half of 2 c. A.D.
Apuleius	born *c.* 125 A.D.
Aristides Quintilianus	? 3 c. A.D.
Aristotle	384–322 B.C.

Aristoxenus	fl. *c.* 318 B.C.
Athenaeus	fl. *c.* 228 A.D.
Caesellius Vindex	2 C. A.D.
Caper	2 C. A.D.
Cassiodor(i)us	*c.* 490–585 A.D.
Choeroboscus	fl. *c.* 600 A.D.
Cicero	106–43 B.C.
Cyril (St)	born *c.* 826 A.D.
Diogenes Babylonius	fl. *c.* 155 B.C.
Diogenes Laertius	? early 3 C. A.D.
Diomedes	4 C. A.D.
Dionysius of Halicarnassus	1 C. B.C.
Dionysius Thrax	born *c.* 166 B.C.
Etymologicum Gudianum	*c.* 1100 A.D.
Eustathius	2nd half of 12 C. A.D.
Galen	131–201 A.D.
Hephaestion	mid-2 C. A.D.
Herodian	2nd half of 2 C. A.D.
Herodotus	*c.* 490–425 B.C.
Hesychius	5 C. A.D.
Ion of Chios	fl. *c.* 450 B.C.
Marius Victorinus	4 C. A.D.
Nigidius Figulus	1 C. B.C.
Pausanias	2 C. A.D.
Plato	427–348 B.C.
Plato Comicus	fl. *c.* 425 B.C.
Plutarch	*c.* 46–120 A.D.
Priscian	5–6 C. A.D.
Quintilian	*c.* 35–95 A.D.
Sacerdos	3–4 *c.* A.D.
Seleucus	1 C. B.C.–A.D.
Sextus Empiricus	fl. *c.* 200 A.D.
Straton	fl. *c.* 280 B.C.
Theodosius	fl. *c.* 400 A.D.
Trypho	1 C. B.C.–A.D.
Tzetzes	*c.* 1110–1180 A.D.
Varro	116–27 B.C.
Wulfila	*c.* 311–383 A.D.

APPENDIX C

The names of the letters of the Greek alphabet

At various points in the main text there have been incidental discussions of the names of some of the letters; but a short overall treatment of this subject may be found useful. I take as a basis the post-Eucleidian (Ionic-derived) Attic alphabet (see p. 17), and begin by simply listing the letters with their names in the 4th century B.C. (and earlier in the case of all but the non-epichoric Ξ, Ψ, and Ω).[1]

Α ἄλφα. Β βῆτα. Γ γάμμα. Δ δέλτα. Ε εἶ. Ζ 3ῆτα.
Η ἦτα. Θ θῆτα. Ι ἰῶτα. Κ κάππα. Λ λάβδα. Μ μῦ.
Ν νῦ. Ξ ξεῖ. Ο οὖ. Π πεῖ. Ρ ῥῶ. Σ σίγμα.
Τ ταῦ. Υ ὖ. Φ φεῖ. Χ χεῖ. Ψ ψεῖ. Ω ὦ.

On the obsolete Ϙ (κόππα) and Ϝ (δίγαμμα) see pp. 17 and 47 respectively.

The Greek alphabet was developed, by around 800 B.C., from a Semitic (Phoenician) model in which basically only consonants were represented (cf. P. K. McCarter, *The Antiquity of the Greek Alphabet and the early Phoenician scripts*); and the order and in many cases the names of the Semitic letters are reflected in the Greek. It is thought that a majority of the Semitic symbols were derived, directly or indirectly, from Egyptian

---

[1] Athenaeus (*Deipn.* 453) preserves the following lines from the iambic prologue to a so-called γραμματικὴ τραγῳδία by Callias, in which apparently a chorus of 24 women represented the letters of the alphabet. I cite these from the text in *Poetae Comici Graeci*, edd. R. Kassel & C. Austin, vol. IV, p. 39:

⟨τὸ ἄλφα,⟩ βῆτα, γάμμα, δέλτα, θεοῦ γὰρ εἶ,
3ῆτ', ἦτα, θῆτ', ἰῶτα, κάππα, λάβδα, μῦ,
νῦ, ξεῖ, τὸ οὖ, πεῖ, ῥῶ, τὸ σίγμα, ταῦ, ⟨τὸ⟩ ὖ,
παρὸν ⟨τὸ⟩ φεῖ ⟨τὸ⟩ χεῖ τε τῷ φεῖ εἰς τὸ ὦ.

Works of the comic writer Callias are attested from 446 to 431 B.C. (cf. Kassel & Austin, p. 38); but doubts have been expressed about the identity of this writer with the author of the 'alphabet play'; and in spite of a possible explanation mentioned by J. M. Edmonds, *The Fragments of Greek Comedy*, vol. I, p. 177 n., these doubts are strengthened by the occurrence of Ξ, Ψ, and Ω, which are very rare in Attic inscriptions before 403 (cf. Threatte, p. 44).

hieroglyphs, on the acronymic principle. To take one example: the hieroglyph for 'palm of hand' was a stylized picture of the object, the Semitic name for which was *kaf*; this symbol would therefore have been adopted to stand for the consonant K, with subsequent simplification of form (cf. Ullman, ch. II).

A number of the Semitic names ended in consonants non-occurrent at word-end in Greek, and in such cases Greek modified them by adding a final α vowel—thus βῆτα for Sem. *bēt*, etc.—in the same way as the exclamations '*st!*', '*pst!*' were conventionalized as σίττα, ψύττα.[2]

We may first consider the Greek consonant-letters and their names. The Semitic languages have no class of aspirated consonants like Greek, but in the case of the dental there was an 'emphatic' (probably pharyngalized) *ṭ*, as in modern Arabic; and the symbol for this (Sem. name *ṭēt*) was adopted for the Greek dental aspirate Θ, with the name θῆτα (cf. p. 29, n. 36). For the other Greek aspirated plosives symbols, and names, had to be invented, namely Φ (φεῖ) and X (χεῖ), of which the origins are disputed; their names were no doubt formed by analogy with πεῖ for Π, which continued the Semitic name *pē*.

Of the letters indicating consonant-groups, the Greek Z [zd], earlier [dz], later [z] (see pp. 56 ff.), derives from the Semitic letter named *zayin*, whose position it occupies; the name may be by analogy with βῆτα and ἦτα. On Ξ and Ψ see pp. 59 f.; their names, ξεῖ and ψεῖ, follow the pattern of Π, Φ, and X. See, however, note on σίγμα below.

About the end of the 4th c. B.C. the phonetic value of ει changed from a close mid vowel [ē] to a fully close vowel [ī], and the resulting confusion of ει and ι in spelling has led, through manuscript traditions, to some words being occasionally misspelt even in modern texts (see p. 70, n. 18). This phonetic change of course affected the letter names πεῖ, ξεῖ, φεῖ, χεῖ, ψεῖ, and these are now commonly spelt and pronounced as πῖ, ξῖ, φῖ, χῖ, ψῖ, perhaps (like other late names: see below) through the medium of Greek teachers of the Renaissance (cf. p. 140).

[2] Forms like ὠόπ, φλαττόθρατ are examples of unmodified onomatopoeia (cf. *AR*, pp. 204 f.).

Though the name of Λ derives from a Semitic *lamd*, the earlier and correct classical Greek form is λάβδα, not the later λάμβδα. The name μῦ for M, of which the Semitic name was *mēm*, is presumably by analogy with νῦ (Sem. *nūn*),[3] perhaps too with an ear to μύζω etc. (Ionic also had the name μῶ, like ῥῶ.) The name σίγμα for Σ may be a derivation from the onomatopoeic verb σίζω (cf. p. 45).[4]

Some of the Semitic letters redundant to the consonantal needs of Greek were utilized in various ways to provide symbols for the vowels. A, E, and O were taken from the Semitic letters named *'alf* (glottal plosive), *hē* (glottal fricative: cf. p. 53), and *'ayn* (voiced pharyngal fricative) respectively. The criterion of selection was evidently the quality of the vowel in the Semitic name: in the case of *'ayn* it is possible that the initial pharyngal consonant induced a back quality of the following *a* which the Greeks could identify with their *o*-sounds (cf. Gelb, p. 292, n. 5; H. Jensen (trsl. G. Unwin), *Sign, symbol and script*, 3rd edn., p. 457, n. 1; A. Schmitt, *Der Buchstabe H im Griechischen*, p. 36; W. H. T. Gairdner, *The Phonetics of Arabic*, p. 48). The Greek I is taken from the Semitic semivowel *yōd*; and whilst the other Semitic semivowel *waw* at first survived in its consonantal value and original position in early Greek (see p. 47), another form of the same letter was used for the Greek vowel Y and placed after the other Semitic-derived letters. For A and I there was already a limited precedent for vocalic use in Semitic.

The Greek H, taken from the Semitic *ḥet* (voiceless pharyngal fricative), was at first adopted in a consonantal value for the aspirate [h] (see pp. 52 f.); but as a result of psilosis in East Ionic it became redundant in this use and was then available to represent at first the vowel [æ] (between [ẹ] and [ā]), which had developed from earlier [ā] in Attic-Ionic[5]—a use still

---

[3] Similarly the occasional ξῦ for Ξ.

[4] An alternative suggestion, first made by Isaac Taylor (e.g. *The History of the Alphabet*, II, pp. 97–102; tacitly adopted by L. M. Jeffrey, *The Local Scripts of Archaic Greece*, pp. 25–8), is that the names and values of the Semitic sibilants were transposed—*zayin* with *tsade* (cf. p. 60), giving, with some corruption, the Greek names σάν and ζῆτα; and *samekh* (cf. p. 59) with *šin*, giving the names σίγμα and ξεῖ. The letter σάν (shaped M) was used instead of Σ in some dialects.

[5] This change probably took place around 900 B.C. (cf. Bartoněk, p. 101); soon after

attested in Cycladic Ionic inscriptions (see pp. 73 f.) even until the 5 c. B.C.—and then the long open mid vowel [ẹ̄] with which it later merged.[6] In parallel with the length distinction thereby indicated, by E and H, on the front-vowel axis, the Ionic alphabet introduced a similar distinction on the back axis by inventing the sign Ω for the long open mid vowel in opposition to O, and this was placed at the end of the alphabet (cf. pp. 79, 90).

The names of the Greek vowels were partly derived from Semitic—ἄλφα, ἦτα,[7] ἰῶτα from 'alf, ḥēt, yōd. The name εἶ for E could derive from the Semitic name hē, but equally it could simply represent the lengthened form of the short vowel [e], viz. [ẹ̄] (cf. p. 90); and this is made the more likely by the non-Semitic name οὖ, at first pronounced [ọ̄], later [ū] (see pp. 75 ff., 90), for the corresponding back vowel O. Similarly the vowel Y was named simply from the long form of the vowel-sound at first pronounced [u], later [ü] (cf. pp. 76 f.); but since all initial υ were aspirated in Greek (excluding psilotic dialects), the Attic name in fact was probably ὗ (like ῥῶ for P: for further evidence cf. Liddell & Scott, Greek–English Lexicon, 9th edn, s.v. Y). The newly created letter Ω was also named from its sound, viz. ὤ [ọ̄] (cf. pp. 75 f.).

For reasons connected with phonetic changes in later Greek, some of these names were altered in post-classical times and the later forms tend to be used in current parlance. In the 2nd c.

this a new [ā] vowel arose by the lengthening of short [a] vowels to compensate for the simplification of certain consonant groups, e.g. acc. plur. fem. τᾱ́ς from earlier τᾰ́νς (as still attested, for example, in Cretan inscriptions).

[6] It seems strange that a letter named ἦτα [hẹ̄ta] should be used, with psilosis, to represent the sound [æ] but not, at first, the sound [ẹ̄]. It is possible, however, that the original Ionic name of the letter was not in fact [hẹ̄ta] but [hǽta] (or in psilotic dialects [ǽta]). For the pharyngal fricative ḥ [ħ] is liable to cause opening of close or mid vowels in its vicinity (cf., on Arabic, Grammont, pp. 214 f., and on Circassian, Trubetzkoy, p. 87; Allen, Lingua 13 (1965), pp. 116 f.). The Semitic name ḥēt would then have been pronounced approximately [ħǽt], the vowel of which was identifiable by the Ionians with their [æ] rather than their [ẹ̄].

[7] Earlier, in its consonantal value (see above), ἦτα: but already in the mid-5 c. B.C., before the official adoption of the Ionic alphabet, Attic inscriptions begin to use H in its vowel value (and to omit it for the aspirate)—so the name ἦτα (unaspirated) may then already have been in competition with ἦτα.

A.D. the diphthong αι developed to a monophthong of the same quality as ε (cf. p. 79), with consequent confusions of spelling. Byzantine grammarians therefore distinguished them as (ἡ) $\overline{αι}$ δίφθογγος and (τὸ) ἒ ψιλόν ('plain ε'). Similarly the diphthong οι developed to a monophthong of the same quality as υ [ü] (cf. pp. 68 f., 81), and these were distinguished as (ἡ) $\overline{οι}$ δίφθογγος and (τὸ) ὒ ψιλόν (by Byzantine times the aspirate had been lost in pronunciation, so this spelling and pronunciation are appropriate as against the classical ὒ).

In the 2–3 c. A.D. the distinction of long and short vowels disappeared in pronunciation, and consequently ο and ω began to be confused in spelling. In differentiating between them grammarians evidently did not find the names οὖ and ὦ sufficiently distinctive, and they came to be referred to as ὂ μικρόν and ὦ μέγα respectively.[8] In addition of course the name οὖ for O, pronounced as [ū] (see above), had long been inappropriate to the sound: the same also applied to the name εἶ for E, pronounced as [ī] by the 3 c. B.C. (cf. p. 90, n. 3).

---

[8] In the *Cratylus*, arguing against the 'conventionalist' theory of language, Plato introduces a *reductio ad absurdum* in the idea of things being given the opposite of their actual names (433 E), and cites as an example: ἐπὶ μὲν ᾧ νῦν σμικρὸν μέγα καλεῖν, ἐπὶ δὲ ᾧ μέγα σμικρόν. But this collocation is a mere coincidence and not a pun on ὦ μέγα (though the Venetus is misled into writing ὦ μέγα). Elsewhere in the same dialogue (420 B) O and Ω are referred to as οὖ and ὦ, and at 393 D Plato expressly states that E, Y, O, and Ω are peculiar in being named by their sound alone. At the end of the 1st century A.D. we still find in the Book of Revelation Ἐγώ εἰμι τὸ ἄλφα καὶ τὸ ὦ—*not* ὦ μέγα in the best MSS: this is confirmed by a citation in Clement of Alexandria, *Strom.* IV.25. §157, around A.D. 200, and metrically guaranteed by Prudentius' hymn *Cathem.* ix (A.D. 405), line 11: 'alpha et Ω cognominatus, ipse fons et clausula' (trochaic tetrameter catalectic). H. B. Swete, *The Apocalypse of St. John*, p. 10, notes that the author may well have had in mind the similar expression found in Jewish works, as in 'Adam transgressed from the *'Aleph* to the *Taw*' (the latter being the last letter of the Hebrew alphabet: cf. above on the placing of Greek Y).

Index of Greek technical terms, etc.

Select Bibliography

(General: for Appendix A see pp. 160 f.)

(Where more than one edition of a work or more than one work by an author are listed, references in the text, unless otherwise specified, are to the first mentioned.)

Abercrombie, D. *Elements of General Phonetics*. Edinburgh, 1967.

Allen, W. S. *Phonetics in Ancient India* (London Oriental Series, i). O.U.P. 1953 (3rd imp. 1965).
  Vox Latina. 2nd edn C.U.P. 1978. [*abbr. VL*]
  Accent and Rhythm (Cambridge Studies in Linguistics, 12). C.U.P. 1973. [*abbr. AR*]

Bartoněk, A. *Development of the long-vowel system in ancient Greek dialects* (Opera Univ. Purkynianae Brunensis, Fac. Philos., 106). Prague, 1966.

Blass, F. *Pronunciation of Ancient Greek* (trsl. W. J. Purton). C.U.P. 1890.

Brosnahan, L. F. & B. Malmberg. *Introduction to Phonetics*. Cambridge, 1970.

Browning, R. *Medieval and Modern Greek*. London, 1969.

Buck, C. D. (*a*) *Comparative Grammar of Greek and Latin*. Chicago, 1933 (8th imp. 1962). (*b*) *Greek Dialects*. Chicago, 1955 (2nd imp. 1961).

Chadwick, J. *The prehistory of the Greek language* (*Cambridge Ancient History*, rev. edn, vol. II, ch. xxxix). C.U.P. 1963.

Chantraine, P. *Grammaire homérique*. 2 vols, Paris, 1948, 1953 (3rd imp. 1958, 1963; 5th imp. vol. i, 1973).

Garde, P. *L'Accent*. Paris, 1968.

Gelb, I. J. *A Study of Writing*. 2nd edn Chicago, 1963 (4th imp. 1974).

Gimson, A. C. *An Introduction to the Pronunciation of English*. London, 1962 (2nd edn 1970).

Grammont, M. *Phonétique du grec ancien*. Lyon, 1948.

Heffner, R.-M. S. *General Phonetics*. Madison, 1950 (3rd imp. 1960).

Jones, D. (*a*) *Outline of English Phonetics*. 9th edn Cambridge, 1960 (5th imp. 1972). (*b*) *The Pronunciation of English*. 4th edn C.U.P. 1956 (3rd imp. 1963; paperback 1966). (*c*) *The Phoneme*. 2nd edn Cambridge, 1962 (3rd edn 1967, repr. 1976).

Lejeune, M. (*a*) *Traité de phonétique grecque*. 2nd edn Paris, 1955.
  (*b*) *Phonétique historique du mycénien et du grec ancien*. Paris, 1972.

Lupaş, L. *Phonologie du grec attique*. The Hague, 1972.

175

Maas, P. *Greek Metre* (trsl. H. Lloyd-Jones). O.U.P. 1962 (2nd edn 1966).

Meillet, A. *Aperçu d'une histoire de la langue grecque*. 7th edn Paris, 1965 (8th edn 1975).

Meisterhans, K. [–Schwyzer, E.]. *Grammatik der attischen Inschriften*. 3rd edn Berlin, 1900.

Newton, B. E. *The Generative Interpretation of Dialect: a Study of Modern Greek Phonology* (Cambridge Studies in Linguistics, 8). C.U.P. 1972.

Palmer, L. R. *The Greek Language*. London, 1980.

Postgate, J. P. *A short guide to the accentuation of Ancient Greek*. Liverpool/London, 1924.

Pring, J. T. *A Grammar of Modern Greek on a phonetic basis*. London, 1950 (7th imp. 1963).

Raven, D. S. *Greek Metre*. London, 1962 (2nd edn 1968).

Schwyzer, E. *Griechische Grammatik*, i (Handbuch der Altertumswissenschaft, II, i. 1). München, 1938 (3rd imp. 1959).

Sommerstein, A. H. *The Sound Pattern of Ancient Greek* (Philological Soc. Publ. 23). Oxford, 1973.

Stanford, W. B. *The Sound of Greek* (Sather Lectures, 1966). Berkeley/C.U.P., 1967.

Stetson, R. H. *Motor Phonetics*. Amsterdam, 1951.

Sturtevant, E. H. *The Pronunciation of Greek and Latin*. 2nd edn Philadelphia, 1940 (2nd imp. Groningen, 1968).

Teodorsson, S.-T. *The Phonemic System of the Attic Dialect 400–340 B.C.* (= Studia Graeca et Latina Gothoburgensia, 32). Stockholm/Göteborg/Uppsala, 1974. (See also p. ix)

Threatte, L. *The Grammar of Attic Inscriptions*, I: Phonology. Berlin/New York, 1980.

Thumb, A. *Handbook of the Modern Greek Vernacular* (trsl. S. Angus). Edinburgh, 1912 (also repr., with 'Language' for 'Vernacular', Chicago, 1964).

Trubetzkoy, N. S. *Grundzüge der Phonologie* (= TCLP, 7). Prague, 1939 (also trsl. J. Cantineau, *Principes de Phonologie*. Paris, 1949; and C. A. M. Baltaxe, *Principles of Phonology*. Berkeley, 1969).

Ullman, B. L. *Ancient Writing and its Influence*. New York, 1932 (repr. M.I.T. 1969).

Vendryes, J. *Traité d'accentuation grecque*. Paris, 1904 (3rd imp. 1938).

Vilborg, E. *A tentative grammar of Mycenaean Greek* (Göteborgs Universitets Årsskrift, lxvi. 2; Studia Graeca et Latina Gothoburgensia, ix). Göteborg, 1960.

West, M. L. *Greek Metre*. O.U.P. 1982.

SUMMARY OF
RECOMMENDED PRONUNCIATIONS

('*English*' *refers to the standard or* '*received*' *pronunciation of Southern British English. Asterisks indicate less accurate approximations.*)

		For discussion see page(s)
ᾰ	As first *a* in Italian *amare*	
	*As vowel of English *cup*	
	(N.B. not as vowel of *cap*)	62 f.
ᾱ	As second *a* in Italian *amare*	
	*As *a* in English *father*	62 f.
ᾳ	As ᾱ	84 ff.
αι	As in English *high* (before vowels see pp. 81 ff.)	79 f.
αυ	As in English *how* (before vowels see pp. 81 ff.	79 f.
ᾱυ	As αυ	84 ff.
β	As English *b*	29 ff.
γ	(1) As English 'hard' *g*	29 ff.
	(2) Before κ, χ, γ, μ (but see p. 37): as *n* in English *ink* or *ng* in *song*	35 ff.
δ	As French *d*	
	*As English *d*	16, 29 ff.
ε	As in English *pet*	63 f.
ει	As in German *Beet*	69 ff.
ευ	See p. 80	
ζ	[zd] as in English *wisdom*	56 ff.
η	As in French *tête*	69 ff.
ῃ	As η	84 ff.
ηυ	As ευ	84 ff.
θ	As *t* in English *top* (emphatically pronounced)	
	*(but see pp. 28 f.) As *th* in English *thin*	18 ff.

SUMMARY OF RECOMMENDED PRONUNCIATIONS

For
discussion
see page(s)

ῐ	As in French *vite*	
	*As in English *bit*	65
ῑ	As in French *vive*	
	*As in English *bead*	65
κ	As French 'hard' *c*, or English (non-initial)	
	k, *ck*, or 'hard' *c* (on ἐκ see pp. 17 f.)	15 ff.
λ	As French *l*, or English *l* before vowels	
	*As English *l* in other contexts	40
μ	As English *m*	33
ν	As *n* in French or *English *net* (on end of	
	word see pp. 33 ff.)	33
ξ	As *x* in English *box*	59 f.
ο	As in German *Gott*	
	*As in English *pot*	63 f.
οι	As in English *boy*, *coin* (before vowels see	
	pp. 81 ff.)	80 f.
ου	As in English *pool* or French *rouge*	75 ff.
π	As French *p*, or English (non-initial) *p*	15 ff.
ρ	As Scottish 'rolled' *r* (on initial, post-	
	aspirate, and double see discussion)	41 ff.
σ	(1) As *s* in English *sing*, or *ss* in *less*, *lesson*	
	(2) Before β, γ, δ, μ: as English *z* (N.B. but	
	not elsewhere)	. f.
σσ	As σσ	12 ff., 60 f.
τ	As French *t*	
	*As English (non-initial) *t*	15 ff.
ττ	As ττ	12 ff., 60 f.
ῠ	As in French *lune*	65 ff.
ῡ	As in French *ruse*	65 ff.
υι	See pp. 80 ff.	
φ	As *p* in English *pot* (emphatically pronounced)	
	*(but see pp. 28 f.) As *f* in English *foot*	18 ff.
χ	As *c* in English *cat* (emphatically pronounced)	
	*(but see pp. 28 f.) As *ch* in Scottish *loch*	18 ff.

		For *discussion* *see page(s)*
ψ	As *ps* in English *lapse*	59 f.
ω	As in English *saw*	75 ff.
ῳ	As ω	84 ff.

DOUBLE CONSONANTS   See discussion   12

ACCENTS   See discussion   127 f., 149

Discussions of POST-CLASSICAL PRONUNCIATIONS appear on the following pages: 23 ff., 30 ff., 53, 58 f., 68 f., 70, 72 f., 74 f., 78 (Table), 79 ff., 85 ff., 93 ff., 130 f., 172 f.